WASHINGTON
GOES TO WAR

David Brinkley

WASHINGTON GOES TO WAR

ANDRE DEUTSCH

First published in Great Britain 1989 by
André Deutsch Limited
105-106 Great Russell Street, London WC1B 3LJ

Copyright © 1988 by David Brinkley

British Library Cataloguing in Publication Data
Brinkley, David, *1920 –*
    Washington goes to war: the extraordinary
    story of the transformation of a city.
    1. Washington, D.C. 1933
    I: Title
    975.3'04

ISBN 0 233 98366 X

First published in the United States of America 1988 by
Alfred A. Knopf, Inc., New York.

Printed in Great Britain by
St Edmundsbury Press, Bury St Edmunds, Suffolk

To Alan, Joel, John and Alexis

Washington in wartime is a combination of Moscow (for over-crowding), Paris (for its trees), Wichita (for its way of thinking), Nome (in the gold-rush days) and Hell (for its livability).

—Malcolm Cowley, "Washington Is Like Hell,"
The New Republic, June 1942

Home of the brave, land of the free
I don't want to be mistreated by no bourgeoisie,
Lord, it's a bourgeois town!

Tell all the colored folks to listen to me,
Don't try to buy no home in Washington, D.C.
'Cause it's a bourgeois town!

—Song by Leadbelly,
black folk singer of the 1940s

Washington the Capital is a symbol of democracy and America. Washington the city is a symbol of almost everything that sincere and thoughtful men know is wrong with democracy and America. Washington the Capital is the hope of world freedom; Washington the city is overcrowded, badly housed, expensive, crime-ridden, intolerant, with inadequate transportation, schools, and health facilities. It staggers under a dilapidated and hopeless governmental organization, and its problems are rapidly getting worse.

—Alden Stevens, "Washington: Blight on Democracy,"
Harper's, December 1941

If the war lasts much longer, Washington is going to bust right out of its pants.

—*Life* magazine, January 1943

Contents

16 pages of illustrations will be found following page 128

Chapter Headpieces

Preface

I am a journalist, not a historian, and while this book is an effort to describe a moment in the past, it is less a work of history than of personal reminiscence and reflection. Essentially, it is an account of my own observations and experiences in wartime Washington, supplemented by material drawn from interviews and other sources. I have tried to create out of it all a portrait of the pain and struggle of a city and a government suddenly called upon to fight, and to lead other nations in fighting, the greatest war in history, but pathetically and sometimes hilariously unprepared to do so.

This is bound to be somewhere close to the last reporting from that period based on firsthand sources. One after another, with unsettling rapidity, those in positions of power and responsibility during World War II are passing from the scene. Several who agreed to recall and describe their experiences in the war years died before I could get to them.

I have not dealt here in any detail with the grand strategy of the war in Europe and the Pacific. Instead, I have tried to report mainly on what I saw and heard and learned in Washington during years now fading into a misty past, the wartime experience of a country two-thirds of whose people are now too young to remember any of it. The result is a sort of *Our Town* at war, the story of a city astonished and often confused to find itself at the center of a worldwide conflict without ever hearing a shot fired. A strange city, set up in the first place to be the center of government and, like government itself at that time, a city moving slowly and doing little.

As the forties began, Washington was mainly a middle-class town grown up around a middle-class government. A Hudson Valley patrician sat in the White House, yes, but he and his appointed assistants presided over a population of government employees of modest incomes and modest ambitions. A town where Raleigh Haberdasher on F Street ran advertisements suggesting that a man in an office job really should own more than one suit. (When the new and radical idea of zippers on men's trousers began to appear, Woodward and Lothrop posted signs in its men's department saying that for $3.50 it would remove the zippers and replace them with buttons.) A town where people routinely bought Chevrolets not new but used.

It was a town and a government entirely unprepared to take on the global responsibilities suddenly thrust upon it. The executive branch, despite its expansion during the New Deal, remained relatively small, its employees more concerned with egg prices and post office construction than with the war clouds gathering in Europe and Asia. And Congress, all its members sent in from other places, was even worse. No one in the Senate even laughed when one of its members, Kenneth Wherry, Republican of Nebraska, rose to declare that after the war China deserved American help so that "Shanghai can be raised up and up until it's just like Kansas City."

A government of drones and paper shufflers simply could not do the job. And so Franklin Roosevelt found that he had, in effect, to recruit an entirely new and temporary government to be piled on top of the old one, the new government to get the tanks and airplanes built, the uniforms made, the men and women assembled and trained and shipped abroad, and the battles fought and won. The war transformed not just the government. It transformed Washington itself. A languid Southern town with a pace so slow that much of it simply closed down for the summer grew almost overnight into a crowded, harried, almost frantic metropolis struggling desperately to assume the mantle of global power, moving haltingly and haphazardly and only partially successfully to change itself into the capital of the free world.

Nothing like it had ever been seen before. Nothing like it is likely to be seen again.

This book is a journalist's attempt to describe it.

David Brinkley
Washington, D.C.
November 1987

Acknowledgments

Washington's agencies and offices produced the weapons and the uniformed men and women to fight and win World War II. They also produced monumental accumulations of paper, much of which has remained stored and largely untouched since the war ended. Nearly eight years ago, Charles Curtis began researching and organizing this material, looking for records of what happened out of the public eye in Washington during the war years. For a part of this time Clifford Sloan also joined in the paper search. The two of them have since gone on to pursue legal careers and may now see this work as less important than what they have done since, but to me it was invaluable. This book could not have been written without them.

Others helped with the interviews and research on a subject so large, so sweeping as to make their assistance indispensable. Mark Powden unraveled the complexities of a number of events in the bureaucracy of wartime Washington. Jonathan Alter conducted with great skill a number of the interviews. Further, I am grateful to Peter Fitzsimmons, Lisa Conniff, Charles Bloche, David Goldberg and James Ralph for their assistance in various stages of the work.

Robert Gottlieb and Ashbel Green of Alfred A. Knopf were extremely supportive and generous with their advice and encouragement, as was Irving Lazar.

Further, I offer my thanks to the splendidly helpful staffs at the National Archives, the Library of Congress Manuscript Division, Washington's Columbia Historical Society, the Washingtoniana Room in the Martin Luther King Library of the D.C. Public Library and the Franklin D. Roosevelt Library in Hyde Park, N.Y.

And foremost, to my son, Alan Brinkley, professor of history. He directed the research, often calling on the aid of his students at Harvard.

And, far more than that, he helped organize and plan these chapters and saved me from numerous errors. If any remain, they are mine, not his. To Alan, my deepest thanks.

WASHINGTON
GOES TO WAR

Prologue

In 1783, the British defeated and the American Revolution ended, the new Congress was already irritated at being forced to move its deliberations from one city to another for the previous six years to escape the British army. Now, settled in Philadelphia, it was infuriated again because it was threatened by its own army, a rowdy mob of its newly disbanded soldiers gathered in the street noisily demanding to be paid. Congress responded with a resolution:

> The authority of the United States having been this day grossly insulted by the disorderly and menacing appearance of a body of armed soldiers about the place within which Congress were assembled, and the peace of this city being endangered by the mutinous disposition of the said troops . . .

It asked the Philadelphia authorities to call out their own militia to remove the soldiers from the street. The troops were, according to James Madison's notes, "muttering offensive words and wantonly pointing their muskets to the windows of the hall of Congress. . . . It was observed that spirituous drink from the tippling houses adjoining began to be liberally served out to the soldiers and might lead to hasty excesses."

Philadelphia responded that it did not believe Congress being disturbed in its labors was sufficient provocation for calling out its militia.

Congress was so enraged it left Philadelphia and held its next session in Princeton, New Jersey. There, Elbridge Gerry of Massachusetts offered a resolution to build a permanent place for a federal government on the banks of the Delaware or Potomac river "if a suitable site can be found."

Everyone agreed that Congress needed a meetingplace under its own control and insulated from local political pressures and from such threats as drunken soldiers, but there was no agreement on where this place should be. There were numerous offers over the next several years. New York State suggested the town of Kingston. Other offers came from Newport, Rhode Island; Annapolis, Maryland; Trenton, New Jersey; Williamsburg, Virginia; and Philadelphia. But Congress rejected them all, out of sectional jealousies, hope for commercial advantage, and for such reasons as South Carolina's dislike of Philadelphia because it had too many Quakers who opposed slavery.

Then two states, Maryland and Virginia, offered both land and money. They would provide between them one hundred square miles of land, on both sides of the Potomac River, and would give $192,000 for new government buildings. An attractive offer, but still not good enough to end the rivalries among the states until Alexander Hamilton, the first secretary of the treasury under the new Constitution, saw a chance to make a deal. He wanted the new federal government to assume responsibility for the debts the individual state governments had run up during the Revolution. He saw that those to whom the debts were owed were mostly wealthy and influential men; if the new central government owed them money, they would be more likely to work for its survival and stability. The Southern states opposed this idea, because most of those who were owed money were Northerners. And the money to pay the debt would have to be raised by increasing the government's only real source of revenue, the tariff on imports, which the Southerners also opposed because they, more than the North, were a rural, agrarian people dependent on imported manufactured goods. Hamilton got his way only by agreeing to support a new capital city in the South, on the Potomac River. On July 15, 1790, Congress voted to remain in Philadelphia for ten years and then move to a new "Federal City" to be constructed somewhere along the Potomac. And so Washington, D.C., was born as it was to live—with a political deal.

Even before it was built, the capital was named for George Washington. Congress gave him the privilege of choosing a site for the federal city, anywhere between the point where the Anacostia River flows into the Potomac and a creek seventy-five miles upstream flowing in through the village of Williamsport, Maryland. Williamsport, expecting to become the great, glittering capital of a new and growing nation, hastily rebuilt its one central street to make it one hundred feet wide, to accommodate the ceremonial processions of kings and princes who would surely be visiting the new American capital. Two hundred years later,

Williamsport still sits there, a remote and tiny village with one enormously wide street.

Within the limits specified by Congress, George Washington located the new capital city as close to his own home, Mount Vernon, as he could. He placed it at the junction of the Potomac and the Anacostia.

As he announced his choice, he warned against greedy land speculators and agreed to pay sixty-seven dollars an acre to buy land from David Burnes for the future White House and from Daniel Carroll for the United States Capitol. He made the same offer to others on both sides of the river: for land in the existing towns of Alexandria, Virginia, and Georgetown, Maryland, and for tobacco farms, swamp, and wasteland— all to make up the one hundred square miles Congress said it needed for protection and privacy. So, on sixty-seven-dollar land—sneeringly described in the New York press as "a tangle of woods and swamps"—rose the capital of the first great republic since Rome.

I

Waiting

Washington in the summer of 1939 gleamed white and green in the sun as if Rome had sent its leftover marble columns, arches, plinths, architraves and friezes to be set down there among the trees. Greco-Roman temples of government rose behind vast ceremonial stairways of a scale and grandeur once intended for emperors and empire, and assuredly they were a grand sight in Rome when Claudius and Vespasian, enrobed and empurpled, descended stairs like these in sedan chairs borne by slaves and guarded by Praetorians. But in a country without emperor or empire nobody ever used them. It was easier to walk under the steps to the street-level entrances close to the elevators.

One of these marble temples, across the street from the United States Capitol, housed the Supreme Court. The justices were fretful and irritable at finding that the Corinthian columns in front had become a roosting place for starlings—nasty little birds long infamous in Washington for soiling the sidewalks, parked cars, pedestrians' clothes, statues of war heroes and the façades of government buildings. The Court asked Congress for money to install electric wires and other devices to drive the birds away. Representative Clarence Cannon of Missouri, high-handed chairman of the House Appropriations Committee, refused. "If they drive the starlings off the court they'll just fly across the street to the Capitol and roost on us."

The temples of government looked out on broad avenues named for places, for a document and for an aspiration achieved with blood—Pennsylvania, Delaware, Constitution and Independence—and on passing streams of Chevrolets, Nashes, Fords, DeSotos, LaSalles, Chryslers and Grahams. At midday, government employees hurried down Pennsylvania to a Childs' restaurant for the blue plate luncheon special of pot roast, mashed potatoes and string beans, served in compartmented platters. Forty cents and no substitutions. Or up Fourteenth Street to Ford's, a counter-and-stool restaurant where customers were asked to examine the menu and write their selections on slips of paper and where the following conversation ensued:

"Yes, sir, what will you have?"

"I wrote it all on the slip."

"Yes, but it's quicker if you just tell me."

"If I'm going to tell you, why do I have to write it all out on the slip?"

"It's quicker."

It wasn't. She was a graying, fiftyish waitress, bearing the marks of strain, struggle and final defeat, along with a knife scar through one ear and down her cheek, inflicted by one or another drunken husband. She told an NBC reporter from across the street that she had ridden the Greyhound up from Danville, Virginia, when she heard the Depression was over in Washington and there were jobs to be had. She evaded the written food orders because she could not read or write.

"I worked in the mills until they went bust. First job I've had since. Now it's this or nothing. Don't you tell them I can't read. Ain't nobody wants a fifty-year-old whore."

Down the Fourteenth Street hill from Ford's was the District Building, headquarters of the city's nearly invisible and nearly powerless local government, run by three commissioners appointed by the president. It dealt with the city's local problems mainly by ignoring them. A woman living in Georgetown telephoned the Sanitation Department and said, "I've had some brick planters for flowers built in my back yard. There were thirty-five bricks left over and I want to get rid of them, but every time I put them in the trash your collectors lift them out of the can and leave them on the sidewalk."

She was told, "Madam, our trucks are not allowed to haul away building materials. If they did, when anybody remodeled a house they'd find a huge pile of lumber and pipe and junk and they're not equipped to handle it."

"Then how do I get rid of these bricks?"

"Madam, do you work somewhere in town?"

"Yes, at the Agriculture Department."

"How do you get to work?"

"On the bus."

"All right. Here's what to do. Each morning, wrap one brick in a newspaper and take it with you and when you get off the bus, leave it on the seat."

Out Massachusetts Avenue and in the Kalorama neighborhood lived the Washingtonians called Cave Dwellers, the earliest residents of the city, mostly rich. Their problems seemed to them to be far more serious than disposing of leftover bricks. They had problems that were almost more than they could *stand*. The city of Washington—*their* city (their ancestors had *owned* it, you know)—had been taken over by a lot of pompous, ill-dressed, argumentative New Dealers, some of whom didn't even shave every day. Maybe they knew about egg marketing and consumer economics, but what else did they know? Just invite one of them to your house in Kalorama, in hope of a little courteous and civilized conversation, and what would he do? He would arrive an hour and a half late, with no apology other than some mumbling about an important meeting. He would walk between the rows of camellias up to the front door, not in dinner clothes or even in a dark suit, but in a baggy brown tweed jacket hanging sloppily over unpressed trousers and with loose threads dangling from where the jacket lining was coming apart. Couldn't a tailor have fixed that in an hour? And that still was not the worst. He would arrive for dinner smoking a pipe, one with the deeply curving stem affected by Baltic sea captains, German sausage-makers and central European professors. He was burning in it some cheap tobacco mixture from People's Drug Store that smelled like smoldering vanilla caramels. At the table his saliva ran down the pipestem to the bottom of the curve and then dripped to his shirtfront. When the wine was served, he asked for milk. That still was not the worst. Eventually, he would knock out of his pipe a black mound of what looked like charred mouse bones, loudly rapping it against the rim of a Lowestoft plate already in use when the family entertained Abraham Lincoln at this same table.

Washington's Cave Dwellers were unhappy with the New Deal. Not entirely for political reasons, although most of them would have voted against Roosevelt had the residents of the District of Columbia been allowed to vote, as they were not. Nor did they admire all his social experiments. But that was not it, either. It was *these people* he had brought to Washington. They were crude, boorish and socially offensive.

This problem was thought to be so severe it merited the attention of the *Saturday Evening Post*. In a 1936 article entitled "Pity the Poor Hostess," it told its readers that

> In the early days of 1933, there was great rejoicing among the [Washington] socially minded. At last, the Nation was to have a President and a First Lady who, having enjoyed exceptional privileges due to family position and wealth, would be able to set a high standard of dignified, gracious living. No occupants of the White House since the Theodore Roosevelts had been so signally favored as to birth and material circumstances. Even the Cave Dwellers dropped their mask of indifference and cheered openly. It was not, they conceded, the fault of other Presidents that they had lacked the opportunities fortuitously granted the Franklin Roosevelts, yet it was nice to have in a position of preeminence again people who were to the manner born.

Nice, no doubt, until the Cave Dwellers discovered that all these professors and thick-knuckled agronomists the Franklin Roosevelts had brought to Washington with them had not been similarly favored with these "exceptional privileges." The *Saturday Evening Post,* valiantly trying to preserve the America of William McKinley, concluded irritably that the effect of the "invasion of the capital by hordes of New Dealers had been to destroy, for the first time in the history of Washington, the incomparably delightful relationship between official and social life. The two are now separate."

How could it be otherwise, the article asked, when your typical New Dealer brushed aside statistics proving him wrong by saying condescendingly that he cared little for figures? Who called everyone who disagreed with him "the enemy"? These newcomers simply did not measure up. And so, the magazine noted, the "mask of indifference" was raised again, clear up to the scalp this time, perhaps never to be lowered, since it now seemed unlikely the American people would ever again elect a president able to meet their standards.

They were called Cave Dwellers because few people in the city ever saw them. Their names appeared on street signs, parks and museums endowed by their ancestors, but seldom in the newspapers. They shrank from publicity and public affairs, stayed in their houses, lived on inherited money and left in June for summer houses in Maine and in January for Palm Beach and Hobe Sound, departing in a trail of cocker spaniels, children with combed hair and shined shoes, maids in uniform and chauffeurs in black leather puttees. They kept track of one another in the social pages of the *Evening Star,* the only paper they considered fit to read.

Most of Washington had been a part of Maryland until 1800, and many of its earliest residents were descended from the first white settlers of the state, including the passengers on the *Ark* and the *Dove,* who had arrived from England in 1634. Since the District of Columbia was placed mainly in their state and much of it on what had been their families' lands, some of them took a paternal, proprietary interest in the government.

One who did was Charles Glover, president of the Riggs National Bank, directly across Pennsylvania Avenue from the United States Treasury. Riggs looked like a government building itself, turned out as it was with the massive stone entrance and vaulted marble interior favored by banks when they felt their architecture had to assure the public they were solid, safe places to keep money, in the days before banks began to look like airline ticket offices. Glover was accustomed to strolling across the street to discuss financial affairs with, and offer advice to, the secretary of the treasury. He was there so often the Treasury set aside a desk for him to use at his pleasure. But in 1915 John Skelton Williams, the new comptroller of the currency, ordered the desk removed: unseemly, he said, for a private commercial banker to have a desk in the Treasury. Glover was so infuriated he struck Williams on the head with his cane. It became, for Washington socialites, a symbolic event. Local historians date from Glover's attack the end of the Cave Dwellers' feeling that since the U.S. Government had been placed on their land, it was their duty to watch over it. They withdrew their attentions from government and from almost everything else in town except the Chevy Chase Club and the downtown Metropolitan and Sulgrave clubs. Oh, they occasionally extended dinner invitations to Calvin and Grace Coolidge (only rarely to Warren and Florence Harding before the Coolidges, since the Hardings *were* a little coarse and Warren preferred whiskey to food) and, for a time, to Herbert and Lou Hoover and a few of their more socially illustrious Cabinet officers. But the New Dealers had ended that relationship, perhaps forever.

How much did the New Dealers mind being dropped from the tables of veal *française* and the apple blossom honey from Winchester, Virginia, hand-carried down to Kalorama? Not much. They considered these people an overprivileged minority living on untaxed money from the robber baron depredations of their forebears, social crimes never to be allowed again.

The New Deal newcomers, with good reason, did not regard themselves as socialites. They were social workers. Roosevelt's closest White House assistant, Harry Hopkins, was a social worker from Sioux City, Iowa, and one of the New Deal's designers. It was he who ran the programs spending government money to put the unemployed to work. It was he who earned an editorial in the Chicago *Tribune* calling him "a bullheaded man whose high place in the New Deal was won by his ability to waste more money in quicker time on more absurd undertakings" than anyone else in Washington. Hopkins had the editorial enlarged, framed and hung on his office wall.

They were social workers, farm economists, liberal lawyers, union organizers, all of them political chiropractors eager to get their thumbs on the national spine, to snap it and crack it until the blood again flowed outward to all the extremities of American life, returning it to health and prosperity. Who gave a damn about these rich socialites? Their day was over. Now it was the people's turn, and the New Dealers were in Washington not to socialize and eat veal but to act for people who could not act for themselves.

But it was a strange town to act in. Since the days of Henry Adams, who was now buried in Georgetown, newcomers had found Washington hard to understand. Adams never understood it. His background had run to Boston, Paris, London, to the drawing rooms of a leisure class in cities already built and already touched with a pleasant air of decay. When Paris and Boston were paved and lit, Washington was still muddy and murky. And beyond that, it was a city conceived and built as a national government factory and nothing else—producing nothing but paper. Paper in the form of laws, currency, reports, postage stamps, rules, regulations. Not so much as a pound of iron or a yard of muslin or a barrel of nails, only paper. And there was the army of politicians sent to decide what messages the paper would carry, assisted by their own army of courtiers and clerks and along with them still another army of paper processors hired at low but steady wages to print, fold, type, bind, file and mail out the paper. This was an army that decamped at dusk and rode the Capital Transit trolleys to small houses bought with $5,000 mortgages at 3 percent interest and modestly embellished with hydrangeas and Atwater Kent radios. For their children, the Washington track was a segregated public school, Strayer Business College and then on into the government paper factory to work and wait for promotion, annual leave, retirement and pension.

It was not a place to look for urban glitter and sophistication. A desk sergeant in the District of Columbia Police Department, in booking the nightly haul of drunks and petty violators, routinely asked their occupations with the question, "Clerk or mechanic?" If the miserable sinner squirming before him protested he was neither, the sergeant only repeated the question. Finely delineated distinctions between government section chiefs, supervisors, lawyers, lobbyists, bricklayers and barbers he found irrelevant: if a man worked with paper he was a clerk, with tools a mechanic. And his two categories did embrace with some accuracy most of the population of a city Henry Adams had labeled "a mere political camp."

The New Dealers now living in this political camp and straining to return jobs and money to a country severely in need of both found the new prosperity slow in coming. A friend had once said to Roosevelt, "If the New Deal is a success, you will be remembered as the greatest American president."

Roosevelt had responded: "If I fail, I will be remembered as the last one."

The slow progress was irritating to all those trying to make the New Deal a success, spending their days at government-issue desks trying to induce the economy to perform, and their evenings lounging with their shoes off in rented houses in Georgetown, pouring whiskey, scratching themselves between the toes and talking half the night about their bureaucratic deals, successes and failures, and about what they might do next to get jobs and money flowing again. There was a good deal to talk about. Social Security had arrived, but what good was that to people in their forties still looking for jobs? Farmers had been helped to save their land from bankers ready to foreclose, but they were making very little money out of it. The Tennessee Valley Authority was showing the private utilities how to sell electric power cheaply, but that was no help to the unemployed who could barely afford to turn on a forty-watt light bulb. The Securities and Exchange Commission had made the crooks and liars on Wall Street tell the truth, finally, about the stocks they were selling, but a cleaned-up stock market was of no interest to those too poor to trade in it. And so there remained the pain in their stomachs, the sickening, aching fact that after all these years the New Deal had failed to end the Depression they had all named in honor of Herbert Hoover. Unemployment was still close to ten million, a third of the blacks were on relief. The New Dealers had, in fact, excised a few of the ugly warts from the face of American society, but clearly something else was needed. What was it?

Some three hundred miles south of Washington, in the small port city of Wilmington, North Carolina, a young part-time reporter for the *Morning Star* poked idly around the Cape Fear River docks. At the foot of Walnut Street, waiting for a ship's winch to lift them aboard, were stacks of wooden bins filled with scrap metal—brake drums, bedsprings, knives and forks bearing the monograms of bankrupt hotels and restaurants, coat hooks, the insides of Big Ben alarm clocks, Chevrolet engine blocks, the long poles grocers used to reach the corn flakes on the top shelves. What was all this junk and where was it going?

"Scrap metal going to Japan," they told him. "So they can melt it down and shoot it back at us."

Was it possible a young man conceived on these bedsprings might someday fight the Japanese and be shot with a weapon made from his own parents' melted-down bedsprings? Nobody on the Walnut Street docks could answer that.

* * *

Franklin Roosevelt sat in his office one day in 1937, took still another Camel from a dented and tarnished silver cigarette case and blew a cumulus of smoke across the desk toward his secretary of state, Cordell Hull, exhaling both words and smoke as they talked about the Germans and Japanese working all night hammering, welding and stamping out weapons. What could we, what could anyone, do about it? Numerous disarmament conferences held at varnished tables in European palaces had produced little more than heaps of paper now yellowing—disarmament agreements ending with dotted lines never signed, or signed and then ignored.

Hull sat stiff and erect in a straight chair. In his black suit, white shirt, black necktie, white hair and black eyebrows he looked like a monochromatic time exposure of the proper Victorian statesman, lacking only an oval walnut-and-velvet frame. And it was a little surprising that when he spoke it was in a high, thin voice with a slight lisp, saying Germany was "hell-bent on war." How did he know? He had a cable from the U.S. consul general in Berlin saying members of the Hitler government were "psychopathic cases and would normally be under treatment somewhere."

The public needed to understand the danger of war in both Europe and the Pacific. It might help, Hull said, if the president were to make a speech explaining that international cooperation was the only reasonable way to meet the danger.

In late September 1937 Grace Tully, one of Franklin Roosevelt's secretaries, traveled with him on a railroad trip across the country for a "look-see," as he called it, at the state of the economy. When the newspapers were put aboard his private car, the *Ferdinand Magellan,* she saw him "glowering" over a report of the September 25 meeting of Adolf Hitler and Benito Mussolini in Munich, a theatrically mounted display of military strutting, belligerent statements, embraces and mugging for the cameras.

"Child," he said to her, "what are you doing tonight?"

He always asked her that when he wanted her to work after dinner; and her answer, true or not, was always the same: "Nothing, sir."

"Grand! You'd better come back and have some dinner, and if you're good I may even give you a little cocktail. Later, we'll do some thinking out loud about my speech in Chicago."

Cordell Hull had urged him to speak somewhere on this trip on the loosely defined topic of "international cooperation." But even a term as fuzzy as that, normally suitable for a polite talk at the Rotary Club, would now be inflammatory, because in Congress and in much of the country "international cooperation" was now seen as a code phrase for sending American troops to Europe again to be killed in another stupid, vicious foreign war. Roosevelt, however, knew the world was approaching some kind of explosion, and sometime, somehow, the country had to be prepared for it. When he and Grace Tully finished "thinking out loud" on his railroad car that night, his speech had gone beyond the pale and cautious words suggested by Hull.

He spoke on October 5 at the dedication of the Outer Drive Bridge, a WPA project in Chicago. The speaker's platform overlooked a large warehouse owned by Colonel Robert R. McCormick, publisher of the Chicago *Tribune,* whose hatred of Roosevelt was venomous and un-yielding. The colonel had sent men out to paint on the side of his warehouse, where Roosevelt could not miss seeing it, the single word "UNDOMINATED," in letters ten feet high. McCormick's would soon be the most strident voice in the isolationist America First movement, intent at any cost on keeping the U.S. out of foreign wars, a movement coming to be enormously vocal and powerful and attracting support in the United States Congress.

Roosevelt's speech infuriated McCormick and the isolationists. "It seems to be unfortunately true," he said, "that the epidemic of world lawlessness is spreading. When an epidemic of physical disease starts to spread, the community approves and joins in a quarantine of the patients in order to protect the health of the community against the spread of the disease."

It was his style to describe steamy and dangerous issues in the language of homely parables. It was a speech that in another place at another time would have left his listeners bored and yawning and looking at their watches. But in this place at this time it was sensational.

Back on the train and leaving Chicago, he said, "Well, it's done now."

It certainly was. The reaction was even angrier than he feared. Hull called it "quick and violent." Six pacifist organizations jointly charged that the president's speech "points the American people down the road that led to the World War." The American Federation of Labor responded,

"American labor does not wish to be involved in European or Asiatic wars." Members of Congress raged and shouted for hours and days and some talked of impeachment. It was many months before Roosevelt again dared to mention the threat of war.

By the winter of 1938–39, Roosevelt knew, but was not yet willing to say, that the New Deal, as a social and political revolution, was dead. The Republicans had gained seats in the 1938 congressional elections. Few New Deal measures of any substance had passed Congress in more than a year. Representative Martin Dies of Texas, one of the great buffoons of his time, was proclaiming his determination to drive out of government such "Communists and fellow travelers" as Harold Ickes and Frances Perkins, the secretaries of interior and labor; he would decide later, he said, if Roosevelt himself should be added to his list.

Nothing Dies said would have mattered if Congress had not urged him on, and if the press hostile to Roosevelt across the country had not quoted and publicized Dies and reported his committee hearings in great detail. He was an irritant and an embarrassment more than a threat, but he took public attention away from the real threats. Adolf Hitler had just moved into Austria and replaced its chancellor with a Nazi gangster. Now he was demanding in public a narrow strip of Czechoslovakia called the Sudetenland and in private demanding the whole country. Who could stop him? The armies of Britain and France were far larger than Hitler's, their navies more powerful. Together, they could stop him. But would they? Britain's Prime Minister Neville Chamberlain, carrying a basket of apples and grapes and an umbrella, boarded a plane for Munich for a meeting with Hitler to discuss a "last last" attempt to save the peace. He and Edouard Daladier of France, with Italy's Benito Mussolini silently looking on, gave Hitler by agreement what he was ready and eager to take by force, Czechoslovakia. It was a deal Winston Churchill called "total and unmitigated defeat." In a choice between war and peace, he said, Chamberlain had chosen war.

In Roosevelt's discussions with Hopkins and Hull, there were more depressing facts to contemplate. The end of his second term was in sight and it was widely assumed he would honor a tradition older than the White House he sat in and refuse even to consider running for a third term. Three years before, he had told his neighbors in Hyde Park, New

York, that he was appearing before them as a candidate for public office for the last time. But among those already talking of running in 1940—John Nance Garner, James Farley, Thomas E. Dewey, Robert A. Taft, Arthur Vandenberg, Wendell Willkie—was there anyone who could be counted on to stand up to Hitler and the Japanese while carrying on what was left of the New Deal? Could any of them deal with the frenzied American opposition to entering any foreign war for any reason? Could any of them make the isolationists understand that if, when the war came, the United States sat there and watched Western Europe go down, watched Hitler continue his increasingly successful campaign to establish and support Nazi movements in South America, watched the Japanese expand all over the Pacific, the United States would stand surrounded in the world? And alone?

Beyond the White House gates, the city slumbered—largely unaware of and uninterested in war and peace and diplomacy, living at the slow pace and with the encrusted traditions that reminded most visitors of a placid Southern town more than of a major world capital.

Nearly a third of the city was black, and the number was rising. Every day, more streamed across the Fourteenth Street Bridge from Virginia: young men alone, with their possessions tied up in bundles carried on sticks on their shoulders; families, with small children in tow, sometimes bringing a few farm animals with them; migrants escaping the poverty of the tobacco lands of rural Virginia and North Carolina or the cotton lands of the Deep South. They were people hoping for something better than long days in the field for low pay and large debts, but—in Washington—seldom finding it.

What they did find was an already substantial black middle class, many of whose members considered them coarse and vulgar and wished they would go away. These established blacks, some of them descendants of the city's nineteenth-century slave population, lived on "the Hill," up Georgia Avenue and along 13th Street, which they tried as best they could to protect from the newly arrived migrants. They went to Dunbar High School. The more successful went on to Howard, by now the leading black university in America, and became physicians, dentists, lawyers, and public school teachers.

But few newcomers had access to this world. And so they did what generations of newly arrived blacks had done before them. They moved to "the alleys."

Pierre L'Enfant, in planning the new city that was to become the capital of the United States, had decided it would be pleasing if on the residential streets all houses fronted directly on the sidewalk, with open space in the back. And that was how residential Washington was built—row houses abutting the sidewalks with gardens and alleys in back and, when the residents were prosperous enough, stables for horses and carriages and small brick or frame quarters for slaves.

After the Civil War, with freed slaves now looking for space to live and work and with black migrants arriving from the South in a steady stream, investors in real estate discovered there was money to be made from the alleys. The tiny houses became valuable as rental property. The stables (particularly once streetcars and automobiles eliminated the need for horses and carriages) could be converted to housing or turned into shops for carpenters, upholsterers and laundries. Prosperous whites all over the city competed to buy alley land and, on virtually every vacant square inch, cram in tiny, shabby new buildings. For a while, new Irish immigrants competed with blacks for space in the alleys. But after a time, the Irish moved on. The blacks remained.

They lived in a squalor that some whites might have found more alarming had it not all been so conveniently out of sight. Alley dwellings often had no plumbing. One water faucet on a pipe rising up from the ground served several houses. Open-ended barrels set down over holes in the ground served as privies—the city health department counted fifteen thousand of them—and were used by as many as thirty people each. The alley shacks themselves were crumbling, unpainted, unheated and filthy.

Social workers and social scientists studied life in the alleys the way anthropologists studied life on the Pacific islands. They found large numbers of households headed by women, shacks known throughout the community as "Jane's House" or "Sally's Place." Unmarried mothers, some of them still in their teens, were common; their babies were known as "social children" or "engagement children." Census-takers came out of the alleys baffled, unable to tell who was married to whom.

For years, some whites and many blacks in Washington had pleaded with Congress to do something about the alleys—to clear them out and move their residents to better housing elsewhere. The first Mrs. Woodrow

Wilson had made the request from her deathbed in 1914, and Congress had agreed to act. But World War I called a halt to everything; and when the war ended and the issue arose again, a more conservative Congress backed away. Yes, of course, these people should be moved, the members said. But where would they go? Public housing did not yet exist. No white neighborhoods, no prosperous black neighborhoods, wanted the alley dwellers. And there was money to be made from alley property. Landowners were pressuring Congress to leave things alone.

In 1939, the New Deal created an Alley Dwelling Authority and gave it ten years to clear the slums and build public housing to replace them. But in Washington, as elsewhere, the black population grew and unemployment increased much faster than the public housing could be built; and so the alley slums remained—a favorite subject for Farm Security Administration photographers, who (when they came back to Washington from the Dust Bowl) took pictures of hideous slums and black children in tattered clothes, with the gleaming dome of the Capitol of the United States in the background.

Wherever they lived—on "the hill" or in the alleys or in the crumbling Georgetown houses that were now being snatched up by New Dealers and converted into expensive housing—blacks looked out on a city that was rigidly and thoroughly segregated. The world beyond the District line did not often take notice of the city's stony race relations, but in 1939—briefly—it did. The Daughters of the American Revolution refused to allow the great black opera singer Marian Anderson to sing in their auditorium, Constitution Hall. And for a moment, the status of blacks in the nation's capital received glaring publicity.

Howard University had arranged for Anderson to come to Washington. Since the university had no adequate space of its own, it requested permission to stage the recital in the two-thousand-seat auditorium of Central High School—an all-white public school attended by the sons and daughters of the city's civil servants and considered a training ground for the next generation of agency heads and office managers. The D.C. school board rejected Howard's request. "It was not just a question of Marian Anderson singing," a Howard professor said bitterly. "It was a question of all those Negroes crowding over there to hear her sing." After a prolonged public uproar, the Board reconsidered. Frank

Ballou, the school superintendent, announced that Anderson could sing at Central as long as the black community understood that such a gracious concession was never to be offered again. Howard rejected this offer as condescending and insulting, and asked for Constitution Hall instead. And as the world was soon to know, the DAR refused, with the explanation that it was only following local custom.

Which it was. Throughout the city, hotels, restaurants, movie theaters, libraries and taxicabs refused to serve blacks. Retail stores, even those in black neighborhoods serving black customers, refused to hire black sales clerks. Dress shops allowed black women to buy clothes but wouldn't let them try them on. White residential neighborhoods were governed by strict covenants forbidding homeowners to sell their houses to blacks (or, in many neighborhoods, to Jews).

For years, the federal government had hired virtually no blacks—a few dozen as janitors and messengers, but not many others. And while things had gotten a little better under the New Deal—with blacks occupying enough significant offices that they were able to form an informal "black cabinet" to try to advance their goals—most of the federal bureaucracy remained under the control of Southern whites from Central High School and the like. Even the middle class in black Washington survived largely by serving the professional and commercial needs of the black community itself, and particularly by providing services whites would not offer blacks even for money. They were teachers, doctors, lawyers, preachers, undertakers. But they formed only a small proportion of the black population as a whole. Most had to accept whatever menial jobs they could find and to tolerate constant belittling from white employers while they did them. Thurgood Marshall, who was eventually to become the first black justice of the United States Supreme Court, recalled years later what it was like to work as a busboy in the 1930s on the Baltimore and Ohio Railroad's dining cars traveling in and out of Washington. Marshall had to wear a white shirt, black necktie, white cotton jacket and trousers. When the B & O issued him a pair of trousers ending six inches above his ankles, he asked the dining car steward for a pair that fit. "No," the steward said. "It's more trouble to find a new pair of pants than it is to find a new nigger."

About the only thing black Washingtonians could do that their counterparts in Richmond or Atlanta or Birmingham could not was ride in the front of the Capital Transit buses—until the buses crossed the river into Virginia, at which point all black passengers had to move to the rear.

For a moment, after the DAR turned down Marian Anderson, the country and the world took notice. And for that moment, there was a response. The Interior Department suggested to Howard that the Anderson concert take place outdoors, on the steps of the Lincoln Memorial. Politicians, actors, artists and other celebrities flocked to be listed as "sponsors"—Eleanor Roosevelt, members of the Cabinet, the Congress and the Supreme Court, Tallulah Bankhead, Heywood Broun, Katharine Hepburn, Kirsten Flagstad, Sol Hurok, Fiorello LaGuardia, John L. Lewis, Leopold Stokowski. On Easter Sunday 1939, more than seventy-five thousand people gathered along the Reflecting Pool and down the Mall to the Washington Monument almost a half-mile away. From all over Washington came black men and women dressed in their finest clothes, little girls in communion dresses, people who had—many of them—never heard an operatic singer before. And they stood rapt, listening to a concert that, for them, was almost a religious experience—a concert that began with "America the Beautiful" (many in the crowd felt tears come to their eyes when they heard the line "And crown thy good with brotherhood, from sea to shining sea") and ended with the spiritual "Nobody Knows the Trouble I've Seen."

Marian Anderson called the recital a "dedication . . . a living witness to the ideals of freedom for which President Lincoln died." Mary McLeod Bethune said of it: "Something happened in all of our hearts. I came away almost walking in the air." But to most of white Washington, the concert was at best a momentary diversion—jarring, perhaps, but not jarring enough to provoke any real change in the nature of things. The *New Negro Alliance* took bitter note of this in its first issue after the concert:

> The golden voice of Marian Anderson poured forth from the front of the Lincoln Memorial as 75,000 citizens, black and white, stood shoulder to shoulder in peace and harmony to enjoy its moving beauty. Leaving the majestic natural setting, this multitude returned to gross discrimination and vicious segregation. . . . Negroes were still unable to attend theaters, use Central High School or Constitution Hall, or to exercise their rights as American citizens. The pent-up emotions of thousands of Negroes were discharged quietly over the Reflecting Pool and then the

strait-jacket of social policy and racial prejudice was quickly
made secure and operative again.

The city's two hundred thousand white federal employees were employed
to do the routine work of government. They were not paid to worry
about its policies. Many had worked there since McKinley, had seen
presidents and ponderous personalities come and go. They remained.

While Roosevelt and Hull worried about the Germans and the
Japanese and the threat of war, local Washington's drowsy life went on as
drowsily as ever, and the citizenry rocked on screen porches and suffered
the summer's heat. When George Washington chose this site for the new
capital city, he chose poorly. He placed it in pastures and malarial
swamps, some below sea level, in a climate consistently damp and
uncomfortable, never more so than in the summers. It was commonly
said that the British Foreign Office had once classified Washington as a
hardship post, meaning that diplomats posted there got a little extra pay
to compensate for the discomfort and that the ambassador, for his
informal daytime duties, was allowed to wear khaki shorts, knee socks,
high-top brown shoes and a pith helmet—the same costume worn by
British diplomats serving in steamy and pungent outposts in Southeast
Asia and central Africa. As pleasing a sight as this might have been, and
as much as it would have amused Henry Adams, Britain's ambassador
actually wore hot, scratchy woolens and bore up.

Some of Washington's business and professional men wore white
linen suits in the summer, with Panama hats and black-and-white wingtip shoes. They looked perfectly splendid for about an hour, until the
linen wrinkled. Others, more willing to suffer, went about in lightweight
white flannel suits—nice, but hot, scratchy and prone to turning yellow.
When they sent their flannels to Mr. Viner at the Sunshine Cleaners on
Mount Pleasant Street, he took each suit completely apart at the seams,
stitch by stitch, hand-washed each flannel piece separately, laid them
all out on the roof to let the sun dry them and bleach out the yellow-
ness and then sewed them back together and pressed the reassembled
suit. All this took one week—longer in cloudy weather—and cost ten
dollars.

Department of Agriculture maps showed that *Magnolia grandiflora*,
the common Southern magnolia with the waxy green-black leaves and
fragrant white blossoms as big as a plate, could be grown successfully

from along the Gulf Coast of New Orleans and Biloxi on across the Southeast to Tallahassee and up the East Coast to Washington, where it grew freely on the U.S. Capitol lawn near the end of its range and the end of the South. Only a river's breadth away lay the old Confederacy. Robert E. Lee's house, Arlington, still stood on the opposite bank, now owned by the federal government and open to tourists. The speaker of the House of Representatives, Sam Rayburn of Bonham, Texas, had not one but five pictures of Lee on his office wall, symmetrically arranged and all facing south. For whites as for blacks, Washington was Southern. Capital of the United States, yes, but Southern in manner, style, and appearance and Southern in climate and culture.

Typical of the local residents' night life in summer was a screen porch and a bridge game. The players found that in the damp heat the cards stuck together and stuck to the table. The wire screening filled with droplets of moisture that splattered to the floor when insects attracted to the light slammed themselves against the screen, drumming and shaking the wire. And there was the iron moan of a trolley car turning a curve out on Wisconsin Avenue, the hum of the black Westinghouse fan with its brass blades rotating on the floor. Upstairs the kids played a radio tuned to station WWDC, and heard the commercial for the New York Jewelry Company on Seventh Street, a seedy shopping area, a commercial Washington must have heard ten thousand times: "Mr. Tash, the manager of New York Jewelry, says [pause] you don't need cash, says Mr. Tash; if you'll take a chance on romance, I'll take a chance on you."

Outside under the elms and sycamores, the street lights showed white, filmy circles in air that seemed one-fourth air and three-fourths water. At the curbs in front of small houses built in the twenties without garages, parked cars accumulated a watery coating of rust and dead insects. When the boys at the Esso station cleaned the windshields, they always said, "Those damn bugs must have been chewing gum."

Local Washington, through presidents, wars, and depressions, had settled into an acceptance of George Washington's poor choice in a sprawling, slow-moving Southern city. People from real cities—Boston, New York, Chicago, cities with factories and immigrants and subways— thought it astonishing. They found few restaurants offering anything not fried in deep fat. On Connecticut Avenue there was a restaurant called Old New Orleans featuring in its front display window a large, plump black woman wearing a long gingham dress and a red bandanna on her head and sitting in a rocking chair, rocking by the hour—the restaurant's trademark. There was one legitimate theater, dark half the time. A baseball team, the Senators, usually in last place in the American League, played in ancient Griffith Stadium, widely regarded as a firetrap. Government employees drove downtown early to seize the free parking spaces on the streets before they were all taken and sat in their cars, eating breakfast out of brown paper sacks and waiting for their offices to open.

Of course, there were enough marble and bronze monuments for any visitor's taste. When Roosevelt announced the plans for the new Jefferson Memorial in 1938, a group of local women led by Eleanor ("Cissy") Patterson, publisher of the Washington *Times-Herald,* opposed it, complaining that clearing land for the Memorial would destroy fifty of Washington's famous Japanese cherry trees. Some of them tried to stop the construction by chaining themselves to the trees and defying the bulldozers. Michael Strauss, assistant secretary of the interior, countered by serving them lunch, with cup after cup of coffee until the women had to unlock their chains and leave for the rest rooms. When they did, the bulldozers moved in, and Jefferson was duly memorialized. But while visitors to Washington found much marble, they found little excitement.

On August 24, 1939, Roosevelt returned to Washington from a vacation cruise aboard the U.S. Navy cruiser *Tuscaloosa.* Cordell Hull met him at Union Station, and they rode together to the White House.

"Only the gloomiest of pictures could I give him," Hull recalled. "The days of peace could now be numbered on the fingers of both hands." Neither of them knew that two weeks earlier, Reinhard Heydrich, of Hitler's S.S., had stationed one of his agents, Alfred Naujocks, in the German town of Gleiwitz on the Polish border. Naujocks was told to await orders to stage an "incident"—a faked Polish attack on Germany. As Roosevelt and Hull rode down Pennsylvania, Naujocks was waiting.

In the next week, Roosevelt and Hull together composed a message to Hitler urging negotiations instead of war. Neither of them thought it would do any good. Its only purpose, they agreed, was to place the blame for war, whenever it occurred, on Hitler.

At 8 p.m. on September 1, Alfred Naujocks was ordered to proceed with the "incident." He brought out twelve German criminals who had all been sentenced to death, and dressed them in stolen Polish uniforms. An S.S. doctor gave them poisonous injections, killing them quickly. Then bullets were fired into their bodies. The story given out was that these "Polish soldiers" had crossed the border into Germany, intent on seizing the radio station at Gleiwitz, and that German soldiers, defending the Fatherland, had killed the attackers. The press was invited to the border to view the bodies and hear the story. Heydrich later boasted, "I started World War Two."

Near 3 a.m. the same night, the telephone rang beside Roosevelt's bed. It was William Bullitt, the American ambassador to France, calling from Paris: "Mr. President, the German army has crossed the border of Poland."

A minute later, the phone rang beside Hull's bed. It was the president. "Cordell, the Germans have invaded Poland."

Shortly afterward, Ambassador Joseph P. Kennedy in London called Hull and said he was confident now that the British would soon declare war. Hull asked: Was he sure? Was there any question they would act now?

"Oh, unquestionably none."

Outside, Washington was suffering the heat, with its politicians and lobbyists, its clerks and mechanics, with a local economy devoted mainly to retail and service trades, with miles of slums filled with shacks without plumbing and black people in poverty, more of them arriving every day. Was it conceivable that the leadership of the Western world in wartime could fall to a city only a few generations out of the mud? A city that still boasted fifteen thousand privies?

II

The Battle for Washington

"They asked, "What did we get out of the first world war but death, debt and George M. Cohan?"

The question being difficult to answer, it was asked repeatedly in the late 1930s by those Americans afraid of being tricked, deceived, stampeded into joining another war to bail out the British and the French. They were called isolationists, but like most sociopolitical labels this one said both too much and too little.

Isolation in the form of a haughty and disdainful withdrawal from a world thought to be unworthy of American attention did appeal to some. Ellis Island had been closed for only fifteen years. Many Americans and the parents of many others had only recently come to the United States to escape the class-based arrogance, the vanities and corruptions of the European kingdoms and their ceaseless wars—wars so stupid that during World War I, when Germany's Kaiser Wilhelm II was asked why his country was at war with half of Europe, he responded, "If only I knew."

Wasn't that war so massively brutal it had planted white crosses row on row across European fields and wiped out most of a generation of young European men? Had not the next generation of Americans learned in grade school to recite the verses "In Flanders fields the poppies blow / Between the crosses, row on row"? Wasn't it a war that had sent Americans home to die in veterans' hospitals with lungs burned out by mustard gas? And the Kaiser didn't even know why it started? And now Americans were expected to join in this madness again?

But the movement called isolationism went beyond that. There were beer hall fascists who, not always secretly, admired Hitler and would not have minded slipping into brown shirts of their own and taking to the streets with flaming torches and swastika flags and truncheons to break the heads of those they despised. There were communists who opposed Hitler until he signed a nonaggression pact with the Soviet Union in 1939 and overnight did a 180-degree turn when the orders came from Moscow. There were the Irish-Americans still unwilling to forget or forgive Britain's exploitation of Ireland. A few industrial tycoons saw Hitler as eminently reasonable in his treatment of business, which was more than they could say for Roosevelt. John L. Lewis of the United Mine Workers Union nearly choked on his hatred of Roosevelt. He told the German diplomats still in Washington that in the 1940 election he would defeat the president by turning American unions against the Democrats. There were those who believed any enemy of Roosevelt's must be a friend of theirs. And still others, many of them in Congress, who felt that Roosevelt had an appetite for dictatorship and that in the strains of a war with Hitler he might become one. In their view, anything he wanted, including going to war, should be denied him.

Those willing to sit back and watch the Europeans fight their own wars made their arguments in speeches, letters, pamphlets, and a few of the hundreds of complaints they offered might be set forth briefly:

Why fight another war to save the Europeans when the French themselves are asking, "Why die for Danzig?" The French sat around drinking wine, allowing their country to slide into decadence, sneering at us, playing with their mistresses and committing vulgar sexual acts, foolishly believing the Germans could be stopped with a concrete wall wide open at one end and with a French army led by generals who looked nice in helmets with feather plumes but couldn't fight worth a damn. The Europeans see Americans as uncouth, and they snicker at our crudities of speech and dress and diet while sending their worthless counts and dukes over here looking to marry rich American girls to bail out their own families. If they are eternally unable to settle their disputes, if they refused to stop Hitler when they still could have, why should we bail them out? George Washington had warned of the dangers of foreign alliances. Our experience has proved him right. We joined their war in 1917, lost our sons, ran up our national debt, lent them money they never repaid, were told we were making the world safe for democracy when it turned out we only made the world safe for Hitler. Do we learn nothing from history? Didn't Senator Robert A. Taft of Ohio say, when Roosevelt talked of aid to Britain, "The president confuses the defense of Britain with the defense of the United States"?

Taft was only one of a squad of senators willing to spend for the defense of this country, but for this country only, not a dime for Britain. Senator Key Pittman of Nevada had cordially invited the British to give it up, to abandon their green islands and to move themselves, King and all, to Canada. Senator Burton K. Wheeler of Montana made the single statement most infuriating to Roosevelt in all his years as president. Recalling a New Deal program to plow under crops and livestock to push up farm prices, Wheeler said Roosevelt's dragging this country into the European war would "plow under every fourth American boy." The senator was said not to know that this phrase had been invented by George Sylvester Viereck, a U.S. citizen working as a Nazi propagandist for the German embassy in Washington. (Viereck claimed to be loyal to the United States, but he was on Hitler's payroll, using money from Germany to set up for the Nazis such front groups as the Make Europe Pay Its War Debts Committee, or to write speeches for Senator Ernest Lundeen, a Republican from Minnesota who delivered them on the Senate floor and who was never heard to say a critical word about the Nazis.)

These were bitter days for Roosevelt. Every step he took to prepare the country for war, every move he made to help the British hang on, provoked bitter, frenzied opposition. In December 1940, he gave a fireside chat calling for full aid to Britain. Senator Worth Clark of Idaho called it "a trick speech, calculated to lead the American people into war and ruin." Burton Wheeler of Montana called the president a "warmonger." A few weeks later, a group calling itself the American

Peace Mobilization began a White House vigil that lasted for 1,029 con-tinuous hours, carrying signs complaining of "warmongering Roosevelt." Representative Luther Patrick of Alabama—isolationism never had much support in the South—said he was tired of attending boring committee hearings and went over to the White House with his own sign reading, "APPEASERS, BUNDISTS, REDS, ETC., YOU KNOW HOW TO PICKET BUT DO YOU KNOW HOW TO WORK?" As Patrick marched outside the fence, he carried a bucket of potatoes, peeling them as he went. Representative Stephen Young of Ohio offered his view of the isolationists: "This blatant group of misguided, misinformed, misdirected and moronic individuals are infringing the personal liberties of the first citizen of this nation. For more than a month the White House has been picketed by a group of mentally unbalanced, publicity-seeking morons."

Two other groups, all mothers, they said, appeared in front of the White House carrying a parchment scroll printed with Roosevelt's numerous promises to keep the country out of war. Ceremoniously, they burned it and placed the blackened tatters in an urn they had bought from an undertaker and labeled "Ashes of FDR's Promises." At the Capitol, Congress had mothers of its own. In the summer of 1941, women in black dresses and veils took over a bench in a reception room near the Senate chamber and sat there, day after day, weeping and moaning and trying to upset the senators about to vote on extending the draft. At night, they were still at it. Vera Bloom, daughter of the strongly interventionist New York congressman Sol Bloom, was home alone one night when she heard an eerie tapping on the windowpanes. She looked out and screamed at the sight of black-clad women standing on the lawn holding lighted candles.

Twelve blocks down Pennsylvania Avenue from the Capitol, at the Raleigh Hotel, the Committee to Defend America First met for a dinner to denounce the encroaching "mad hysteria" and to hear Senator Wheeler say, "By setting the United States on fire we will not help put out the fire in Europe." Protestant churches around Washington began accepting applications for registration as conscientious objectors. John L. Lewis offered the opinion that the draft equaled dictatorship. Eight antiwar organizations rented the Belasco Theater on Lafayette Square for a massive rally against joining the war. The speakers included Senator Arthur Capper of Kansas, widely known among women staff members as the Senate's most tireless fanny patter. When he was not busy with that, he found time to propose a constitutional amendment saying the United States could never enter any war until the question had been put to the American people in a national referendum. In 1940 he voted against the draft and asked, "Why turn this country into an armed camp?" A year later, shortly before Pearl Harbor, he voted against it again, and said, "There is no reason why we should not have peaceful relations with the world if we cease playing the role of international Meddlesome Mattie."

Congress in 1940 had voted, slowly and reluctantly, to draft young men for one year only. Now, in 1941, the draft law was about to expire. The isolationists had been so effective that the opposition to renewal was substantial. But if the draft were not renewed, all those young soldier-draftees, after just one year in uniform, would have to be discharged and sent home.

One member of the House Armed Services Committee was a young, gangling Texan, all squeaky shoes, Adam's apple and cold-molasses drawl, named Lyndon Johnson. On the morning before the vote he and Speaker Sam Rayburn closed the door to Rayburn's office and calculated how the vote might go, examining the reports brought in by the party whips, whose job it was to find out in advance how many members would vote for and how many against whatever was before the House so the leadership could manage the legislative business. In this case, the whips reported the vote would be close and the draft extension could easily lose.

Rayburn and Johnson called Secretary Hull and asked for a letter in support of extending the draft, one as dramatic as he could make it. They suggested a few points they thought might persuade some House members still wavering. One was that the country needed military power for its own defense whether it joined the war or not, regardless of what happened anywhere else in the world. And they asked Hull to move fast.

Rayburn sent a messenger to the State Department to pick up Hull's letter, and he read it on the floor. Its message was that whatever happened in Europe, the great and glorious American republic must be ready to defend itself, and that—a clause that caught them emotionally—"the American flag is too precious to endanger."

It worked. There were even a few tears among members. It appeared that some votes might have been changed and so Rayburn called the bill up quickly, before the effect of Hull's words could wear off. It squeaked

by. The vote was 203 to 202. Four months before Pearl Harbor the United
States had decided, barely, to keep its armed services.

In July of 1914, the British and German ambassadors to Washington lived
in houses facing each other across Connecticut Avenue, the bathroom
window of one looking over through the trees into the bathroom window
of the other. In the mornings, as the two of them shaved, each looked
out across the avenue at the other and smiled and bowed—old colleagues beginning the day with ivory-handled straight razors and badger
shaving brushes in porcelain mugs. A month later, their countries were
at war. The bowing and smiling stopped. Each refused to look out the
window while he shaved.

Woodrow Wilson had presided over the drafting of the peace treaty
at Versailles in 1919, changing a few European borders and proclaiming a
new philosophy he thought would avoid military viciousness in the
future. But the treaty left much of the old order intact. And in the next,
last years of royal courts and government by aristocracy, European
countries in peacetime still chose to send rich men abroad as their
ambassadors, on the assumption that those who lived in palatial style
and entertained without regard for expense at home would have the
presence and the polish and the money to do the same in foreign
capitals. Diplomats in the 1920s and 1930s were social figures and not
much more. Theirs was a generation—the last—when the titled and
wealthy and well-born actually did run their countries, and when their
ambassadors found little reason to associate with anyone not of their
class. Few in Washington were. If President Roosevelt was a New York
patrician, the vice president, John Nance Garner of Texas, was a country politician who lived in one room in a medium-priced downtown hotel
and went to bed at eight o'clock at night in his long woolen underwear.

British ambassadors in the earlier decades of the twentieth century
saw little need to visit any of the country beyond Washington, midtown
Manhattan, Newport, Southampton and Palm Beach, and no need to see
or know anyone beyond those in Washington who had power and those
in other cities who had money and social status. The Spanish embassy in
Washington never did anything much more serious than have parties and
dinners—in summer, outdoors among Moorish fountains. The ambassador of Mexico, notably rich even in this company, moved about Washing-

ton in a stately procession led by his green Mercedes limousine accompanied by footmen in velvet uniforms dyed to match his car.

World War II changed it all. The ambassador of Poland, Count Jerzy Potocki, was as rich as the others; and when his country was overrun by the Germans in 1939, he continued to operate his embassy by paying the expenses out of his own pocket. Shortly before, he had said, "We ambassadors of countries about to be invaded ought to organize a bridge club. We now have precisely enough for three tables and the fates are dusting off the chairs for a fourth." But eventually, he wearied of financing the embassy himself and, seeing little hope for his own or his country's future, bought a plantation in Peru, his wife's native country, and moved there to raise tea.

By early 1940, nearly every country maintaining an embassy on Sixteenth Street or Massachusetts Avenue, the embassy rows, was involved in the war or about to be. Some ceased to exist as independent nations, and the Germans demanded the keys to the Washington embassies of countries they had invaded and occupied. They got only one, Austria's. All others refused. The Czech ambassador, Vladimir Hurban, said, "I will not hand anything over to the Germans." Henrik Kauffmann, ambassador of Denmark, announced: "I am not prepared to take orders from the German government. I represent Denmark and the king of Denmark and nobody else." Since the U.S. Government upheld and supported the ambassadors, the Germans could do nothing.

The displaced diplomats remained in Washington, most of them having nowhere to go. The State Department maintained them on its diplomatic lists and invited them to its receptions. Some managed more successfully than others. The Dutch kept their embassy open with revenues from their colonies and supported the Luxembourg embassy as well. But the ambassador of Rumania, cut off from all income and refusing to represent the Fascist government now in power in his country, remained in Washington as a private citizen trying to sell insurance, while his wife worked as a sales clerk in a downtown department store.

Social life among the diplomats became increasingly awkward. But it continued, now described by Hope Ridings Miller in the Washington *Post* as "more serious and purposeful," though what was serious about it, or purposeful, was difficult to see. The Roosevelts had in the past held annual diplomatic receptions and entertainments, splendid evenings with the U.S. Marine Band in scarlet and gold playing in a White House filled with diplomats wearing red sashes across white shirtfronts, medals glazed with diamonds and emeralds flashing under the chandeliers and throwing little spangles of light on the walls and ceilings, military attachés from the European monarchies in court uniforms ornamented with leopard and bearskin, the Poles and the Hungarians the most gorgeous of all. But with Europe at war none of this worked any longer. Diplomats from the subjugated countries pushed and elbowed to stay on the far side of the East Room and away from the Germans and the Italians, who were still invited as a requirement of protocol since the United States was not yet at war with them. Guests gathered in hostile little groups, staring coldly at each other across the room. Some diplomats refused to speak to the Germans or the Italians and would not allow them to dance with their wives. It was all so messy and strained that the Roosevelts quietly ended their diplomatic receptions.

In 1940, after France was conquered and Paris occupied by the Germans, there arrived in Washington Gaston Henry-Haye, who proclaimed himself the new French ambassador. He represented a puppet regime set up by the Germans in the town of Vichy, which was openly cooperating with the Nazis while pretending to be a real government. At its head was Marshal Henri Pétain, an elderly and honored French general in World War I. His deputy head of state and foreign minister was Pierre Laval, a nasty little man with a sordid record of political deception and betrayal. After the war the French shot Laval, but in 1940 he was happily assisting the Nazi occupiers. It was he who had sent Henry-Haye to Washington.

On arrival, he took over the French ambassador's handsome residence on Kalorama Road, settled in, and waited for invitations to diplomatic and social functions. None arrived. Instead, he was ridiculed, snubbed, attacked in public. A group of prominent American writers paid for a newspaper advertisement denouncing him as a Nazi stooge. The FBI told the State Department that he was a devoted Nazi and that three of Hitler's agents were working out of his embassy, spreading messages of "defeatism and isolationism."

When Henry-Haye showed up at an occasional diplomatic reception uninvited, demanding the attention due an ambassador of France, he was treated with condescension and contempt. He called on the secretary of state. Cordell Hull later described him as "a little man with ruddy cheeks and a truculent moustache," who tried to deny any Nazi associations. The secretary questioned him about the rumors that Vichy planned to give its navy to Hitler for his use, saying, "It is impossible for the American people to understand why the French government would hand to Hitler a loaded gun with which to shoot at their friends."

Henry-Haye then sent Roosevelt an oily, self-pitying letter about his mission to Washington: "Allow me, Mr. President, to compare the mission with which I am entrusted by the French Republic with that which, in 1776, was confided to the great Benjamin Franklin." Then he called on Sumner Welles, the Undersecretary of State, and complained about his "cruel martyrdom."

It was bizarre. An ambassador from America's oldest ally, claiming to represent France but in fact representing the Fascist government of Pierre Laval, who looked in news pictures like a likely candidate for a rat trap. An ambassador who had turned his embassy into a base for Nazi spies. He failed to persuade the Washington political and diplomatic community that he actually was the ambassador of France, as he failed in everything he tried. He remained in the embassy, his telephones tapped, his mail opened and read, his radio circuit monitored, his agents watched. In November 1941, Vichy broke relations with Washington, and Cordell Hull sent him home—a ludicrous little man, warmly despised.

In these months before the United States entered the war, Washington's French, German and Italian diplomats had little to do. The State Department had nothing to say to them and had no interest in anything they had to say, and so they were left to pursue their own private purposes, which ranged from the corrupt and sinister to the merely lazy and self-indulgent. Their first purpose was to remain in the United States and away from the intrigues and dangers of their own countries at war, to remain in a foreign capital that, however small-townish, still had plenty of food, and where, if French and Italian wines were scarce and expensive because of trans-Atlantic shipping problems, there were acceptable wines to be had from California. Washington had well-stocked stores, interesting women, Cuban cigars, docile black servants willing to work at low pay—in all, a far more pleasant life than they could hope for in their own countries.

Then there were the expense accounts. The Berlin office of the Abwehr, the German intelligence agency, grumblingly suspected its people in Washington were cheating on their claims for expenses. They were claiming to have spent handsome sums entertaining Washington political leaders. They were claiming to have paid for information they had actually picked up free from party gossip or had imaginatively rewritten from the newspapers.

Otherwise, their only real purpose in Washington was to encourage, however they could, the America First and other isolationist groups trying to keep the United States out of the war. And so they remained—a gaggle of fascists representing rulers who deserved the gallows, enjoying life in a city where that was still possible, spying and propagandizing while swindling their own governments on the side.

The German embassy was on a block of Massachusetts Avenue where some of Washington's nineteenth-century architectural errors still survived. The embassy itself was one of them: a hideous, pigeon-stained pile of dark brownish-red brick, its stubby parapets lined with the familiar black cast-iron ornamental railings, the exterior prospect gloomy and foreboding.

In November 1938, Nazi hoodlums in Germany, in a night of orgiastic frenzy, smashed windows and looted stores owned by Jews, beating and intimidating their owners and leaving the streets strewn with broken glass—an event known thereafter as *Kristallnacht*, "Glass Night." Cordell Hull recommended that the American ambassador to Germany, Hugh R. Wilson, be ordered home for "consultation," as a mild, not to say weak, gesture of protest. Roosevelt agreed and issued a statement saying he "could scarcely believe that such things could occur in a twentieth-century civilization." Adolf Hitler then called his ambassador in Washington, Hans Dieckhoff, back to Berlin to deny Roosevelt the pleasure of ordering him out.

Dieckhoff, to his regret, then had to give up his beautiful Massachusetts Avenue residence, a mile from the embassy and built in the 1920s by one of the Vanderbilts. Shortly before he left, never to return, he called on Cordell Hull for a conversation bordering on the surreal. He complained that an American official had said in a speech that Hitler had killed more people than Charles II, king of England during the Restoration. Dieckhoff demanded an apology for this outrageous slander.

Hull said he had never thought of Charles II as a particularly notorious killer and asked, "How many people did Charles Second kill?"

Dieckhoff fidgeted, squirmed in his chair and said, "I'm afraid I don't recall." With that contribution to diplomacy, he left for Berlin.

On his departure, the German embassy fell into the hands of a *chargé d'affaires,* Hans Thomsen, an operator of some skill. He was tall, blond, handsome, of Norwegian ancestry, so polite to everyone and particularly to critics of the Nazis, they were misled into thinking Thomsen agreed with them. His wife, Bebe, cultivated Washington women by bursting into tears on carefully selected occasions and swearing she would never return to Germany while "those awful Nazis" were in power. She played this role with such high theatrical skill it encouraged her women friends to pour out gossip and information which her husband sent out each night in his reports to Berlin.

On the second floor of the embassy was the office of the military attaché, General Friedrich von Boetticher. He had been sent to Washington in 1933 when Hitler resolved to ignore the Versailles treaty's prohibition against posting German military attachés abroad. A short, plump man of porcine features, with horizontal creases across the back of his neck, his reddish hair kept in a brush cut, he was often seen strolling the streets in full uniform with riding breeches, boots, monocle, his thick chest heavily ornamented with Nazi medals and insignia. He bought bundles of domestic and foreign newspapers and magazines and burrowed through them looking for items he hoped would catch Hitler's eye. His job was to unearth and report whatever military information Berlin might regard as useful and whatever fact or fiction about American Jews and their sinister influence that Hitler himself might find titillating.

Boetticher had the perfect situation. No one in the United States saw his reports. No one had any idea what he was sending to Berlin. Hitler liked what he read. And so no one in the German government dared argue with him. He was free to invent any lie or distortion he liked. When Henry Stimson and Frank Knox, both Protestants, were appointed secretaries of war and navy, Boetticher reported that they were Jewish. Occasionally, he embellished with fanciful details a widely circulated rumor that President Roosevelt was of Jewish ancestry.

When after the war the Allies rummaged through the German files in Berlin, they found that in his years in Washington, Boetticher had filed only one report that was both accurate and clearly of great value to the Germans. In 1936 he had described an American invention that the German military took seriously while the American military should have and did not. He had reported on the work of Dr. Robert H. Goddard,

developer of the first long-range, liquid-fueled rockets. All his findings
were published in American technical journals in full detail. Boetticher
lifted it all and sent it to Berlin. Eight years later the Germans and Dr.
Wernher von Braun were using Goddard's findings to send V-1 and V-2
rockets across the Channel to explode in London. After the war, von
Braun was asked how the Germans developed their rockets and he
responded in surprise, "We got it all from *you,* from your Dr. Goddard!"

Hans Thomsen, pretending to be a diplomat carrying on in the
ambassador's absence from Washington, spent most of his time and
some of Hitler's money trying to influence American politics and public
opinion. He cabled Berlin, for example, that he had persuaded Senator
Gerald P. Nye of North Dakota, the fiery isolationist and Roosevelt-
hater, to mail out under his own name and on congressional stationery
one hundred thousand copies of a Senate speech by Nye that the
Germans thought was effective propaganda. Thomsen further claimed
to have paid for advertising in the New York *Times* urging defeat of the
Democratic party "war machine," the advertisement written by George
Viereck. And Thomsen reported to Berlin he had "financed" a group of
Republicans in Congress who inserted an antiwar plank in the party
platform at their 1940 political convention, and his cable said, "Nothing
has leaked out about the assistance we rendered in this." This last claim
and perhaps all of them were almost certainly lies. Writing a plank cost
nothing, and in 1940 it would have been impossible to keep an antiwar
plank out of the Republican platform.

In any case, whoever paid for them, antiwar advertisements and
speeches covered the country, causing venomous letters to flood the
White House in such volume that Roosevelt's advisers urged him to give
the mothers of America still another assurance that their sons would
not, ever, be sent off to fight and be killed.

He was irritated. "How many times do I have to say that? I've said it a
thousand times. It's in the Democratic platform."

But his political managers and speechwriters, including Robert
Sherwood, pushed him to say it again in a major speech he had
scheduled in Boston on October 30, 1940. They wrote out a paragraph
for him:

> And while I am talking to you mothers and fathers, I give you
> one more assurance. I have said this before, but I shall say it

again and again and again: Your boys are not going to be sent into any foreign wars.

Here was the president of the United States saying in a political campaign what he feared was not true and saying it because of public pressure generated by speeches in Congress, churches, union halls, hostile editorials and advertising; some of this pressure actually had been bought with Hitler's money, dispensed through the German embassy six blocks from the White House.

The Italians were ensconced in a splendid Renaissance embassy at Sixteenth and Fuller streets, designed for them in 1924 by the same architects who had planned New York's Grand Central Terminal. But this extravagance was not carried forward into their 1939–40 budget for Washington espionage. While Hans Thomsen was spending millions, the Italians' budget for this work was five hundred dollars a month. Their military attaché, General Adolfo Infante, discovered that the newsreels in the movie theaters on F Street often had pictures of American military exercises and war plants turning out new tanks and airplanes. Infante spent most of a month's allowance to buy a print of a newsreel with military pictures and ship it to Rome along with a letter explaining that many more were available if the Italian military found this one useful. The response was yes, the information was extremely valuable but, regrettably, the cost of buying the film and shipping it to Rome was too high. Couldn't Infante simply go downtown to Loew's Palace Theater, buy a ticket, sit in the balcony, and take notes?

Frank O. Lowden of Illinois was elected to Congress in 1906. His wife was the daughter of George M. Pullman, the sleeping car tycoon. Mrs. Pullman assumed her daughter and son-in-law would remain in Washington indefinitely and so would need a proper residence. She ordered a mansion built for them at 1125 Sixteenth Street. It was in the eighteenth-century Italian-French cupid-and-swag architectural idiom, its interior richly ornamented in gilt, marble, bronze and mahogany. But poor health forced Lowden out of Congress, and in 1913 czarist Russia bought the house for an embassy. During the years after the 1917 Bolshevik revolution, while the United States refused to recognize the Soviet Union, the building was occupied by a lone caretaker who stayed on even though the new Moscow government refused to pay him. He supported himself with a small job in the U.S. Government. When Roosevelt finally opened relations with the Soviet Union in 1933, the new Russian diplomats wanted the interior of the embassy done over in the art deco style then fashionable. They called in Eugene Schoen, of a New York architectural firm whose previous work included a theater in Rockefeller Center, the Dunhill pipe stores and the passenger liner *Leviathan*. Schoen looked at the magnificent gold-leafed walls in the grand salon and refused to touch the building. He said he would leave all of it "to the last hair of the last Cupid." And so it remained.

By 1939 it was occupied by Soviet ambassador Constantine Oumansky, perhaps the most offensive diplomat ever sent to Washington. He despised the United States, missed no opportunity to say so in the most insulting manner, and talked of almost nothing else. During his years as ambassador, the Soviet embassy became the most detested diplomatic mission in town. Invitations to Oumansky's dinners were rejected by everyone able to do so. But out of diplomatic necessity the State Department occasionally asked officers from its Russian desk to accept. One of them, a staff member named Edward Page, Jr., later recalled a perfectly miserable evening at the Soviet embassy. The ambassador spent the entire time delivering a ranting, abusive tirade about real and imaginary American indignities to his country and about the essential rottenness of American society, its political and economic system and all its people without exception. Page, the diplomat, kept silent. Guests from other embassies, who also were there because they had been ordered to come, squirmed, perspired and waited for the ordeal to end.

Cordell Hull described Oumansky after a visit to the secretary's office: one of the most difficult foreign diplomats.

>...[He was] insulting in his manner and speech, and had an
>infallible faculty for antagonizing. Overbearing, he made demands
>for concessions as if they were his natural right.... In my opinion,
>he did much to harm Russian-American relations.

Oumansky's previous career had been in police work. He had also worked in journalism, as practiced in the Soviet Union, writing in the combative, argumentative, propagandistic style the government required of its newspapers. Why his behavior in Washington was so boorish no one ever knew—his successors often were pleasant and agreeable. But Oumansky never changed. He was furious even when the Americans did him favors. In January 1941, U.S. intelligence told Oumansky it had learned Hitler was planning to attack his country in violation of their nonaggression treaty. Oumansky's response was anger at the United States, not Hitler, and he called Hans Thomsen to tell him the Americans were spreading vicious gossip and trying to undermine German-Russian friendship.

In this period Russian undercover activities in America were about as widespread as the Germans'. In 1941, Walter Krivitsky came to Washington trying, he said, to avoid being killed by Josef Stalin's gunmen. He was an ex-NKVD agent and a follower of Leon Trotsky, who had been murdered in Mexico City by a Stalin agent who split his skull with an axe. Krivitsky had defected from the Soviet Union and had written a book, *I Was Stalin's Agent,* which had been read with extreme displeasure in the Kremlin. Now he had been running and hiding for years. On the night of February 10 he tried to hide in the Bellevue Hotel, a small place near the U.S. Capitol. On the following morning he was found dead, shot through the head. The District of Columbia police examined the body and the hotel room and pronounced it a suicide. No one believed it, but nothing further was ever proved.

There were other nasty episodes. The State Department discovered two blundering Soviet military attachés, one of them Major Constantine Ovchinnikov, exploring aircraft plants and loudly demanding that the plant managers hand over plans and technical drawings. They were ordered out of the country. As soon as this got into the papers, Mrs. Willard West of suburban Chevy Chase wrote a furious letter to the State Department. Ovchinnikov, she said, had rented the top floor of her house and always kept the door locked. When he left, she found he had kept carrier pigeons in her maid's room and in the attic. "I have never seen such filth in my life," she wrote. "It was like a barnyard." But by the time her letter arrived, Germany had invaded the Soviet Union and the Russians suddenly were potential allies against the Nazis. Ovchinnikov and his colleague were pardoned while they were still in San Francisco awaiting a ship to take them home. They both returned to the Washington embassy. As for Mrs. West's complaint about the pigeon droppings, a

State Department memo from Edward Page said, "It seems rather suspicious that a military attaché should keep carrier pigeons. But perhaps it is a hobby."

The British, in their upper Massachusetts Avenue embassy styled after an English country mansion, had Franklin D. Roosevelt himself as their first advocate in the United States, and so had less need to turn their embassy into a spy center. What spying they did in America was aimed largely at the Germans, Japanese and Italians still in Washington before the United States entered the war in December 1941, and at secret Nazi agents, who remained during the war. This work was not handled through the embassy but from an office in Rockefeller Center in New York City and called by a cover name, BSC, British Security Coordination. Its director was Sir William Samuel Stephenson, a famous flying ace in World War I, a pioneer in electronics and an intelligence officer most of his life. His code name was "Intrepid."

He recruited his agents skillfully. One he brought into BSC was a beautiful young American woman named Amy Thorpe, who had been a Washington debutante in the 1929 season. Her father was a marine corps colonel and her mother, Cora, was nearly consumed by the flames of social ambition, both for herself and for her strikingly beautiful daughter. She pushed and shoved Amy into any and every situation likely to improve their social status, down to picnics in Rock Creek Park for the city's embassy attachés. Attachés got little attention in the mainstream of social life, being regarded as mere functionaries. But as peripheral as they were, they were part of diplomatic society; and Mrs. Thorpe believed the prospects and possibilities were worth the effort.

Amy's beauty and manner made her a great success at the picnics. One admirer she attracted was a junior naval officer in the Italian Embassy named Alberto Lais, who called her his "golden girl." Another was Arthur J. Pack, an attaché at the British embassy, an outwardly dull man, but with enough energy and spirit to get Amy pregnant. In those years, pregnancy required marriage, nothing less. Near hysteria, Pack demanded a wedding at the earliest hour, fearing a baby born too soon after a marriage would be embarrassing and damaging to his career. Amy's mother was even more insistent.

Amy and Pack were married in 1936 at the Church of the Epiphany. But even after the wedding Pack was fearful that somebody in the British

Foreign Office would count the months and discover his guilt, and so he insisted that she ride horseback in Rock Creek Park, over jumps where possible, in the hope of inducing a miscarriage. The effort failed. The baby was born five months after the wedding.

Amy was bored with Pack from the first hour of the marriage, but she went with him when the Foreign Office posted him to its embassy in Poland. There she found Pack as flaccid and dull as she had found him in Washington. He was away a great deal, sick a great deal. Eventually she learned that he was involved with another woman. He no longer mattered in her life. During this period the attractions of Amy's green eyes, her auburn hair, her wit and liveliness aroused a sexual frenzy in some of the highest officers in the Polish Foreign Service, including the personal aide to the foreign minister, Josef Beck. She enthralled them all.

By the winter of 1937, Stephenson's BSC was aware of Mrs. Pack's activities in Warsaw. It also was aware of and in pursuit of the Enigma coding machine, a piece of hardware first developed commercially in Germany for recording secret business records and figures. But it had since been improved and refined to send and receive secret messages in codes the Germans were totally confident could not be broken by even the cleverest cryptographer, unless he had his own Enigma machine. The British were determined to possess one. It was for this job that Stephenson asked Mrs. Pack to work for British intelligence. Polish mathematicians and engineers had worked on Enigma, and the Warsaw government might be persuaded to supply drawings and mechanical details, perhaps even information about where a machine could be found, stolen and flown to London. And who in Warsaw other than Mrs. Pack had such genuinely intimate access to high levels of the Polish government?

Stephenson appealed to her sense of patriotism and taste for adventure. He never overtly suggested that she use her bedroom skills to gather information from the Poles, quietly leaving her to make that decision herself. She agreed to work for BSC, and with her enthusiasm and skill she persuaded the Poles to give her the drawings, documents and other information that helped the British to steal a machine and then to figure out how to use it. This would be known to the Allies—the tiny handful allowed to know of it—as ULTRA, the greatest secret and most spectacular intelligence achievement of the war. All the way to the German surrender, it allowed the British to read Hitler's most secret messages, and to read orders he sent out to the Nazi generals even before the generals read them.

After Amy's success with ULTRA, the Foreign Office sent Arthur Pack to South America, mainly to get him out of the way of his wife's work. And by the time Poland was attacked in 1939, Stephenson had moved Mrs. Pack to Washington, where he had further plans for her. He gave her the code name "Cynthia" and set her up in a house in Georgetown at 3327 O Street.

Alberto Lais, the Italian naval officer whom Amy had first met at a diplomatic picnic several years before, was now an admiral and the naval attaché at the Italian embassy on Sixteenth Street. Rome had sent him to Washington in 1940 to arrange the sabotage of twenty-seven Italian merchant ships lying idle in American ports, unable to return to Italy because of the British blockade. Mussolini—convinced that America would soon join the war and seize the Italian ships—ordered Lais to Washington to keep the ships from the Americans by blowing them up at their docks. Lais's credentials were impeccable. He was a handsome figure, sixty years old, with a clipped moustache, an American wife and perfect English. Formerly the head of Italian naval intelligence, he was experienced in organizing undercover schemes.

Lais was busy in his office one afternoon when his telephone rang. A woman's soft voice said, "Alberto, it's your golden girl. Can we meet?"

Lais tried to resist. "No. I'm afraid that is impossible. We are enemies now. At least, my country is an enemy of yours. Maybe it will be possible when peace comes, but not now."

Despite his pious refusal, Amy knew he would call back. No man had resisted her yet. In a few days he telephoned and agreed to come to her house. It was impossible, he said, to meet at his house or at the embassy or even at a hotel. The risk of discovery was too great. He arrived in civilian clothes and after the briefest of preliminaries she had him in bed, telling her in whispered intimacy how he had arranged for the merchant ships to be sabotaged. Bombs had been planted aboard with their fuses in place, and when the bombs went off the ships would be so heavily damaged that if the Americans seized them they would be useless. She pretended a concern that he was staying too long, said she would feel guilty if his visit caused him trouble, and politely suggested he should leave. The instant she closed the door behind him she telephoned the Office of Naval Intelligence with all the details, including precisely where to find the bombs. It was too late. Most of the twenty-seven ships, plus some others blown up by the Germans in an attack coordinated with the Italians, went up in flames that night. But a few were saved and the Americans, as Mussolini had feared, seized them.

When Lais's hand in the explosions became known, Cordell Hull ordered him out of the country. But before he left, Lais arranged for Amy to have the Italian navy's code books. The British used them to plan a carrier-based air attack on the Italian navy base at Taranto in the Ionian Sea, where they sank three battleships with airborne torpedoes.

(Navy Secretary Knox studied the Taranto attack with great interest and wrote to War Secretary Stimson, suggesting that "precautionary measures be taken immediately to protect Pearl Harbor against surprise attack in the event of war between the United States and Japan." Neither Knox nor anyone else in the U.S. Government knew that Admiral Yamamoto, commander of the Japanese navy, had also been impressed by the British success at Taranto, so much so that he was encouraged to go on with plans for airborne torpedo attacks on Pearl Harbor. Nor did Knox know that his warning would be ignored.)

Finally, Cynthia was asked to penetrate the Vichy French embassy of Henry-Haye. There, employing her familiar methods, she arranged to have the French navy's code books passed out a window of the embassy in the middle of the night to FBI agents waiting outside, who copied and returned them within an hour, wiped clean of fingerprints. Knowledge of the French codes later was credited with saving Allied lives in the landings in North Africa.

In all, even though never well known to the public, Cynthia's career in espionage was among the most brilliant of the war, perhaps of any war. Her career ended when she married Captain Charles Brousse, the French embassy's press attaché, who had helped her steal the code books. When peace came they moved to the south of France and lived there until she died in 1963, a genuine heroine never sufficiently honored.

In the last months before the United States entered the war, the hardest and most important diplomatic mission fell to the British ambassador. His task was to solicit, as openly as he dared, American help in the war—help with money and arms and with American troops if possible. As early as the spring of 1940, Churchill's government saw it could not forever stand against Hitler alone, and it could only turn to Washington for help. There was nowhere else to turn.

It was not easy. A 1939 Elmo Roper poll found 67 percent of Americans saying the U.S. should remain neutral. Only 12 percent were willing even to aid the Allies while staying out of the war. Those eager to declare war and join the fight: 2 percent. Not only was there the intensity of American isolationism. There was the person of London's ambassador, Sir Ronald Lindsay. He was an old-school-tie product of the British Foreign Office, with manners fit for the days of dominance. He was six feet nine inches tall and had the bulging eyes, walrus moustache and austere arrogance of the English clubman. He had little interest in anyone in Washington: a boring and provincial town, he thought. He associated with almost no one but the socialites of New York, Newport and Palm Beach. He infuriated the Washington establishment during the visit of Britain's king and queen in the spring of 1939 — a visit the British arranged in the hope of improving their relations with America, believing, correctly, that while Americans wanted no royalty of their own, they would fawn on Britain's. But when Lindsay gave an embassy reception for the king, so many invitations went to his friends among the out-of-town socialites that most Washington political figures were ignored. The ambassador's wife gave the newspapers an icy, tight-lipped explanation: "I cannot be concerned about the nine hundred thousand people who think they should be invited. I have to draw the line somewhere."

She drew her line at nine hundred, and it took urgent appeals from the State Department to get a few invitations for members of the Senate. Her behavior was not only arrogant but stupid. Whatever Britain might need from the United States could be had only with the approval of Congress. Not a great many tanks or fighter planes were likely to come from their socialite friends in New York and Palm Beach. Lindsay's performance as ambassador was so obviously doing more harm than good that the Foreign Office, though unaccustomed to considering the views of aliens and colonials, replaced him.

The new envoy at first seemed little better. He was Philip Kerr, Marquess of Lothian, Lord Newbattle, Baron LongNewton and Dolphinston, Viscount Brien, Baron Kerr of Newbattle, and was normally addressed as Lord Lothian. Along with his chain of titles, he brought with him a reputation as an appeaser, as a Neville Chamberlain ally, and as a former member of Britain's Cliveden set, a group of vaguely fascist apologists for Hitler, led by his close friend and fellow Christian Scientist Nancy Astor.

Early reactions were hostile. The Hearst press savagely caricatured him and all his titles. Other newspapers said that England, having bungled its way into war through its policies of appeasement, now sent an agent of its failed policy here to trick the United States into bailing it out, to save itself from its own folly by exploiting Americans. A book by Quincy Howe published several years earlier, *England Expects Every American to Do His Duty,* increased its sales. When the new ambassador visited the Midwest, he was greeted with banners reading "Let the Cliveden set fight the war."

But Lothian rallied and surprised his critics. He tried, as his predecessor had not, to understand the Americans and their attitudes. When he called on Roosevelt to present his credentials as ambassador, he avoided the convention of top hat, cutaway coat and striped trousers and instead wore a shapeless business suit that looked more Salvation Army thrift store than Savile Row, clothes so rumpled and ill-fitting they did not appear to be his own. After the visit, he stopped to talk to the press outside the White House; and as he chatted, somebody's black cat appeared and rubbed itself against his trouser leg. He picked up the cat and placed it on his shoulder, making an engaging picture for the newspapers. Americans found this an improvement over the starchy, irritating Lindsay. Journalist William Allen White remarked that Lothian looked like "a professor at a teachers college . . . apparently fighting a middle-age tendency to be heavy-set and not succeeding."

Lothian encouraged all this by ridiculing the imperial hauteur of the British embassy, showing visitors the oil portraits of King George III and calling him "one of the founders of the American republic." He eliminated the red-coated, bearskin-hatted, black-booted guardsmen from the embassy entrance. Shortly after his arrival, *Time* announced, "The chill is off."

Lothian had used the American taste for informality and the unstuffed shirt to win some points with public and press, but as he passed sunny mornings on his Georgian portico looking out over the embassy's acres of immaculate English gardens, he knew his problems were still severe. Neville Chamberlain encouraged him not to push the Americans too far, since in Chamberlain's view, "It is always best and safest to count on nothing from the Americans but words."

But when Winston Churchill became prime minister on May 11, 1940, he sent new instructions: Do nothing to discourage Americans from speculating that if Britain fell, its fleet would fall into the hands of the Germans. That would give Hitler dominance in the Atlantic, which the Americans saw as their prime protection from Europe's war. Said Churchill, "We have no intention of relieving the United States of any well-founded anxieties on this point."

Yet even after Hitler had overrun Poland, Denmark, Norway, the Low Countries and France, Lothian had to move carefully. If he exaggerated the danger, the response among isolationist Americans might be that since Britain was going to lose the war anyway, why pour men and money into its lost cause? If he understated the danger, he would hear it said that the British could take care of it themselves.

Throughout 1940, he worked every day in support of Roosevelt's destroyers-for-bases deal, the first of the president's clever and arguably illegal tricks to evade the neutrality laws and to help the British, even while the country and the Congress were rigidly and loudly opposed. He got away with it with only a few bruises, but even when Britain had been in the war for almost a year, Congress continued to demand that any further aid must be "cash-and-carry," Britain paying in full and hauling the goods home in its own ships. This went on until Churchill found his money running out. "We shall go on paying dollars as long as we can," he wrote Roosevelt, "but I should like to feel sure that when we can pay no more, you will give us the stuff all the same."

On December 3, 1940, Roosevelt summoned the navy's cruiser *Tuscaloosa* to take him on a ten-day cruise through the Caribbean, alone but for a few staff members and Hopkins. In these quiet days at sea, Hopkins saw him lounging on the deck, withdrawn and silent, staring outward. His thoughts, it was later learned, were of how to help Britain and how to persuade Congress and the American people to agree. He settled on a plain-sounding but deceptive phrase he thought would go down well in a country still isolationist but possessed of a strong sense of fairness and decency. He settled on the term "lend-lease."

Lord Lothian worked secretly with Roosevelt and Churchill to develop a plan for lending and leasing war supplies to Britain, based on the fiction that they could be returned after having been used and somehow paid for at some unstated time in the future. But Lothian by now had worked himself into exhaustion. He fell ill on December 7, 1940, the day after a letter came from Churchill offering suggestions on how a lend-lease program could be explained and sold to Congress. Sick and weak, Lothian continued to work on a speech to the American Farm Bureau Federation. On December 12, he died, without seeing the lend-lease deal completed. An autopsy, required by law since as a Christian Scientist he had had no physician attending him, showed that he died of uremic poisoning. His death was listed on the District of Columbia police blotter as "Philip Kerr, 3100 Massachusetts Avenue." His successor as ambassador commented on Lothian's death in a diary: "Another victim of Christian Science."

Lothian's last speech, delivered by a deputy shortly before he died, said:

> I have endeavored to give you some idea of our present positions and dangers, the problems of 1941 and our hopes for the future and what support you will give us in realizing them. We are, I believe, doing all we can. Since May, there is no challenge we have evaded, no challenge we have refused. If you back us, you won't be backing a quitter. The issue now depends largely on what you decide to do. Nobody can share that responsibility with you. It is the great strength of every democracy that it brings responsibility down squarely on every citizen and every nation. And before the judgment seat of God, each must answer for his own actions.

He was buried in Arlington National Cemetery.

Even before Lord Lothian's funeral, speculation was rampant about the identity of the new ambassador. Many Washington socialites hoped for the Duke of Windsor. Older politicians hoped for Lloyd George. Almost no one was pleased at first with the man they got: Lord Halifax, a protégé of Chamberlain widely branded as an appeaser. On January 24, 1941, President Roosevelt, in a gesture of support for the British, traveled to Chesapeake Bay (a few reporters in tow) to greet Halifax as he was secretly put ashore from H.M.S. *George V.* But even the president must have wondered about the new ambassador's judgment over the next few weeks—particularly when Halifax went fox-hunting in Virginia, reviving images of the aloof and imperious Lindsays. He began to collect derisive labels: "Lord Holy Fox," "the praying mantis with an umbrella."

Beneath the Eton-Oxford exterior, however, was a hard, shrewd, energetic diplomat who turned his embassy into a fountainhead of propaganda for England. By mid-1941 there were over three thousand British businessmen, military officers, and Foreign Office officials working in Washington to promote their country's cause. At one point, Halifax had a truck that had been dented by German bombs shipped over from London, placed signs on it saying "Buy British," and sent it off around the city. The British in Washington were a stiff-lipped, close-knit group who talked little about themselves but constantly about their country's needs. They had the satisfaction of watching, and helping to create, a shift in American opinion that ultimately left the isolationists and Anglophobes a powerless minority and turned England into America's most revered ally.

A great deal of Roosevelt's almost magical talent for persuading and manipulating the American people lay in his ability to state his thoughts in simple, homely phrases, in the language of the working neighborhood where visitors sat in the kitchen, with puppies frolicking under the stove, husbands wearing working clothes and wives their one-dollar cotton housedresses. Seldom in his whole career did Roosevelt offer a poetic allusion or a stately or monumental phrase. More commonly, his public speech was rambling, wordy and even ungrammatical, not far above the level of informal discussion at the kitchen table. But it was effective. While he was not by any definition the common man, he certainly knew how to talk like him. When he spoke to the American people by radio, he called it not a speech or an address but a "fireside chat," even though he broadcast not from a fireside but from a small White House radio studio cluttered with wires and microphones and network technicians in coveralls carrying pliers and screwdrivers.

His skills at informal speech were displayed at their best on December 17, 1940, when at his press conference he thrust the United States deeply into the European war with his first public word on lend-lease. A formulation he had planned meticulously was offered as if he were thinking it up as he went along, with pauses, the appearance of groping for words, a little calculated stumbling. "Well, let me give you an illustration. Suppose my neighbor's house catches on fire, and I have a length of garden hose four or five hundred feet away. If he can take my garden hose and connect it up with his hydrant, I may help him to put out his fire. Now what do I do? I don't say to him before that operation, 'Neighbor, my garden hose cost me fifteen dollars. You have to pay me fifteen dollars for it.' What is the transaction that goes on? I don't want fifteen dollars. I want my hose back after the fire is over. All right. If it goes through the fire all right, intact, without any damage to it, he gives it back to me and thanks me very much for the use of it."

That was how he told the American people of his decision that aid to Britain should no longer be cash-and-carry but should be lent or leased, that the U.S. should take over the role of arms supplier, inject itself into the war against Hitler, drop all pretense of neutrality, take the risk that Hitler would see this as a declaration of war. It was his way of selling a program that, however necessary and desirable, was totally fraudulent as he described it. But it worked, even though Senator Taft, his voice sounding like chalk on a dry blackboard, replied immediately: "Lending arms is like lending chewing gum. You don't want it back."

As for chewing gum, no doubt Taft was right, even though he later voted for lend-lease. As for weapons, his wisecrack was irrelevant, since it was clearly understood by both Roosevelt and Churchill that what was lent would never be returned and what was leased would never be paid for. Roosevelt had done slyly what he was not able to do openly— decided that a German defeat and occupation of Britain would be an historic disaster for both the British and the Americans, that it could not be allowed to happen, and to prevent it the United States had to help the British survive. Roosevelt had decided to push the United States— sideways—into the war.

III

Bureaucracies at War

Leon Henderson was an economist who could not control his weight, his shirttail, his hair, his shoelaces or his temper. When he lost a bridge game, he threw the cards across the room and slammed his fist through the table. He got into fights with taxi drivers and truck drivers. On hot days, he sat behind his desk wearing shorts and nothing else, his two hundred pounds bulging and sweating. His daily habit was to find the tenderest toes in Washington and step on them.

But even those he infuriated would, with some encouragement, admit that he was brilliant—a little crazy, yes, but brilliant. And perhaps that was why, in 1940, with the war in Europe going badly, he was one of the few true New Dealers still involved in the frantic, desperate, often clumsy effort to transform the United States government from a collection of half-formed bureaucracies accustomed largely to handing money out to states, cities, farmers or the unemployed into an efficient instrument capable of managing a wartime economy that, well before Pearl Harbor, most of the world knew would make the difference between victory or defeat for the Allies.

In the summer of 1940, Henderson was working for one of the predecessors of the Office of Price Administration, trying to bring some order into the use of raw materials in a country still making toasters and automobiles but also expanding rapidly into the building of military hardware. Shortages and black markets were already beginning to appear. Prices were rising too fast even for an economy still struggling to recover from depression. Something had to be done.

Henderson arranged for an appointment with the president to discuss these weighty matters. He arrived at the White House with a younger colleague: David Ginsburg, a twenty-eight-year-old lawyer who, in contrast to Henderson's look of a walking rummage sale, was neatly and immaculately dressed. They walked into the Oval Office carrying notebooks crammed with proposals for economic action, neatly typed in dense, single-spaced elite type. The stacks of paper were huge and intimidating, interlarded with grainy charts and graphs; intersecting lines, traced with wooden styluses on stencils and then mimeographed, rose and fell in chaotic patterns.

Roosevelt glanced briefly at the papers they were carrying and paid no attention to them whatsoever. Instead, he pushed himself back from his desk and pulled out papers of his own—rolls of architectural drawings. These, he told Henderson and Ginsburg, were sketches for temporary office buildings that, to his regret, had to be built along the Mall for the defense agencies now growing so fast that Washington had no room for them. He had written orders that these buildings, soon to be known as "tempos," must be of such flimsy construction that they "will be guaranteed to last less than ten years." He knew that shabby and hideous buildings that were called temporary had a way of staying around. Some erected for World War I still stood now, more than twenty years later, because there was always some reason, real or contrived, for temporary buildings to become permanent—the real reason being that it simply was not in the nature of governments to shrink. And Roosevelt was determined that would not happen this time.

"These," he said to Henderson and Ginsburg, "are the buildings they want me to approve along the Mall. Tell me what you think of them."

Dutifully, they laid aside their own papers and studied the drawings, knowing little of how to read blueprints but feigning some interest. Roosevelt wondered if they should be two stories high or three? How about this entrance door? Should it be here—he pointed with his cigarette holder, spilling ashes—or should it be moved over there?

Yes, they agreed. The door should be moved, and the buildings should be so ugly no one could possibly want to keep them standing and so flimsy that if they were not torn down in a few years they would fall down. For an hour, Roosevelt rigorously held them to a discussion of this and nothing else, while Henderson scratched and squirmed and watched the time allotted for their appointment run out. When he and Ginsburg left, their papers were untouched, their proposals unheard, their questions unanswered.

That was Roosevelt's way of operating. He did not want to discuss copper allocations, he did not want to discuss the price of steel. These questions bored him. He did not feel qualified to answer them, and if they came to be critical, he would find someone else to deal with them. But issues like Henderson's kept coming to his desk because while he enjoyed piddling with blueprints for tempos, he otherwise wanted to make only the great, historic decisions, yet was always reluctant to delegate power to those who could relieve him of tedious details. And so issues remained unsettled until they became more troublesome, more expensive, and finally had to be dealt with, usually hurriedly. This weakness would in time be costly to Roosevelt and to the country, and the cost would be counted in the coin of delay, confusion and waste. The United States eventually was prepared for war, but at far greater cost than if presidential leadership had been more exacting and if administrative power had been delegated quickly and firmly.

In the end, the preparations for war succeeded only because the country had manpower, skills, resources and industrial capacity enormous enough to succeed in spite of itself. And because a nation coming out of ten years of deep depression had a great pool of men and women who had been unemployed for so long that they were hungry for jobs and eager to work anywhere, anytime, doing anything. And because the government applied to the civilian economy the old philosophy of the U.S. Army—if enough men and weapons are poured into a confused battle situation, an enemy can be overwhelmed rather than defeated; and if masses of manpower and equipment are sent in, the probability is that sooner or later, by the grace of God, somebody will do something right.

But by the spring of 1940, almost no one had done anything right. Some, like Leon Henderson, had tried, but generally with little success. Congress, mired in its strange mixture of timidity and arrogance, had so intimidated Roosevelt that he was reluctant to move more than a few millimeters ahead of public opinion, his reluctance reinforced by a powerful segment of the American press so consumed by its hatred of him it could find no ink black enough or adjectives vicious enough for its tirade of abuse and invective.

Congress and the press had been able to intimidate and discourage Roosevelt because he had been through several bad years. After his enormous landslide of 1936, almost nothing had gone right for him. In 1937 he had sought to enlarge the Supreme Court and give it a liberal majority more likely to support his New Deal programs. The old Court had knocked those programs down, one after another. But his attempt to expand the Court was a fiasco. Congress and the public and the press saw the Supreme Court as one of the majestic pillars of American government, not to be tampered with, and they objected angrily to "Court-packing," as it came to be called, and defeated it. Further, in the fall of 1937 the economy, after making what had seemed to be modest progress from the depths of the Depression, fell backward into another severe recession. Unemployment, already high, rose again. The stock market crashed again. Production declined again. And then the 1938 elections brought a new group of conservatives to a Congress that was now even less willing to approve anything Roosevelt asked.

But despite Roosevelt's political difficulties, despite the persistence and increasing loudness of the isolationists, despite the government's slowness to act and its uncertainty about what to do when it did, despite all this, the American economy was converting to war production with remarkable speed. Demand from abroad (from the British and, later, the Russians) for war matériel and for the consumer goods the belligerent nations could no longer make brought factories that had been running at half-speed for a decade back to full production. Workers who had spent years unemployed or underemployed found their services in demand again. And so, as Leon Henderson and others tried constantly to remind

the president, the economic problems of recession—stagnation, unemployment, deflation—were replaced by the more welcome but still dangerous problems of a boom.

Washington responded in the only way it knew—by improvising.
Business leaders informed the president that, even at full production,
existing factories would not be sufficient to build all the weapons the
Allies (and the American military) were demanding. New plants would
have to be built, and private industry was not willing to build them. No
corporation, they said, could afford to construct new armaments factories at its own expense. What would happen when the war ended and the
demand for weapons ceased? Roosevelt responded by creating the Defense
Plants Corporation, which spent over five billion dollars erecting new
factories, mills and shipyards, then leased the new plants to private
industry. (After the war, demand for the products of these plants did not
decline. And the government sold them, at bargain prices, to the private
industries that were operating them—a remarkable windfall that defenders
of "free enterprise" seldom acknowledged.)

The Defense Plants Corporation solved only a small part of the
government's difficulties. Washington wanted private industry to convert
more quickly to war production—to stop making waffle irons and start
making weapons. But the economic recovery of 1940 was suddenly
increasing demand for waffle irons, and industrialists were reluctant to
stop making them. Factories trying to buy steel and other raw materials
to make rifles and tanks and airplanes were competing for those raw
materials with factories that were continuing to make consumer gadgets.
The government's critical task, therefore, was to control the allocation
of raw materials—to make sure war production would get what it needed
and that civilian production would shrink down to producing only what
was necessary. Everyone knew that the government had to act. But,
except briefly during World War I, the government had never done
anything like this before. So few agreed on what to do.

The first group to try to step into the vacuum was the military. In
another country or in another time, that might seem natural. What other
arm of government could compete with its size and experience? Who
else should know better what was necessary in preparing for war? But
the American military entered the 1940s as weak and divided as most of
the rest of the government, and its efforts to seize control of war
preparations were never entirely successful. The army and navy were

only slowly recovering from the effects of years of neglect and even indifference from the White House and Congress. They were only just beginning to order substantial amounts of new weapons, for the first time since 1918, in the meantime trying to make do with ancient and obsolete equipment. And, beginning in 1940, they were absorbing thousands of new draftees without much idea yet what to do with them. They were in a state of unreadiness that at times seemed hilarious but that actually was pathetic.

In the spring of 1941, a supply sergeant in the army's 120th Infantry lay on his bunk at Fort Jackson, South Carolina, smoking Old Golds and listening to radio station WIS in nearby Columbia playing Benny Goodman records and commercials for Carter's Little Liver Pills (" . . . starts the flow of our most vital digestive juice. When this juice flows at the rate of two pints a day, most folks feel like happy days are here again"). His Philco radio sat crookedly on a pile of worn and stained olive drab blankets that had been made for the army in 1917 and, after surviving that war, stacked in a leaky canvas supply tent awaiting service in another. Some had come down the years from the 1918 Armistice still stained with blood, God knew whose. Stacked on shelves above the blankets were a dozen ancient objects made of black painted tin, brass and glass, and not even the oldest officer in the regiment had any idea what they were. They appeared to be some sort of lanterns or signaling devices left from some earlier war. Each was stamped on the bottom, "Mfg USA 1863."

They, and an accumulation of other ancient military equipment, were charged to the supply records and had to be stored and hauled around every time the company moved, loaded into trucks and unloaded again, because there was no way to get rid of them. Every article of junk was charged to the company commander personally; and if anything was discarded as useless, he could be forced to pay the army for it, in cash. The officers thought there must be some prescribed procedure for disposing of obsolete military goods, but no one knew what it was. Inquiries to division headquarters went unanswered; presumably an army kept on starvation budgets since 1918 clung to its ancient junk because it had nothing else, and the procedure for disposing of it had simply faded away from disuse.

Captain Joseph E. Cheek, Company I's commander, recalled that in the early thirties his infantry company on maneuvers had seen one of its pack mules stumble and fall down a hillside into a river and disappear in the current. While he regretted the loss of the mule, he was delighted to clear up his supply records by filing a report claiming that the load swept away in the river had included every piece of the company's equipment lost or stolen since 1918. If anyone had checked the report, they would have discovered that one spindly mule was carrying three tons. Cheek would have liked to use this method again in 1941 but, regrettably, he no longer had pack mules.

First Sergeant Ira Kelly pushed into the supply sergeant's tent and said, "Get off your ass. The president's coming."

"What president?"

"The president of the United States. Franklin D. Roosevelt. Ever hear of him?"

"What's he coming here for?"

"How the hell do I know? All I know is the captain wants the company street cleaned up. Get a detail and get it done."

The president had begun a series of visits to army and navy bases around the country to draw the public's attention to the military's expansion, to get out of Washington occasionally, and—his stated purpose—to see the troops and show them his support. One day he came to Fort Jackson in a black convertible with the top down, wearing his felt hat, cigarette holder tilted upward, smiling and waving as he rode quickly around the fort's few paved roads. The soldiers should have saluted, but most of them had never seen a president before and were busy with their Kodak box cameras.

Roosevelt never stopped to examine his army. Had he paused for a closer scrutiny he would have seen some unsettling sights. He would have spotted a U.S. Army tank of truly horrendous design—it had no periscope and the soldier driving and steering it could see nothing in any direction. Whenever the tank was moved, its commander had to sit in the open hatch on top, exposed from the waist up to enemy fire, resting his feet on the driver's shoulders. To guide the tank in battle the officer had to kick the driver on the left shoulder for a left turn and on the right shoulder for a right turn. In battle, an officer so exposed might, if he was lucky, survive for a minute or two. And even though it lacked all the essential features, the army's tank did boast—no one knew for what purpose—a siren.

When George Patton arrived at Fort Benning, Georgia, as a brigade commander in the 2nd Armored Division, he found most of his 325 tanks in disrepair and in need of nuts and bolts simply to hold them together. When ordered, the nuts and bolts never arrived, probably because the army did not have them. So he bought them from Sears, Roebuck, & Co. Sears delivered, and Patton was never reimbursed.

Had Roosevelt stopped to look closely, he would have seen that the army not only still had horse cavalry but had just ordered twenty thousand more horses. A cavalry commander at a post in Texas said he had just been given a thousand new men who had never seen a horse and a thousand horses who had never seen a man, and he was trying to make a combat unit out of them. He was not troubled by the recent news that Poland's cavalry, the best in Europe, had been destroyed by Hitler's tanks in about a week.

Still, General John Knowles Herr, chief of cavalry, sat before a congressional committee in 1941 and said with great confidence that four mounted cavalrymen, spaced one hundred yards apart, could charge half a mile across an open field and destroy an enemy machine gun nest without injury to themselves. His testimony suggested that not only was a good deal of the military's equipment obsolete but so were many of its officers. But the army loved its horses and wanted to keep them. Whatever their value in battle, the horses were always available for the officers' Sunday afternoon polo games. One of the army manuals issued to officers in the 1930s was a guide to the care and feeding of polo ponies. And horses were believed to be essential for parades. An officer in dress uniform with medals, his guidons flapping smartly in the breeze, looked far handsomer proceeding down Pennsylvania Avenue on a horse than if he were riding in a tank. In a tank he looked like a construction worker on his way to excavate a basement.

Roosevelt, had he looked, would have seen army divisions on maneuvers in the Southern pine woods, sleeping on the ground, begging for ammunition for their rifles to protect themselves against rattlesnakes, and being refused. Much of the ammunition was left over from 1918, made for Springfield bolt-action rifles manufactured in 1910 and still in use. As Sergeant Kelly put it, "Firing a round that old in a rifle that old might hurt you more than it hurt the snake."

Between the wars, the army had diminished to little more than a social club for officers commanding the two hundred thousand enlisted men, most of whom had signed up to escape civilian unemployment. The fault lay partly in Congress's refusal to vote money in peacetime and partly in the attitudes of the army itself. A businessman who served as a reserve officer between the wars wrote: "In general, I found the individual officers more concerned with their personal ambitions, their personal aggrandizement, than with the success of the Army's mission. I found a good deal of arrogance, of intolerance and contempt for views other than those held by the all-powerful General Staff."

In 1938, General Albert Wedemeyer returned to the United States after spending two years as an exchange trainee at the German War College, the *Kriegsakademie* in Berlin. This was a tradition among most of the world's larger armies, a professional courtesy between nations that was honored until the war started. He reported to the chief of staff on what he had seen of the tremendous and aggressive growth of the military in Germany. No one was interested. "They seemed busy with the details of their offices. They didn't seem to grasp what I was trying to bring out." What little interest they displayed was in the privileges and perquisites enjoyed by German officers. What ranks got limousines? Were their officers' clubs better than ours? What about the social lives of Goering and the others? When he told them the Germans were building a huge, deadly, war machine, the high ranks thought he was exaggerating. There were even private suggestions that because he had a German name, he was too easily impressed. No one listened.

Under a similar exchange program in Japan, Captain Maxwell D. Taylor trained with an artillery regiment. He bought Japanese military manuals sold in shops near the training camps and kept them. When the war began, these were the only Japanese military guides the U.S. Army had.

General George C. Marshall, soon to command the largest military operations in history, said later, "During this period I commanded a post [Fort Leavenworth, Kansas] which had for its garrison a battalion of infantry [normally about five hundred men] . . . but a battalion only in name, for it could muster barely two hundred men when every available man, including cooks, clerks and kitchen police were present for what little training could be accomplished." Thus the future commander of over seven million men and women spent the prewar years aimlessly maneuvering two hundred soldiers, cooks and potato peelers about a dusty parade ground in Kansas.

On the military posts surrounding Washington and on many others, the unwritten but well-understood rule was for officers to leave West Point or Annapolis and immediately pursue one of the principal requirements for a successful career in the professional military: marrying money. Money was essential for the kind of entertaining that led to promotion. It was essential for the proper houses and grounds for lawn parties, the white gloves and silver tea services, the well-tailored uniforms, the well-dressed wife able to play her role and defer charmingly to the higher ranks, the Irish setter romping handsomely on the lawn, and the other elements of military success—facility with a bridge hand, a golf club, the fox trot at the officers club and the side-by-side double-barreled shotgun, preferably a Purdey, for bird-hunting. Promotions were so slow for younger officers that whenever one finally rose in rank, a celebration was called for, usually a small party with a bar and buffet and snacks in a chafing dish. Gradually, Woodward and Lothrop and Washington's other department stores announced that chafing dishes, once bought, could not be returned; too many young officers were having their promotion parties, using the chafing dishes and then taking them back.

In a budget hearing in Congress, a senator asked a general why the army needed money for enlisted men to do household chores for the officers.

"Sir," came the reply, "would you like to see a general in the United States Army out pushing his own lawn mower?"

"Well, I am a senator of the United States and I push my own lawn mower."

Symbolic of the 1940 army were its offices in a creaky wooden structure on Constitution Avenue called the Munitions Building, one of the temporary buildings erected during World War I but still standing and now crumbling and sagging. The ceilings were water-stained. When an officer walked down a corridor, his footsteps rattled the bottles in the Coca-Cola cooler. But somehow the building seemed appropriate to the army's civilian leadership. The secretary of war, Harry Woodring, had been named by Roosevelt in 1936, an appointment they both agreed was temporary, since Woodring's qualifications for the job were not readily visible. He came from Elk City, Kansas, where, after a one-year course in business and commerce, he had gone into banking, and eventually served a term as governor of Kansas. He brought a fierce Midwestern isolationism to Washington. After the war began in Europe in 1939, Woodring was so obstinate in opposing any and all aid to Britain that Roosevelt began ignoring him and turning to the State and Treasury departments instead.

But Woodring did display one talent—the ability to hang on. Roosevelt kept saying, "Harry is a nice fellow, but . . . " and, typically, refusing to replace him. Instead, also typically, he appointed an assistant secretary of war named Louis Johnson, an energetic and politically shrewd Washington lawyer who would, Roosevelt hoped, compensate for Woodring's failures. Johnson, of course, quickly came to covet Woodring's job. A good deal of his time and energy went into leaking reports to the press that Woodring had been found incompetent and was about to resign, each report followed routinely by Woodring's denial. This went on and on while Roosevelt did nothing to resolve it, and while the army awaited World War II barely equipped and trained to march tamely down Main Street in a holiday parade. Until, finally, nearly a year after the war had started in Europe, Roosevelt fired Woodring and replaced him with a pillar of the American Republican establishment, Henry Stimson, who had been William Howard Taft's secretary of war and Herbert Hoover's secretary of state. His classic Republicanism, Roosevelt hoped, would reduce some of the complaints and criticisms from the Republicans in Congress and perhaps even help in the November 1940 election.

Once the military started to get money in amounts it had not seen before, it began displaying surprising skills in assembling a real army and navy. And it soon proposed that it be given total supervision of industry, of weapons production, of allocations of scarce materials. Roosevelt refused—"fascistic," he said. Instead, he began giving these powers to civilians and installing them behind desks and chrome water carafes in an endless progression of new war agencies. One of the first was the War Resources Board, staffed by business leaders, mainly because Roosevelt thought Congress would hold to the common wisdom of the men's luncheon clubs that businessmen could be trusted where bureaucrats could not. Louis Johnson chose the board's members and made a remark that showed clearly how little the Washington establishment understood the bureaucratic turmoil that lay ahead, the rapid turnovers and the revolving doors, in the war agencies: He would pick members of the War Resources Board carefully, he said, because "after the war it will be hard to get rid of them." He named Edward Stettinius, Jr., chairman of U.S. Steel; Walter Gifford, president of American Telephone and Telegraph; General Robert E. Wood, chairman of Sears, Roebuck & Co.

Roosevelt soon came to dislike everything about the War Resources Board, and abolished it almost before the new members were settled at their desks. There were complaints from the isolationist crowd in Congress that it should have been called the Defense Resources Board. And the president disliked all those anti–New Deal businessmen holding all that power. He thanked them for their willingness to serve and sent them all home. So it was that with Hitler overrunning Europe and the Japanese expanding aggressively in Asia, Washington had no plan to mobilize war production, no plan to manage the economy, prices, materials, rationing, no plan to prepare the country for war.

Roosevelt's next move, on January 7, 1941, was to set up another new agency, the Office of Production Management, headed by two men who assuredly could never work effectively together—William Knudsen, former president of General Motors, and Sidney Hillman, president of the Amalgamated Clothing Workers Union. Knudsen was a Danish immigrant who had gone to work in the automobile industry, first at Ford and then at Chevrolet, and had eventually become president of General Motors, still speaking with a heavy accent. Roosevelt admired his record as a production specialist and the fact that he had no understanding of and no ambition in politics. Hillman was an immigrant from Lithuania who had gone to work in the clothing industry and then into socialist and union politics and had become the first president of the Clothing Workers Union and later a founder of the CIO. Conservatives in Congress viewed him with deep suspicion, suspecting that the CIO was a nest of communists, and that he had been appointed merely because he was a Roosevelt sycophant.

At a press conference, Roosevelt was asked, "Why is it that you don't want a single, responsible head?"

"I have a single, responsible head. His name is Knudsen and Hillman." Under the Constitution, he said, "you cannot set up a second president of the United States." He would tolerate no "czar" or "Poobah" in Washington. The newspapers began referring to the leaders of OPM as Mr. Knudsenhillman.

Knudsenhillman's OPM had little real power. It could not require industry to convert to war work. It could only argue and try to persuade. And so, like the War Resources Board before it, OPM found itself with no choice but to ask the businessmen themselves to take charge. It invited industrialists and corporate lawyers to join its staff for a token payment of one dollar a year to act as advisers. More than a thousand accepted while continuing to be paid by their own companies or law firms. Many New Dealers were skeptical about placing control of war production in the hands of people still on the payrolls of private industry. Would such people not argue that the way to save the free world was to buy more of whatever their regular employers were selling? No, as it turned out. The record of the dollar-a-year men was better than many expected. As for promoting their own companies' products, a maker of war supplies did not need promotion. His problem was not to make sales but to produce the stuff fast enough.

But Roosevelt remained dubious about bringing in so many business people, almost all of them Republicans. At a press conference, he described a conversation with Knudsen, who was recruiting executives to work for government. "In about the fourth or fifth list of these dollar-a-year men," Roosevelt said, "they were all listed as Republicans except a boy who graduated from Yale last June and had never voted. And I said, Bill, couldn't you find a Democrat to go on this dollar-a-year list anywhere in the country? And he said, 'I have searched the whole country over. There is no Democrat rich enough to take a job at a dollar a year.' " (Laughter.)

Some of his critics asked why he insisted on creating virtually an entirely new government establishment on top of what already existed. Why not send wartime problems with food production to the Agriculture Department? Union problems to the Labor Department? Business to the Commerce Department? Why bring in all these new people who didn't even know how to find the men's rooms? Roosevelt's answer, never publicly stated, was that the old-time Washington agencies were simply not up to dealing with the upheavals a war would demand. Many of them had gone along for decades resisting change, taking weeks to move a paper from one office to another, following encrusted habits and iron routines even if no one any longer remembered why, pursuing whatever policies they thought would protect and expand their staffs and their budgets and resisting everything else. The German sociologist

Max Weber had argued long before that a large bureaucracy, once established, turned away from whatever task it was supposed to do and instead worked mainly at administering itself. And so when employees of Agriculture and other departments were invited to move over to work in their fields of experience in the new war agencies, most of them resisted, fearing any kind of change and fearing the loss of their places in line for promotion, retirement and pension. This saved them from conflicts with Congress that might endanger their budgets and saved them from the danger of unwelcome attention in the press.

While all that was true, it also was true that the federal bureaucracy in 1941 simply was not large enough, or experienced enough, to handle the enormous job of managing preparations for a war. Some agencies had been in existence for only eight years, since the New Deal expanded the old federal offices and created new ones. And no existing agency of the government had ever been asked to regulate the steel industry, or any industry, or to allocate materials or set production quotas. In 1941, government was moving into areas it had never touched before, and its bureaucracies simply did not know how to deal with them. And so most of the existing government had to sit on the sidelines and watch while the new agencies were run by the dollar-a-year men, the only people in the country who knew how to do it.

Roosevelt considered the new people temporary, as they considered themselves. Men working for a dollar a year had no interest in government careers. They had no civil service status and so could be fired anytime without ceremony or protests or hearings and appeals. They were simply asked to resign, given a letter of thanks for their contributions and allowed to return home quietly with their reputations intact.

While the newly recruited businessmen were skilled in dealing with industrial production, they were guileless in dealing with Congress, the military and the press; guileless about spending vast amounts of money without the discipline of a corporate profit-and-loss statement; and careless in dealing with contractors who had suffered huge losses in the Depression and now, at last, saw a chance to make money.

The first, early warning came from Missouri in the form of piles of mail to a Missouri senator, Harry Truman, saying that there was tremendous waste in the construction work at Fort Leonard Wood. There were complaints that defense contracts were going mainly to companies represented in Washington by the dollar-a-year men. Truman looked into it and found the waste was even worse than reported. Early in 1941, he won passage of a bill to set up a Senate committee to investigate waste and corruption in the awarding of contracts by the war agencies. His committee became famous for running one of the straightest, cleanest, least political investigations Congress had ever seen. Truman found hundreds of millions of dollars wasted in the building and enlarging of nine army camps—poor workmanship, outrageous overcharges. He found that army-navy rivalry led to wasteful duplications in building two of everything, needed or not. He found "negligence and willful misconduct" in the navy's Bureau of Ships, sloppy construction of military aircraft, cheating by labor unions. His committee labeled Knudsenhillman's Office of Production Management a "hopeless mess."

Truman's unsettling discoveries went on and on, his reports of waste and corruption, lavishly covered in the press, making upsetting reading for Roosevelt. It was such reports, among other things, that placed increasing pressure on the president to come up with somebody who could run the economy honestly and efficiently to support the war abroad and civilians at home. The word "czar" began to be heard, a single person to have absolute power to decide who got the copper and steel, and which manufacturer would make what and how many. The job would carry such great power and generate so much publicity it was assumed that whoever held it and did it well would be regarded after the war as a great American hero.

"The amusing part of the whole business," Harry Hopkins said, "was that everybody was a candidate. [Vice President Henry] Wallace, I am sure, hoped the president would ask him. [Financier] Bernard Baruch was in a hotel room spreading propaganda for himself. A great many of my friends were pushing [Supreme Court Justice] Bill Douglas. [Secretary of the Treasury] Morgenthau wanted it worse than anything in the world. So did [Secretary of Commerce] Jesse Jones."

Roosevelt was uneasy because the only people equipped to do such a massive job were people he distrusted—managers of big industries, all Republicans, all opposed to his New Deal. Wasn't there a danger that a man like this, taking charge of war production, would push on and on and try to control the domestic economy and domestic life? And trample the New Deal to death? But what was the alternative? Roosevelt was equally unwilling to hand over this power to a politician, who might use it to turn himself into a heroic figure and possibly even a presidential challenger.

Well, there was always Bernard Baruch. He was so eager for the job he was pulling every string in town, applying pressure through the newspapers and his friends in the military and in industry. He had won fame as an economic "czar" in World War I, when he served as chairman of the powerful War Industries Board. He had made himself rich in Wall Street long ago; he was seventy now and had many friends in Congress, most of whom were now pushing him for the big job as hard as he was pushing himself. Perhaps his hunger for money had been satisfied, but his hunger for power had not.

But what had Baruch actually accomplished in World War I? He had, some argued, simply recruited the leaders of big industry and given them and the armed services control of war production. Roosevelt's opinion was that these people had turned out to be greedy profiteers who had manipulated the spending to fill their own pockets and had provoked a series of ugly congressional investigations in the 1920s that called some of them "merchants of death." And ultimately, in Roosevelt's view, these were the men who had brought on the Great Depression. Beyond that, the idea Baruch was touting now was a return to his World War I plan. Roosevelt did not want it. He had not spent eight years building his New Deal only to let his enemies come in and tear it apart.

Finally, in September 1941, with almost the entire American economy now mobilizing for war and the production crisis growing worse by the hour, Roosevelt acted—after a fashion. OPM was in disarray, but he neither disbanded it nor reformed it. Knudsen and Hillman had proved ineffective both in cooperating with each other and in forcing the military and the corporate world to cooperate with the government, but Roosevelt did not fire them. Instead, he created a new agency with a new director, to operate alongside the agencies that already existed. It was called the Supply, Priorities and Allocation Board (SPAB); and its director was Donald Nelson.

Nelson had spent nearly thirty years as a buyer for Sears, Roebuck and by the late 1930s had risen to become its executive vice president and chairman of its executive committee. He had come to Washington in June 1940 to coordinate purchases for one of the early war agencies, recruited on the assumption that anyone who could buy for a tremendous operation such as Sears could buy for anyone. He was good at his job. In purchasing clothing for the armed services he had found one man in the textile industry who had cornered the market in a particular type of cotton fabric used in uniforms and was intent on profiteering. Nelson bankrupted him by changing the specifications to another type of cotton, leaving him with a monopoly on a fabric nobody wanted. And he used methods he had used at Sears, such as sending orders to factories in the off seasons when demand was slack and they were willing to accept lower prices.

His work was unspectacular but effective. I. F. Stone in *The Nation* called him "one of the ablest and most public-spirited of the dollar-a-year men . . . the one leading businessman usually prepared to uphold the rights of labor . . . bargaining as firmly in buying for his country as he would have in buying for his company." Nelson himself, like his work, was unspectacular. He was overweight, balding, smoked a pipe said to smell like a sulfur sink in Yellowstone National Park, sat at his desk for long hours and was patient, slow-moving and easygoing. He liked to say to reporters that he had edited a publication with a larger circulation than any of their newspapers—the Sears, Roebuck catalogue. Above all, he was a survivor. Through the months and years when new war agencies were created quickly and then quickly abolished and one of Washington's larger industries was the printing of new letterheads, Nelson stayed on. He held one job after another, mainly because nobody had any reason to object to him. He spoke in the folksy language that Roosevelt himself so often favored. "The housewife wants to buy to the best advantage," he was fond of saying. "We have the same objective." He was pleasant, patient and conciliatory. He ruffled no feathers, and no one—including, most important, the president—considered him a threat.

Nelson served as chairman of SPAB for only a few months. The new agency was crippled from the beginning by its lack of real power and by the confusing lines of authority that Roosevelt's patchwork efforts had created. Critics of the president continued to carp until Pearl Harbor finally forced him to act. Early in 1942, he abolished OPM, SPAB, and a number of other agencies and created the War Production Board, which would, he promised, have vast powers over the entire economy. Donald Nelson would be its chairman.

Just a few days after Nelson assumed his new post, his easygoing manner led a WPB staff member to observe: "One of these War Department generals will stick a knife into Nelson and he pulls the knife out and hands it back and says, 'General, I believe you dropped something.' And the general will say, 'Don, thanks. I believe I did,' and right away he sticks it back in again." *Fortune* magazine called Nelson "patient, kindly, decent, honest and patriotic." He was, but these were not the qualities it took to survive in the bureaucratic shark tank of wartime Washington.

The military had wanted Baruch, not Nelson, and tried again and again to turn Roosevelt's appointment around. Lieutenant General Brehon Somervell, head of the Army Supply Services, was an experienced bureaucratic guerrilla fighter. He and his staff began a series of leaks to the newspapers about Nelson's WPB being too slow, which it was. It had started out with a set of priorities to determine who should get scarce materials first, the top priority being "A-1a," but so many arms plants had priorities, Nelson had to invent such "super priorities" as AA-1 through AA-4, and on up to AA-2X, whereupon it all became nonsense.

He admitted the problem and responded by trying to conciliate the armed services. He sent several of his top executives over to army and navy headquarters to work as civilian advisers trying to help the military officers with their problems. Somervell flattered them, put them in uniform with military ranks high enough to impress their grandchildren and got them to work for him, leaving the WPB with a row of empty offices. Nelson complained to Roosevelt. Still suspicious of the military's taste for power, the president overruled Somervell.

But there was damage. Soon, Congress was complaining about Nelson's ineffective system of priorities, the press was saying he was too nice, too tolerant, too indecisive for the job. Nelson, uncharacteristically, was furious. He announced, "From now on anybody who crosses my path is going to have his head taken off. I am tough enough to get this job done and the job will be done."

Tough or not, he was in serious trouble. His system of priorities had collapsed. War plants across the country were running at as little as 50 percent of capacity because they could not get the materials they needed. Members of Congress were shouting their complaints at full throttle. Seven committees in the House and Senate, having not much else to do, drew up seven plans for new boards, new leaders including a real "czar," new bureaucratic structures they assumed would be more effective than the old.

But Roosevelt would not have it. "You know what it is," he said at a press conference. "I can take two blueprints of exactly the same kind of organization and those two blueprints won't like each other at all."

"Well, sir, is there anything in the works on giving one man overall power?"

"No. It's just like sitting down and drawing—what do they call it when a fellow sits and draws a figure?"

"Doodling?"

"Doodles, that's it. Now they are just engaging in doodles . . . a very good word for it."

The press wanted to know about the disputes between Nelson's WPB and the armed services, routinely leaked to the newspapers. "Who has the final say?"

"I guess the answer is that they work it out together. Everybody has a say."

"But who has the final authority?"

"I would say they all do, mutually, and they are supposed to agree. And if they don't agree, then I'll put them in a room and I'll say, 'No food until you come out in agreement.'" (Laughter.)

But Nelson and his deputies went on fighting with each other and fighting with the armed services. Nelson tried to stop it through traditional bureaucratic means. He got out a pencil, paper and a ruler and drew a new set of boxes with new lines of authority running back and forth from one box to another until it looked like the plumbing diagram for a twelve-room house. He passed this out and called it reform. It wasn't. As with all such charts, the lines of authority were clearer on paper than they were in the daily struggle for power.

The fight for power was so vicious because for middle-aged civilians working in the war agencies for one dollar a year, there was nothing else to fight for. While soldiers would be coming home from battle with medals attesting their valor, the agency managers going home after the war would be able to claim only whatever victories they had won in the paper wars; and it was difficult to win much when somebody else controlled the paper. Further, a good record in Washington with a little favorable publicity might be helpful when they went back to their home towns and their old employers. This was particularly important to those in the dollar-a-year corps who were already a little uneasy over their employers' willingness in the first place to hand them over to serve in the government. Had their bosses donated to Washington those they felt they could most easily do without? The Depression and unemployment were still very fresh in memory, and few Americans could feel casual and confident about jobs and future prospects.

The new undersecretary of war, Robert Patterson, continued the attacks on Nelson, calling him a failure who was unable to give the armed services what they needed, and by early 1943 the military leaders were determined to get rid of him. Even an old friend, Felix Frankfurter, told Roosevelt that Nelson was "an utterly weak man incapable of exercising authority or making decisions."

On February 14, 1943—Valentine's Day—Nelson's telephone rang just before midnight. A staff member was calling to say he had learned Nelson was to be fired the next day and replaced by Bernard Baruch. The army had maneuvered it and had drawn up for Roosevelt's signature a letter ordering this. A meeting in the president's office was set for two o'clock the following afternoon, when the secretaries and under-secretaries of the War and Navy departments would watch the president sign it.

That morning Nelson called the president, who refused to take the call. In fact, Roosevelt had already sent a letter of his own, hand-carried by messenger across Lafayette Park to Baruch in his suite in the Carlton Hotel, asking him to replace Nelson at the WPB.

Whereupon Nelson displayed a combativeness never seen before. He put out a press release announcing he had asked for and accepted the resignation of his deputy, Ferdinand Eberstadt, a financier and friend of the military—too friendly, in Nelson's opinion, and the source of much of WPB's subjugation to the army and navy. Eberstadt first heard about this, as was not unusual in Washington, when he read it on the Associated Press wire.

When this news of yet another nasty little battle in the paper war reached the White House, Harry Hopkins told Roosevelt that if he gave in to the army on this bureaucratic fight, he would look weak, the military would have won, and Baruch would emerge as the conquering hero. Hopkins said he should keep Nelson. Roosevelt agreed. Nelson stayed.

But no one told Baruch. Two days later, he walked over to the White House, ready to take over the War Production Board. He later recalled the episode:

In the hall outside the president's office, I met [Roosevelt aides] Sam Rosenman and Pa Watson. They took me aside hurriedly and said, "The president has changed his mind." They had no chance to explain further before I was summoned inside.

The president leaned back in his chair and puffed on a cigarette stuck in an uplifted holder. He greeted me in his customary genial fashion. He showed no sign of embarrassment or uneasiness.

"Mr. President, I am here to report for duty," I said. My salutation went unacknowledged. It was as though he had not heard me.

"Let me tell you about Ibn Saud, Bernie," he said confidentially. And he launched into some general observations about the Middle Eastern monarch. Then he suddenly interrupted himself. "Forgive me. I have to go to a Cabinet meeting," he said, and rolled off.

As for the chairmanship of the War Production Board, which he had offered Baruch only a few days before, it was never mentioned again.

While the civilian agencies grew, the military was expanding even faster. By early 1941, the army alone had grown from seven thousand civilian employees to forty-one thousand, spread through twenty-three buildings in the District of Columbia and nearby Maryland and Virginia. A new War Department building was already going up on Virginia Avenue, in a dreary part of town known as Foggy Bottom. Stimson hated it, said it was too small, and complained that the façade looked like the entrance to a provincial opera house. He announced he would never move into it. He never did. (The building became, and remains, the Department of State.)

And so began a movement to build a new colossus for the military, a building so enormous there was no room for it in the city. It was to rise across the Potomac River in Virginia on a site near Arlington National Cemetery, and to have three times the floor space of the Empire State Building. It would hold the War Department in a mammoth, five-sided agglomeration of concrete corridors and offices a mile in circumference, filled with the military secretariat, officers and enlisted men and civilian clerks and all their desks, file cabinets, cafeterias, mimeograph machines and mechanical typewriters that, in time, would turn out the notices to families that their sons, brothers and fathers had been killed in battle.

Congress was asked to put up thirty-five million dollars for the monstrous new building but would not do so until it had a good deal of conversation about it. Representative Fritz Lanham of Texas explained the problem on the House floor: "One of the high officers of the War Department testified that his offices are now in four different places in the city and that he loses two hours a day going from one to another. . . . So, by all means, I say it is feasible to pass this legislation" to spend the money.

But Robert Rich of Pennsylvania still insisted that if the country was sensible it would stay out of war and therefore would not need a new building for the military. "Where are you going? Where are you taking this nation? No place except to national bankruptcy and ruin. . . . I am opposed to it in every way I can be. War in Europe or Asia for us spells ruination of America."

Others wondered how a building so huge could possibly be used after the war. Everett Dirksen of Illinois said, "Here is a building proposed to house thirty thousand people, to stand over across the Potomac River. You can ride [by taxi] to the present War Department for twenty cents. It will cost you at least sixty cents to go over to this new building and sixty cents back. We may not need all that space when the war comes to an end. . . . What will we do with the extra space?"

Clifton Woodrum of Virginia responded that when the war was over the new building could be used to store military records, or some other civilian agencies of government could be moved into it.

August Andresen of Minnesota rose and said, "I understand that the report is quite current around here that they want these big buildings so we can police the world after the war is over. . . ."

After receiving the most solemn assurances that the total cost of the new building would be thirty-five million dollars including all furniture and fixtures, Congress voted the money. The final cost would be eighty-seven million dollars.

Reluctantly, Roosevelt agreed to allow the building of the Pentagon, as it quickly came to be called, but he would not agree to the location. In his view and that of the press and public, it would desecrate a hallowed place, Arlington National Cemetery. Only twenty years after the previous war, with many of its veterans still in hospitals, people were deeply emotional about Arlington, and the outcry was so fervent that the military and its architects could not ignore it. They chose another site, farther from the cemetery, partially occupied by warehouses and a public dump.

Roosevelt agreed to the new site but said he disliked the building. Why not, he asked, build a huge, square, concrete monolith without windows and with entirely artificial light and ventilation? Then, he said, after the war when the military was back down to its peacetime size, the building might be useful for storage. When Stimson heard this, he was appalled and said—out of Roosevelt's hearing—that he would never work in a building designed like a cold-storage warehouse for bananas.

At a press conference in August 1941, a reporter asked, "Mr. President, can you say anything about the new War Department in Arlington?"

Roosevelt recalled that in the fall of 1917 he was assistant secretary of the navy and his department needed more room. He talked with President Woodrow Wilson about a new temporary building across the lawns from the White House. Wilson asked, "Why did you select that place?"

"Because it would be so unsightly right here in front of the White House it would just have to be taken down at the end of the war."

Wilson thought for a moment. "Well, I don't think I could stand all that sawing and hammering right under my front windows. Can't you put it somewhere else?"

Roosevelt had told the 1917 contractor to put it on the Mall about a mile from the White House where Wilson could not hear the hammering and now, twenty-four years later, it still stood and still housed many of the offices of the navy, uglier than ever. "It was a crime. I don't hesitate to say so. It was a crime for which I should be kept out of heaven, for having desecrated the whole plan of, I think, the loveliest city in the world. . . . " He was willing, he said, for the War Department to build something, but what the Pentagon now proposed was too big and would spoil the city planning of a hundred and fifty years.

Two months later, in late September 1941, while Roosevelt still wavered about the location, the army just went ahead. General Somervell, not yet busy fighting Donald Nelson, was a West Point engineering graduate whose previous projects had included New York City's LaGuardia Airport. He simply told the contractor to start work. By the time Roosevelt found out about it a month later, the foundations were already in place.

The construction moved ahead with incredible speed. At one point, thirteen thousand men were working around the clock, with enormous banks of arc lights burning through the night. Accident rates were 400 percent higher than average. Three hundred architects worked in a large, abandoned airplane hangar near the construction site. They were trying, and failing, to design the building fast enough to keep up with the workmen. Construction foremen were snatching blueprints off their desks even before they had finished drafting them. Alan Dickey, one of the architects, recalled another architect asking him, "How big should I make that beam across the third floor?"

Dickey answered, "I don't know. They installed it yesterday."

By May 1942, half-a-million square feet were ready for occupancy, and the army began moving in. Military guards lined the route from the old Munitions Building on the Mall, across the Fourteenth Street Bridge and through the muddy fields to the half-finished structure. Armored trucks rolled in with secret files. Movers carried in office furniture so hurriedly that workers the next day deluged their supervisors with complaints about broken lamps and damaged desks. For months more, Pentagon workers had to fight construction barriers, wet cement, noise, and dust so thick, one remembered, "you could write your name on any desk with your finger."

By early 1943, the Pentagon was complete—a building big enough to house forty thousand people and all their accoutrements, the largest building in the world, conceived, funded, designed and constructed in a little more than a year. And on the day it was finished, it was already too small. The army was once again spreading outward over the city, renting office space in hotels, apartments and downtown office buildings.

Jokes about the Pentagon quickly became a staple of bureaucratic humor. It was so huge people were said to spend days and even weeks wandering its endless corridors trying to find their way out. One woman was said to have told a guard she was in labor and needed help in getting to a maternity hospital. He said, "Madam, you should not have come in here in that condition."

"When I came in here," she answered, "I wasn't."

Less than a mile away, on the Virginia banks of the Potomac, another symbol of Washington's sudden transformation was rising from the mud. A new airport, built with funds appropriated by Congress, was nearing completion. It replaced the old Hoover Field, which was being displaced in turn by the Pentagon and its enormous parking lots. Hoover Field had been the city's only airport for years—a simple place, but not without its charms. It consisted of little more than a grassy field between an amusement park on one side and a warehouse and dump area on the other. A county highway, Military Road, ran directly across the only runway.

The airport authorities, fearful of a collision between a car and an airplane, once asked the Arlington County government to close the highway for safety reasons. The county refused. The airport manager, on his own, installed a red light to stop automobile traffic when planes were landing and taking off. He was hauled into court, charged with installing a traffic signal without authority, and found guilty. The light was removed. For years, pilots flew in and out of Washington timing their landings to coincide with breaks in the traffic on Military Road, while using Hoover Field's only navigational aid, a wind sock nailed to a pole on top of the amusement park's roller coaster.

Now the soldiers, sailors, businessmen, politicians, diplomats, statesmen and lobbyists who were streaming in and out of Washington every day could land at what the city proudly called "the most modern airport in the world"—National Airport, whose runways were so close to downtown that passengers could look across the river and see the Capitol Dome and the Washington Monument as they taxied to the gates. National had a tower, navigational signals, restaurants, newsstands and parking lots. Airplanes no longer had to dodge automobile traffic. Washington was coming of age.

In the country's last months of peace, the city's population was increasing at the rate of more than fifty thousand a year. People arrived from all over the country and wandered bewildered out of the crowded waiting room of Union Station into strange, crowded streets, looking for jobs and—in this labor-starved town—usually finding them.

In their wake came the inevitable gaggle of drifters, con men, pickpockets, prostitutes, robbers and general-purpose hoodlums, and with them an alarming increase in crime. A sleepy Southern city accustomed to drowsing among the magnolias and slapping at mosquitoes looked up to find itself labeled, in Newsweek, the "Murder Capital of the U.S." Its homicide rate was now two-and-a-half times New York City's. Perhaps equally alarming was a 1942 headline in the Washington

Daily News: "Enough VD Cases in D.C. to Overflow the Stadium" (Griffith Stadium seated thirty thousand). But according to the director of Washington's venereal disease bureau, "There are fifteen thousand more cases than there are seats."

Washington was poorly equipped to deal with these big-city problems. Its municipal government had no answers, because it was more joke than government. It consisted of three commissioners appointed by the president—if he remembered to do it and had nothing better to do at the time. They were usually aging hacks (their combined age in 1941 was well over two hundred years), and they had so little power they could do little more than fill potholes and replace burned-out street lights without asking Congress for approval.

The official head of the city government in the early 1940s was J. Russell Young, formerly a reporter for the *Evening Star* and now chairman of the district commissioners. His office carried such limited powers and required so little work that Roosevelt was unable to stifle his laughter when he announced Young's appointment. Young could often be found conducting municipal business in the Mayflower Hotel bar, there usually being little business to conduct.

The city government had been marginally adequate in earlier years when hardly anything ever happened and Washington could afford to wait for Congress to respond to its modest requests. In one chapter from the annals of democracy, the Senate of the United States had spent hours debating the necessity and wisdom of replacing the linoleum on the floor of the city fish market. But the fish market floor could wait. Other problems could not. The city government was barely able to continue the minimal services it had always provided: collecting trash, licensing shoeshine parlors and hot dog stands, pumping the water, lighting the streets. The new problems—crime, disease, housing shortages, transportation breakdowns—it had to leave to Congress. And Congress was not much interested.

That was partly because the House and Senate district committees, the real powers in the city, were among the least desirable assignments in Congress. They were filled either with very junior members struggling to make a name elsewhere and move up or with congressional pariahs shunted off to a place where the leadership believed they could do the least harm. That explained why Theodore Bilbo of Mississippi was for many years a member of the Senate District Committee and, beginning in 1944, its chairman—known, ludicrously, as the "Mayor of Washington."

Bilbo was a short, strutting, bantamlike man, with gold-rimmed glasses, slicked-back, thinning hair, an unpleasant face, and the flamboyant wardrobe of an aging dandy, his bright ties set off by a diamond stickpin, his plump body loosely encased in a white suit now yellowing and three sizes too large. He seemed to hate everyone: communists, Jews, union leaders, union members, anyone who could, by any definition, be called a foreigner, and above all, of course, blacks. And Bilbo never hesitated to make his hatreds known. When he ran for the Senate in 1934, he denounced an opponent as "a cross between a hyena and a mongrel . . . begotten in a nigger graveyard at midnight, suckled by a sow, and educated by a fool." When he received a hostile letter from a woman named Josephine Piccolo in New York City, he wrote back and addressed her: "Dear Dago."

As one of the nation's most outspoken racists, Bilbo hated the fact that nearly half the residents of the city he helped administer were black. "If you go through the government departments," he once said, "there are so many niggers it's like a black cloud all around you." He repeatedly introduced a bill to deport all Negroes to Africa and once suggested that Eleanor Roosevelt be sent with them and made their "queen." Throughout his tenure on the district committee, Bilbo judged almost every proposal on the basis of its effect on race relations. Anything that might benefit blacks—and in a city whose black population was growing rapidly, that was most things—he opposed. Nothing outraged him more than the effort in 1941, by blacks themselves, to confront racial discrimination in employment.

Almost no one in government—either in the Congress or in the administration—was eager to confront the racial problem in 1941, even if few were as openly racist as Bilbo. But the growth of war industries and the increasing federal role in the economy was creating demands that the president, at least, could not evade.

Even in peacetime, the New Deal had taken little interest in racial issues. Roosevelt had always refused to support any legislation (the anti-lynching bill most prominently) that might antagonize Southern Democrats and jeopardize what he considered his more important programs in Congress. And while a number of blacks received appointments to significant posts around the administration, the total was always small.

Alfred Edgar Smith later recalled what it was like trying to represent blacks in the Washington of the 1930s. He entered the government a few years before the war to help advise Harry Hopkins, head of the WPA, on how to deal with racial issues in administering relief. Hopkins had no particular interest in a black adviser. The need for jobs, housing and opportunity was the same for everyone, he believed. Relief programs did not need to worry about race. But he was under such constant pressure from black leaders to appoint someone to represent them that finally, if only to shut them up, he hired Forrester Washington, dean of the School of Social Work at Atlanta University, and gave him the title "Negro adviser." Washington took on Smith, a graduate student at Howard, as his assistant. Smith described his experiences:

A Negro assistant in government, a race relations adviser, was new, a new concept, and Forrester Washington didn't know what to do himself.

He showed me a room with a big table like a dining table with all the leaves in and piled high with envelopes. He told me all those letters were from Negroes addressed to President Roosevelt, that the president had made a tactical error and actually gave a Negro family selected somewhere down in Mississippi forty acres and a mule. . . .

I got pushed into the room and was told, "Do something with these letters." Forrester Washington then resigned from government and went back to Atlanta, shaking his head. Harry Hopkins didn't know another black and so one morning I read in the paper I was the new Negro assistant to Harry Hopkins. Pretty soon I got all the calls about the black folks no one else knew anything about. One call said, "Smith, go down to Mississippi and see what the hell's going on down there with the sewing projects."

Sewing projects? It turned out to be a work relief program hiring women to work at sewing machines, and the complaint coming up to Washington was that black women were paid only a third as much as white women doing the same work. Smith went to Mississippi and told the project director, "You have to pay all these women the same or the federal government is going to snatch all this money away from you." Smith recalled, "He said he couldn't do it. I said he had to do it. So they raised the pay of a few black women in places where they could be seen. These things always became a compromise, never done right."

But there were achievements:

If it had the word "Negro" on it, they called me because they didn't know a damned thing about it. Take Morgan University over here in Baltimore. It used to get a few hundred dollars from the government, but it was a private school and not supposed to get any government money. But it wanted a stadium and I got a call from upstairs from whoever was in charge of allotting federal projects. He asked me, "Morgan University over there in Baltimore—is that a state school?"

I said, "Uhh, err, ahhhh . . . "

"All right. Thank you."

He took it I was saying yes. It became a state school. So it got a beautiful stadium built with WPA labor, and I didn't even get invited to the dedication.

Later, Smith had a visitor—Mary McLeod Bethune, perhaps the most admired black woman in America, friend of Eleanor Roosevelt and head of Bethune-Cookman, a small, struggling, debt-ridden junior college for black students in Florida. She was wearing a fur coat that reminded Smith of his dog, a Newfoundland retriever, and the coat's lining was torn and hanging out.

She asked, "How can I get government money for my school?"

Smith took her in to see Aubrey Williams, head of the National Youth Administration. It had plenty of money. In his office Mrs. Bethune took off her coat and after a talk with Williams he promised financial help.

Smith said, "I helped her back into her coat. She deliberately put her arm in so as to catch the torn lining, not the sleeve. She put on a little performance, pulling her arm out of the lining and then finding the sleeve. As Aubrey Williams sat watching this, she said to him, 'I have to wear this old coat because every cent I have goes to my school.'

"It was a beautiful act. She deserved an Oscar. She came out of Williams' office smiling and asking, 'How'd I do?' "

She did so well she got enough money to make her school totally free of debt.

The WPA had hired some black workers, never many but enough to convince black leaders that the Roosevelt administration was at least not hostile to them. That goodwill was stretched thin quickly, however, soon after war mobilization began. Some war plants operating on government contracts, paying their workers with government money, hired a few blacks to sweep and carry out the trash and drive the trucks. But most industries maintained, without pretense or apology, an uncompromising policy of hiring whites only. In Washington, the war agencies—preoccupied with their internal bureaucratic problems and with the needs of the American and Allied armed forces—showed no interest in using their power to challenge such practices. Several black leaders decided to force them to do so.

A. Philip Randolph, president of the Brotherhood of Sleeping Car Porters (the only black union in the American Federation of Labor), remembered what had happened after World War I. Blacks had volunteered to serve in a segregated army for a segregated government, confident that after the war their sacrifices would be rewarded. When black veterans returned in 1919, they got a nice parade through Harlem and nothing else—no jobs, no challenges to segregation, no progress. Randolph and others were determined that the same thing would not happen again. And the time to ensure that, he believed, was at the beginning of the war, not at the end.

In the spring of 1941, Randolph went to the White House with what he called a proposal but what was, in the president's eyes at least, really a threat. In the booming voice of the opera singer he had once been, Randolph said that even in armament plants so burdened with orders they could not find enough labor, there were only a few menial jobs for blacks. The president of North American Aviation had inadvertently supported Randolph's case a few months before when he had said, "While we are in sympathy with the Negro, it is against company policy to employ them as aircraft workers or mechanics, regardless of their training. But there will be some jobs as janitors for Negroes." And the federal government, Randolph said, was just as bad. It too hired blacks as janitors but not much more. There had to be changes.

In particular, there had to be a fair employment practices commission, with the power to investigate discrimination in government agencies and in companies working under government contracts and to ensure equal employment opportunities for blacks in both. Obtaining congressional approval of such a measure would be difficult, he realized. But the president could create a temporary committee by executive order. To demonstrate the importance of this demand, he said, he would bring a hundred thousand blacks to Washington on July 1, 1941, for a massive protest march.

Roosevelt was aghast. He tried everything he could think of to talk Randolph out of what he considered a rash and dangerous plan with the potential for great political embarrassment to him. But Randolph was adamant and returned to New York to continue planning for the march. The president then sent his wife and Fiorello LaGuardia, the mayor of New York, to visit Randolph at his union headquarters to try again to change his mind. They did their best. They told Randolph that Washington's police force was filled with white Southerners who could not be trusted to protect the marchers. There was danger of violence. "There's going to be bloodshed and death in Washington. . . . You're going to get Negroes slaughtered," LaGuardia told him. "If you bring a hundred thousand people there," Eleanor Roosevelt added, "nobody will be able to control them."

Randolph was undeterred. Blacks were already serving in the armed services, he argued, and they had earned a right to jobs in war plants as well. "But they won't get employed by merely wishing for it." And so LaGuardia and Mrs. Roosevelt left, and Randolph went back to work. As he later recalled it:

> We began forming the groups. I had a program of going down the avenue, going into all the stores on that avenue, the barber shops, the saloons, the pool rooms, and saying to the men, "Are you satisfied with the jobs you've got?" They said, "No!" I said, "Do you want more jobs? Are you willing to march to Washington for them?" And the response would be, "Yes! We'll go anywhere." That was in New York, Baltimore, Washington, St. Louis, Chicago, Detroit. I, myself, went to all these places.

Roosevelt was in a quandary. He did not want the march, but he did not want an employment commission either. Southerners in Congress were already opposing him on almost everything he tried to do, and even whispering the idea of a fair-employment rule would set them off like Roman candles. In the House, John Rankin of Mississippi had already made sixteen speeches denouncing the idea, each more vituperative than the last; Representative Arthur Miller of Nebraska had called Randolph "the most dangerous Negro in America"; Theodore Bilbo, of course, was nearly apoplectic every time the idea was mentioned. Besides, Roosevelt argued, if he issued a fair-employment order for Negroes, every other group would want one: the Poles, the Italians, who knew who else? But a march on Washington, Roosevelt feared, could be even worse. "It would make the country look bad in wartime," he told Randolph at another White House meeting, this time before the entire cabinet. "It would help the Germans."

Randolph refused to yield, and Roosevelt finally had to make a choice: a march or a commission. He chose the commission. The president sent a message to a young lawyer on his staff, Joseph L. Rauh, Jr.: "We need an Executive Order for a Fair Employment Practices Commission, and we need it in a few hours." It became the famous Executive Order 8802—the first of many to deal with racial discrimination. It included a phrase, coined by Rauh as he worked hastily against his deadline, that was to become one of the most powerful and familiar in American life: "No discrimination on grounds of race, color, creed, or national origin."

Randolph cancelled the march.

So it was that a small, provincial town prepared itself for the greatest war in history. Crowded, confused and stubborn, mired in its own customs and prejudices, relying on slipshod, haphazard improvisations, Washington struggled to transform itself into the capital of the free world.

IV

"Locked in Deadly Struggle . . ."

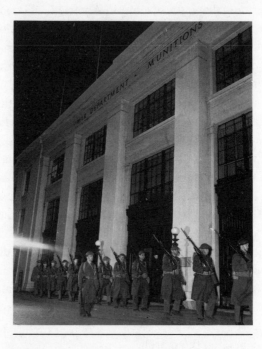

It was still possible in 1941 to walk through the White House gate and into the grounds without showing a pass or answering any questions, since the White House was not yet considered much different from any other public building in the city. Until a few years before there had been no gates at all, and on summer days government employees had lounged on the White House lawns eating picnic lunches out of paper sacks. In the mid-thirties, a Washington resident was driving his Ford convertible down Pennsylvania Avenue with the top down when it began to rain. He turned into the White House driveway and drove under the portico for shelter, put his top up, and went on. Only twenty-five years before that, in Taft's administration, tourists looking around inside the White House had been allowed, when the president was absent, to go into his office and sit for a moment and bounce in his chair. It was all casual, easy, open and trusting.

And so just after noon on Sunday, December 7, 1941, the thirty guests Eleanor Roosevelt had invited for lunch in the Blue Room strolled in casually from Pennsylvania Avenue. They were a group of friends, relatives and New Deal functionaries, some from the Army Medical Corps. One was Mrs. Charles Hamlin, a Roosevelt friend from the Hudson Valley who had spent the night of December 6 as a house guest, sleeping in Lincoln's bed, and who in the late morning had walked alone across Lafayette Square to services at St. John's Church. One of the guests looked over the group and said, "Mrs. Roosevelt's secretary is cleaning up the edges of her social list."

Outside of Washington, in Olney, Maryland, Harold Ickes, Roosevelt's secretary of the interior, maintained a working farm stocked with chickens, cattle and pigs. More than once it had led him into embarrassing little scandals when the Washington *Times-Herald* had caught him using Interior Department trucks to deliver eggs from his farm to be sold to Larimer's, a fancy grocery on Connecticut Avenue. On this Sunday he was entertaining Donald Nelson of SPAB, Supreme Court Justice Hugo Black and Senator Tom Connally of Texas, chairman of the Senate Foreign Relations Committee. They lazed about after lunch, skimmed the newspapers and carried on a fitful discussion of the international situation. All agreed that whatever Roosevelt thought, or others thought, they foresaw no imminent American involvement in the war.

They were more optimistic than the president was. The U.S. Navy was already effectively at war with Germany in the Atlantic, convoying supply ships to England and attacking German submarines when they threatened. One American ship, the *Sussex,* had been sunk. In the Pacific, American embargoes on shipments of oil and other supplies had embittered relations with Japan. Roosevelt had read coded Japanese cables Ickes and his guests had not seen and had information they did not have.

Earlier in 1941, Undersecretary of State Sumner Welles had spent a month touring Europe and talking to the national leaders still accessible, to assess the prospects for war and peace. He returned with the message that in his conversations with kings and prime ministers and the Pope, the chances for peace were seen to be poor. Roosevelt listened privately to Welles's report and concluded he saw "scant prospects" for peace.

A few weeks before, he had invited the ambassadors of the Western

Hemisphere countries—from Canada to Argentina—to a White House meeting where he said he believed they were in danger. "The war is approaching the brink of the Western Hemisphere itself," he said. "It is coming very close to home. But we will not accept a Hitler-dominated world."

Now, on December 7, his wife's guests filed into the Blue Room for lunch. Roosevelt was invited to join them, but declined. He had a cold, sinus congestion and a headache, and did not feel up to affecting the convivial gaiety that would be expected of him. He remained upstairs, wearing a turtleneck sweater, sitting with Harry Hopkins and having lunch on a tray. When the tray was removed from the small rack that attached to his wheelchair, he idled over his stamp collection. Hopkins lounged on a couch.

The day before, the Japanese government had sent its Washington embassy a long and angry message to be given to Roosevelt. The embassy had not yet delivered it but he had already read it. Since the Japanese diplomatic code had long since been broken, American officials routinely read Tokyo's communications with its Washington embassy even before the Japanese ambassador read them. And when this message, belligerent and threatening, was shown to the president he said, "This means war."

It did—much sooner than he thought. At Radio Washington, the U.S. Navy's communications station, the Sunday watch had just changed when chief radioman Frank A. Ackerson was called to the Hawaii circuit by an alert to stand by for an urgent message. It came: AIR RAID PEARL HARBOR. THIS IS NO DRILL.

This message, and the few details following, went to the watch officer, Lieutenant William L. Tagg, and from him to Rear Admiral Richmond K. Turner of the navy's War Plans Division, then to Admiral Harold Stark, chief of naval operations, and from there to Frank Knox, secretary of the navy, who responded, "Those little yellow bastards!" Knox telephoned the president.

It may be that at historic moments of stunning surprise or extraordinary stress, great leaders utter stately and sonorous phrases suitable for future preservation on granite slabs. But Roosevelt's response on hearing the Japanese had attacked Pearl Harbor was a good deal less than stately. His response was, "No!"

J. Edgar Hoover of the FBI, in New York for the weekend, took a telephone call from his Honolulu agent-in-charge, Robert L. Shivers, who said he knew Japanese airplanes when he saw them, and he saw fighters called Zeros, built by Mitsubishi. "You can hear the bombs yourself! Listen!" He held the telephone out his office window while Hoover sat in New York listening to the explosions.

Roosevelt called Secretary of State Hull, who was at that moment receiving the Japanese ambassador in his office at the State-War-Navy Building next door to the White House. He told Hull the news and instructed him to treat the Japanese coolly.

Japan's ambassador, Kichisaburo Nomura, arrived at Hull's office late because, it was learned later, his embassy staff had been drinking Scotch whisky all night and the translators were still drunk the next morning. They had to struggle to get Tokyo's message into English for Hull to read. When the ambassador and an aide came in, Hull did not treat them coolly. He called them "bastards" and "pissants." They left, running awkwardly down the corridors trying to escape the press and the photographers.

Roosevelt dictated a short statement of the news and asked his press secretary, Stephen Early, to announce it to the public. Early arranged a conference call to the Associated Press, the United Press and the International News Service: "This is Steve Early at the White House. At 7:30 a.m. Hawaiian time, the Japanese bombed Pearl Harbor. The attacks are continuing. No, I don't know how many are dead."

Mrs. Roosevelt's guests, their lunch over, left the Blue Room and walked out to Pennsylvania Avenue knowing nothing of the news. Donald Nelson, driving down Georgia Avenue from the Ickes lunch in Olney, heard it on his automobile radio. In the air between Fort Bragg, North Carolina, and Hunter Field near Savannah, Georgia, a Douglas A-20 bomber, army air corps pilot Paul W. Tibbetts at the controls, was about twenty minutes from landing. Tibbetts navigated by tuning in a Savannah radio station and steering by his radio compass, a simple device then commonly used. The station he was homing in on interrupted a Glenn Miller record to broadcast the news. Tibbetts knew war had started; just over three-and-a-half years later, he would help end it by piloting the *Enola Gay,* named for his mother, over Hiroshima and dropping the atomic bomb.

About twenty-seven thousand people, not yet having heard the news, were watching the Washington Redskins' last football game of the season. They were playing the Philadelphia Eagles in creaky old Griffith Stadium.

* * *

It was a modest place, used for Redskins football and Washington Senators baseball. There were green-painted steel-and-wood grandstands and bleachers, a lighting system that faded dangerously toward near-darkness in the far outfields. On the scoreboard in right field small boys changed the numbers by hand. There was not enough parking for the players and none at all for the customers. Griffith Stadium stood in the midst of one of the city's worst slums and looked as if it belonged in one of the minor leagues.

The first word of Pearl Harbor came to the stadium when the Associated Press sent out the news and ordered its sportswriter in the press box to "keep it short," meaning that the news wires that night would be far too jammed to have room for much sports news, if any. Pandemonium broke out in the press box and when the spectators nearby overheard it, the news began to spread down the seats, becoming more and more garbled as it traveled from row to row. Then the stadium loud-speaker started a series of announcements asking one general or admiral after another to report to duty immediately. The stadium announcer then said newspaper circulation managers and delivery boys were wanted at their jobs without delay. Then the ambassador from the Philippines. Other ambassadors. Radio news people. Newspaper reporters. The football crowd was bewildered and confused, but the stadium management refused to announce the news on the public address system, saying, "We don't want to contribute to any hysteria." The wife of a newspaper reporter heard the news on her radio at home and dispatched a telegram to her husband sitting in the grandstand: "DELIVER TO SECTION P, TOP ROW, SEAT 27, OPPOSITE 25-YARD LINE, EAST SIDE, GRIFFITH STADIUM: WAR WITH JAPAN! GET TO OFFICE!"

At the Japanese embassy on Massachusetts Avenue, crowds gathered and saw smoke rising from diplomatic papers being burned in the rear garden. Reporters walked inside and watched the embassy staff quietly and solemnly filing out a rear door carrying cardboard boxes, each carefully wrapped and each with a fuse protruding from the end, like a big, square firecracker. Each box in turn was set down and lit with a kitchen match. The fuse sizzled, and then the box burst into flame. It almost seemed as if the Japanese had prepared fireworks to entertain children at a lawn party. But it was all quiet. The Japanese said nothing, the crowd standing around said nothing, and the only sound was the sizzle of the fuses and the crackling of burning paper. As the news spread and the crowd grew, the embassy called the Burns Detective Agency for a crowd-control detail, but the District of Columbia Police and the FBI soon arrived and took over, coughing a little in the smoke.

Two months earlier, in October, the FBI had begun to notice an unusual number of Japanese embassy staff people quietly drifting out of Washington, many of them on airplanes to Argentina. It had also observed new and more elaborate radio antennas appearing on the embassy roof. But otherwise, nobody had paid much attention to the Japanese. Unlike the Germans, they were almost invisible on the diplomatic social circuit. Usually they were seen only when they came out of their embassy in a little phalanx of pinstripe suits and bowler hats to call on Cordell Hull, tell him that day's lie about their devotion to peace, and return home.

On network radio, H. V. Kaltenborn reported the attack on Pearl Harbor and offered his analysis, based on no information whatsoever, but speculating about how many days and hours, depending on the winds and current, it would take the U.S. Navy to sail across the Pacific and "devastate the home islands of Japan."

Roosevelt called a meeting of his Cabinet to discuss a speech to Congress. A declaration of war, yes. But what else should he say? The Cabinet's consensus was that Congress and the public were steaming in fury. Even Roosevelt's oldest enemies were saying that nothing else mattered now, and everyone should fall in line behind the military forces and behind him, their commander-in-chief. Therefore, they agreed, his speech should do no more than ask a formal declaration of war and try to direct this rage toward the Japanese. A speech saying this and little else was written in haste, and it was announced that the president would address Congress the next day at noon.

Early Monday morning, Mike Reilly, chief of the White House Secret Service detail, began looking around for an armored, bulletproof limousine for the president's protection, but he ran into a federal regulation against buying any car that cost more than $750. Then he found that the U.S. Treasury owned a huge armored limousine it had seized in its income tax evasion case against the notorious gangster Al Capone. Reilly had it washed, lubricated and driven to the White House. Roosevelt asked what it was and when told said, "I hope Mr. Capone won't mind."

It was the vehicle he used thereafter, until the Ford Motor Company offered to build him an armored car and to avoid the regulations by leasing it to the White House for $500 a year.

Among the guests invited to the Capitol to hear Roosevelt's speech on Monday was Mrs. Woodrow Wilson, who still lived in the same house at 2340 S Street into which she and her husband had moved after they left the White House. She arrived in black dress and white gloves to hear Eleanor's husband ask for a war her own husband had hoped, and for a time believed, would never come. Just before the United States entered her husband's war, Wilson had come to this same building and said in a speech to the U.S. Senate, with more foresight than he could have known, that World War I must end in "peace without victory." Otherwise, he said, "victory would mean peace forced upon the loser, a victor's terms imposed on the vanquished. It would be accepted in humiliation, under duress, at an intolerable sacrifice, and would leave a sting, a resentment, a bitter memory upon which the terms of peace would rest, not permanently, but only as upon quicksand."

So quick had been the sand that a German corporal, as if he had memorized Wilson's speech, seized power by appealing precisely to these stings, resentments and bitter memories among the German people. And as Roosevelt came to the Capitol, Hitler was already promising the Japanese he would soon join them in war against the United States. Within a day the German embassy was burning its code books and Hitler was praising Japan for striking without warning and without wasting time with a formal declaration of war.

And so quick had been the sand that some of the same men who served in the army as second lieutenants in Wilson's war would now serve as majors and colonels in Roosevelt's.

Edith Wilson's husband's war had led to Eleanor Roosevelt's husband's war in a historical fabric twenty-three years long and with hardly a seam, even though Wilson had told Congress in 1918, "This is the culminating and final war for human liberty." She may, must have, remembered all of that when Roosevelt came into the House Chamber to ask for another. Some may even have remembered the bitter remark by David Lloyd George, Britain's prime minister in World War I: "This war, like the next war, is the war to end all wars."

Roosevelt's speech to Congress and the American people attracted, according to the Hooper ratings, the largest audience in the history of radio, sixty million people. What all those people heard was a statement about five minutes long, short and simple because of the decision that since the nation's fears had already been so cruelly aroused, oratorical flourishes were not needed. Within a few days nobody could remember much of it except one grammatically dubious phrase in the opening sentence, "a date which will live in infamy. . . . " There was none of Churchill's rolling thunder and lightning about fighting them on the beaches, nor any calling of the country to its finest hour. Instead, there was a fairly flat statement of the facts, a careful omission of any detail about the great losses suffered at Pearl Harbor, an unembellished call for a declaration of war on the Japanese empire. Forty-eight minutes after the president arrived, the Senate declared war, by a vote of 82 to 0. Thirty-two minutes later the House followed with a vote of 388 to 1.

The one was Representative Jeannette Rankin of Montana, who had also voted (but not alone) against World War I. She cast her "no" vote and then ran into an anteroom, closed herself inside a telephone booth, and sat there crying. The police insisted that for her own safety they would have to escort her across the street to her office. Her state reacted with a burst of fury and telegrams poured in accusing her of "staining the honor of Montana." It was the end of her career in Congress.

Military officers stationed in Washington were ordered to report on the morning of December 8 in full uniform. Their peacetime dress, on duty and off, generally had run to outfits like brown tweed jackets and gray trousers, and the higher ranks had worn uniforms only on ceremonial occasions. Some barely owned any. And so on Monday morning the corridors of the army and navy buildings were filled with officers who looked a mess. Some wore uniforms and parts of uniforms dating to 1918, many of them now two sizes too small. Majors were in outfits they had bought when they were second lieutenants. Others were dressed in clothes partly military and partly civilian. There were wool leg wrappings from the 1918 war and other outfits equally outlandish and topped with garrison caps (leather bills), field caps (the "overseas" cap folding open like an envelope) and campaign hats (wide brimmed, as worn by forest rangers and Boy Scouts). It was a rummage sale called to war.

Even before Roosevelt spoke, all over Washington the hoarding had begun. Nobody knew what the war's effects would be. Some foods certainly would soon be scarce, but no one knew which ones. So people crowded the grocery stores on Monday and bought whatever was there. Because the geopolitical analysts among the shoppers knew that Pearl Harbor was in Hawaii and Hawaii meant pineapple, the canned pineapple shelves emptied fast. A Ford station wagon left a Connecticut Avenue store so grossly overloaded with canned foods the rear end sagged down and rubbed on the tires, causing black smoke and a horrible odor as it crept slowly toward Chevy Chase, the front end so high in the air the driver could hardly see ahead, his headlights shining upward into the trees. Had the driver only known, most of the foods he had stacked in his wagon would remain reasonably plentiful while the tires he was destroying would not. Hoarders would have been better off if they had bought new cars, spare tires, whatever gasoline they could store, cigarettes, coffee, sugar, liquor and household appliances, especially radios. Not knowing, people rushed to buy anything and everything and by nightfall on December 8, the markets looked as if a high wind had blown them clean. The following spring, heavy rains flooded some Washington basements, and the *Post* reported that rainwater had poured into a basement stacked full of hoarded canned goods, soaked the labels off the cans and left the owner to guess which ones held cranberry sauce and which held green peas.

On the evening of December 8, Mrs. Atherton Richards had planned, and declined to cancel, a dinner in honor of Colonel William ("Wild Bill") Donovan, head of COI (Coordinator of Information), which was soon to become the OSS (Office of Strategic Services) and eventually the CIA. None of the guests knew much about the events at Pearl Harbor until one of them, Arthur Krock, head of the New York *Times* Washington bureau, went out to take a telephone call. He came back to say, "My God! Ninety percent of our fleet was knocked out at Pearl Harbor!" Asked if Krock was right, Donovan said, "Arthur has very good sources."

For months, the public learned almost nothing of what had happened. When Roosevelt was asked at a press conference about reports that the Japanese had done far more damage than the American people had been told, he answered that the best description of these stories was "R-O-T," that Washington was the worst rumor factory in the United States and the source of more lies than any other city. The truth was that Roosevelt and his military advisers were afraid that if the Japanese knew how thoroughly they had devastated American naval power in the

Pacific, they might consider an amphibious assault on Hawaii. The truth continued to be concealed.

The day after the United States declared war, the Japanese in Washington had other troubles. Their envoys, Nomura and Korusu, after delivering Tokyo's message to Secretary Hull, had been ordered to remain in rooms rented for them at the Washington Hotel under twenty-four-hour guard. Nomura asked that his samurai sword be sent over from the embassy. Fearing that he was preparing to commit suicide, the State Department refused; it did not want to be accused of murdering a diplomat, even an enemy.

Out at the Japanese embassy, with the burning finished, fifty staff members were held under guard in a building with overnight accommodations for only ten. On Monday, they sent the Woodward and Lothrop department store an order for 26 mattresses, 72 cartons of Ivory soap, 101 pillow cases and 47 pillows. They called other stores to order Scotch whisky, beer, oysters, French bread and 500 aspirin tablets. It all arrived with bills stipulating that only cash would be accepted—no Japanese checks.

While the Japanese were confined with their oysters, aspirin and whiskey, German and Italian diplomats moved about Washington freely for several days, until Hitler declared war on the United States on December 12. Hans Thomsen rode over to the State Department to deliver his country's declaration of war. As he stepped into his black Buick, he said cheerfully, "Anybody want to buy a nice car?" He used it for the last time to call on Cordell Hull, who deliberately kept him waiting an hour. Thomsen finally sold the car for a thousand dollars to Olivia Davis, owner of a nightclub a block from the embassy. Thomsen's wife, Bebe, was busy trying to sell her horse. "Leaving the United States," she said, "is like leaving a second home. It is so sad! I shall come back here after the war is over. Goodbye."

During his last days in Washington, Thomsen was asked about "a fine mist of ashes" coming out of his embassy's chimney. He said most of his secret material was already back in Germany, "but there are always a few confidential papers." Visitors were still greeted at the door by a guard clicking his heels and offering a Nazi salute, arm extended upward at thirty degrees and a brisk "Heil Hitler!" One of the embassy's Gestapo officers, Hans von Gienanth, working with the diplomats of friendly countries—Italy, Spain, Vichy France, Argentina—carried on their joint programs of espionage as if nothing had happened. But the FBI, listening to everything around town, found the Germans were hand-carrying messages to the Spanish embassy to be encoded and sent to Argentina, where German diplomats received them for unencumbered delivery to Berlin. That, finally, was enough. The State Department announced that all enemy diplomats would be removed from Washington forthwith and confined elsewhere until they could be exchanged for American diplomats interned in Europe and Japan.

On December 29, a police motorcycle escort rolled up to the Japanese embassy at the head of a column of four buses, three limousines and five trucks for baggage. All the Japanese were driven to Union Station and put aboard a special train to the Homestead Hotel, a mountain resort in Hot Springs, Virginia, where, after a good deal of confusion and complaint, they were assigned to rooms and the hotel kept under guard.

The hotel management asked the State Department to promise to pay for any damage the Japanese did to the hotel and to get them out by April 1, in time for the hotel's spring season. State was evasive.

The first request from the Japanese was from a second-level diplomat who wanted books. He asked for Albert Schweitzer's *The Quest of the Historical Jesus,* Sandburg's *Abraham Lincoln: The War Years,* and the works of Shakespeare. The second demand was for prompt shipment to the Homestead of a stock of whiskey left in the basement of the Washington embassy—five cases of Old Paar and five of Johnny Walker Black Label.

The Germans and Italians were settled at the Greenbrier Hotel in White Sulphur Springs, West Virginia. The hotel complained their dogs were ruining the carpets and their children were roller-skating in the hallways and playing in the elevators. At first they were all confined indoors until they objected to being cooped up like animals and demanded access to the outdoors and fresh air. Eventually, a small area of the hotel grounds was opened to them, including two tennis courts. Then they discovered the hotel's souvenir and gift shops and bought up huge supplies of soap, coffee, tea, radios, canned foods, cigarettes and sports clothes. They piled all this in the basement in sealed boxes to be taken home when the time came. Then the State Department spoiled it all by saying that each interned diplomat, on returning home, would be allowed two trunks and no more.

At first, relations among the interned diplomats were cordial enough. They dined together, danced with one another's wives, played bridge.

Then it all began to come apart. The Italians complained about the food, and the Germans complained about the Italians. There were sneers and disparaging remarks and jokes about the Italian navy. And when Rumanian and Hungarian diplomats began arriving at the hotel, the conversations fell to the level of ethnic slurs and screaming arguments about how countries should share in the spoils when the war was over. The different nationalities withdrew to themselves and refused to speak to one another. Since they were denied newspapers and radios and all information from outside, each group circulated poisonous and insulting rumors about the others' countries and leaders, their wives and daughters. Lies and slanders floated all over the hotel, which became a steaming, rancid swamp of snobbery, hatreds, insults and cross-cultural loathing. A German officer fingered his monocle and announced in icy tones that he could not possibly share a hotel "with these swarthy and barbaric people from the south of Europe." Had the diplomats not been stripped of personal weapons and sharp instruments, they might have started still another war among themselves right there in the mountains of West Virginia.

By March 1942, the hatred had risen to such a dangerous level that the State Department feared the diplomats would soon be stabbing each other in their beds with sharpened knives stolen from the dining room. To avert the possibility of violence, it moved the Italians and Hungarians to the Grove Park Inn in Asheville, North Carolina, another mountain resort. A State Department agent on the scene reported back to Washington, "The Italians were very happy to leave, having no great affection for the Germans."

To fill the space left by the Italians' departure, the Japanese were moved to the Greenbrier from the Homestead, further irritating the Germans. The Nazis complained they were insulted by being housed with Orientals, while the Italians now at the Grove Park Inn complained of the food, the maid service, and of accommodations "inadequate to the rank and family conditions of the members of the staff." Most furious of all were those housed, because the hotel was overcrowded, in the servant cottages.

In May 1942, a solution was reached. The Germans were to be exchanged for the interned American diplomats. They traveled by train to New York City and boarded a Swedish passenger liner, the *Drottningholm,* bound for Lisbon. Through the packs of American, British and German submarines, in the only ship on the ocean fully lighted at night, with the word DIPLOMATS painted in huge lettering on the sides, they crossed the Atlantic. It was a trip the majority of them probably did not welcome.

Meanwhile, back at the Greenbrier, the farce continued. The Japanese, who had now replaced the Germans, came to Edwin Poole, a State Department officer, and demanded 133 additional rooms. Poole said these had to be reserved for future arrivals. The Japanese spokesman flew into a rage, called it racial discrimination and insisted on precisely the same accommodations the Germans had been given. Poole did move a few people around, trying to shut them up, while reminding the Japanese they were in no position to demand anything.

Henry Morgenthau, Jr., was secretary of the treasury even though he had wanted to be secretary of agriculture, his background having been that of an apple grower in upstate New York and a neighbor and worshipful friend of Roosevelt's. The Secret Service, now charged with protecting the president, was an old government service originally established to protect against counterfeiting of U.S. currency, and so it was always an agency of the Treasury. Now it was under Morgenthau's direction. Within hours of the news of Pearl Harbor, he was pacing the White House looking nervously out of the windows and scanning the skies for German bombers. He insisted that the Secret Service pile sandbags at all White House entrances and place machine guns at every door. Mike Reilly thought this was not necessary, but all staff members were issued gas masks, Roosevelt's hanging from the arm of his wheelchair. The White House architect, Lorenzo Winslow, was put to work designing a bomb shelter. It included a tunnel under the street to the basement of the Treasury Department next door and, under the East Wing of the White House itself, a shelter forty feet square with a concrete ceiling nine feet thick, enough to withstand the blast of a five-hundred-pound bomb. There were diesel engines to generate electricity and to bring in filtered air. The design was recommended by the British, who were by now experienced at surviving bombs.

The Secret Service urged the army also to place antiaircraft guns on the roofs of government buildings. The army agreed, but it was later discovered it had so few of them that some were replicas made of painted wood. A few real guns were installed, but since none was ever fired, it was not known until years later that the ammunition stacked up beside them was the wrong size.

Throughout Washington there were fears of sabotage and enemy attack. If Japan had bombed Hawaii from aircraft carriers, who could be sure it could not do the same to Washington? When you make war on a country, you attack its capital city, don't you? And how about the Germans, who were much closer than the Japanese and whose submarines were already active along the Atlantic coast? These worries were addressed, after a fashion, by a new Civilian Defense Committee, headed by a retired colonel, Lemuel Boles. He was full of confidence and reassurance, saying, "Washington has nothing to worry about at the present time." He already had a third or more of the volunteer air raid wardens he needed, he claimed. He invited others willing to serve to a meeting in the fire department training school. There they would be sworn in, issued identification cards and given instructions on how to patrol the streets during blackouts, fight fires with their buckets of sand and report suspicious behavior to Colonel Boles.

Three thousand people showed up at a building big enough to hold two hundred. Those who could not get in were packed so densely on the outside that those inside could not get out. They waited. But no one rose and walked to the microphone. Nothing happened at all. There was bedlam. Where was the training? The ID cards? No one could answer. Finally, Clement Murphy, a fire department battalion chief, climbed to a table, threw up his hands in despair and said he would now swear in everyone in the room and everyone outside, and would they all please go home and wait for their ID cards to be sent to them? Thus did Washington begin preparing to defend itself against the rain of bombs no doubt soon to fall.

A week after Pearl Harbor, Colonel Boles, or "Lem," as he was called, addressed a group of volunteers in the DuPont Circle neighborhood and gave them instructions that directly conflicted with those being given other groups. Asked about this, Boles said, "These are the directions you are getting today. It is only fair to tell you, however, they may be changed tomorrow. I would not be surprised if they were changed again a week from tomorrow. And ten days later they may be changed back to the directions you are getting now."

The District School Board ordered its teachers to serve as wardens to protect their school buildings at night. But no one was sure what the buildings were to be protected from or what to protect them with. One teacher was ordered to remain in the school all night and maintain communication with her principal through a telephone inside a locked closet to which she was denied a key. The buildings being unheated at night, the teachers were told to report for duty with blankets and heavy coats. One teacher spent the nights in a chair on the front steps of Eastern High School bundled in blankets, a shotgun in her lap and a German shepherd lying on each side. Another, ordered by her principal to report for duty, agreed and politely asked what she was to do. His response, in the tones of some tough drill sergeant he must have seen in the movies: "This is war. It is not the time for subordinates to ask questions."

Out in the streets, there were complaints that some of the street-corner air raid wardens were "behaving like fascists." For no reason, they stopped people on the sidewalks and demanded to know who they were and where they were going and why. At night, they aimed flashlights in their eyes and examined them as if they were a robbery squad questioning criminals.

An air raid drill, the city's first ever, was called for December 21. A disaster. Washington's only air raid siren was left over from World War I and was mounted on top of the electric power company's building downtown. Newspapers and radio stations had warned the citizenry for days in advance that they would be required to take cover, keep away from windows and stay inside until the all-clear sounded. Everyone was ready and waiting, a little excited, some with beer and sandwiches for sustenance while they hid under their beds. They had not seen all those newsreels and Hollywood movies about the bombing of London for nothing. The moment came. A city officer threw a switch. Nothing. The old siren was so rusty and creaky it could put out no more than a modest squawk, its volume about equal to that of a chicken with her neck caught in the henhouse door. It could not be heard across the street. Everyone had expected a chilling, frightening but secretly pleasing scream. What they got was an undulating, croaking wheeze. Police telephones were jammed with callers asking what had happened to the air raid drill? Was that the best we could do? What will we do if the Germans come?

Their air raid drill an embarrassing failure, the city fathers felt the need to do something that might work. They announced that on the night of December 30, there would be a blackout drill. How could that fail? It required nothing, after all, but flipping light switches. This time, they arranged for the police and fire departments to blow their sirens, and said that other noisemakers to alert the city would include church and school bells. The city's factories would blow their whistles, even though no one knew of a factory of any kind in Washington, and certainly none with a whistle. This time it was a little better. Most of the lights did go out. But it did seem that spending days, even weeks, advertising and organizing all this noise would present difficulties if German bombers were already on the horizon.

There were other unexpected problems. On the night of the first blackout, a radio station with studios in the Raleigh Hotel downtown made careful plans for an announcer to describe the darkening city by walking around the hotel roof with a portable microphone and reporting which neighborhoods were the first to get all their lights out and which were the laggards and how many violations were visible. In its promotional announcements, the station said, "It's going to be an exciting program." It might have been, if the management had remembered that when the hotel janitor pulled a switch in the basement to black out the hotel, he also cut the station off the air.

There were still more problems. Farmers growing cabbage near the seacoasts floodlit their fields at night to stop the sea birds from eating their crops. Their neighbors complained to Civil Defense that the lights made an easy target for enemy bombers. The Agriculture Department's county agent responded, "How in the name of God do they expect to win a war without cabbage?"

New York's Mayor Fiorello LaGuardia wrote to Roosevelt urging a new national office for civilian defense:

Now, Mr. President, as I see it, what is needed is something more than just another Board, Bureau, Commission, Committee or Volunteer Firemen's Association. God knows, you have enough of them now. Please bear in mind that up to this war, and never in our history, has the civilian population been exposed to attack. The new technique of war has created the necessity for developing a new technique of civilian defense. It is not just community singing, sweater knitting and basket weaving that is needed.

* * *

Roosevelt's response was to set up a new federal government agency, the Office of Civilian Defense, and to put LaGuardia in charge of it while he continued as mayor, commuting back and forth between New York and Washington.

After the fall of France, Eleanor Roosevelt had offered to go to Europe to help in relief work for war victims, but Roosevelt refused. His security people said it was unthinkable for the president's wife to risk being captured by the Nazis. So she turned to civilian defense as her favorite volunteer work and applied to it her enormous energy, generosity and kindness, along with a degree of unworldliness always puzzling to her admirers. For example, her hiring of a dancer named Mayris Chaney to be "National Sports Coordinator" for employees of the OCD. Her duties were to lead them in dancing and exercise to music from a portable record player on the flat roof of the OCD building at DuPont Circle, and to organize "volunteer coordinators" across the country to plan bowling, archery and other diversions to keep women employees mentally alert and physically fit.

Among the first signs of trouble was a letter in a Washington newspaper from a man asking to be made "volunteer coordinator for stud poker." The real outcry came when it was discovered Miss Chaney was being paid $4,600 a year, more than most military officers. Roosevelt's enemies in Congress, ever eager to ridicule him and his family, could not have been happier. They denounced Miss Chaney as a "fan dancer" and "burlesque queen." She was neither, but the charge alone was enough to set newspaper cartoonists and editorial writers to howling with glee about a fan dancer making $4,600 a year while a new private in the U.S. Army was paid $21 a month. Nothing was known of Roosevelt's reaction to all this, but the speculation was that he said, "Goddamn it, Eleanor, what will you do to me next?"

What she did next was to announce she would appoint the movie actor Melvyn Douglas to some unspecified office in the Office of Civilian Defense. That set them off again, since Douglas was a vociferous liberal, frequently charged with having vague communist connections. Conservatives in Congress were outraged in public and secretly pleased in private. It gave them material for more speeches, especially when someone pointed out that Douglas's name was actually Hesselberg, suggesting he was of German ancestry and therefore not to be trusted. Whatever appointment Mrs. Roosevelt had had in mind for Douglas, he never got it.

LaGuardia suggested that air raid shelters be equipped with decks of playing cards to help people pass the time while waiting out the air raids. Rural clergymen, for whom a deck of cards was the handmaiden of gambling and certain to unravel the players' moral fiber, wrote to their congressmen demanding that the air raid shelters be stocked with Bibles instead. More editorials and cartoons. More speeches in Congress. It was just too ridiculous to be allowed to go on, and Roosevelt's advisers were urging him to get rid of LaGuardia. He agreed and asked Budget Director Harold Smith to invite LaGuardia to the White House to be fired. When he arrived, there was only a long, aimless conversation without substance or purpose. Roosevelt was faced with having to look across his desk at a man he genuinely liked and tell him he was fired. He simply could not do it. Smith recalled, "They talked all around the lot but it ended with LaGuardia staying on as OCD director."

When the embarrassments continued—LaGuardia seemed to spend all his time flying around town in OCD cars with sirens screaming and being photographed in funny hats—Roosevelt gave in halfway. He summoned the mayor again and used what Smith called "a favorite FDR dodge": instead of firing him, the president went around LaGuardia sideways and appointed a deputy, with the understanding that the deputy would do all the work. He asked LaGuardia to take on James M. Landis, dean of the Harvard Law School, as his assistant.

Within a few months Landis was running the agency, and LaGuardia and Mrs. Roosevelt had bowed out. Landis did bring some order to the place, and along with it some bureaucratic language. At a press conference Roosevelt tried to read some of it but could not get through it without laughing. It was the OCD's instructions for blacking out office windows: "Such obscuration may be obtained either by blackout construction or by terminating the illumination."

Reporters laughed, asking, "Did Steve Early write that?"

"No, Steve didn't write that. The dean of Harvard Law School wrote it."

Roosevelt handed the paper to press secretary Steve Early and asked him to rewrite it. "Tell them the buildings that have to keep their work going, put something over the windows. In buildings that can afford it, so that work can be stopped for a while, turn out the lights."

* * *

In the late, reddish, half-dark afternoon of December 24, 1941, as always, the National Christmas Tree on the lawn south of the White House was to be lighted by the president, at the push of a button. The public was invited. The White House gates would be open, and the U.S. Marine Band in its red coats would play *Adeste Fidelis* and more. Washingtonians knew it would be beautiful. This Christmas would be much like those that had gone before, with trees and ornaments and lights and gifts and their families all at home. But when would there be another? Where would their sons, brothers, fathers, husbands be a year from now? How many would even be alive? Draft calls were increasing, and there were long lines of volunteers at the recruiting stations now open twenty-four hours a day. How many of the men in their lives would be home for Christmas in December 1942? How many would never be home again?

They also knew this: When Roosevelt pushed the button this evening, the tree would leap into shining life, he would speak, he would be optimistic and reassuring in those distinctive tones of his, and when he finished he would introduce a visitor—Winston Churchill. Few names on earth, few names in history, so stirred them. It was routine now in the letters to the newspapers for people to say the British so loved Roosevelt and the Americans so loved Churchill the two allies could exchange national leaders and both would be happy—possibly even happier.

Barely two hours after he had returned to the White House from asking Congress to declare war, Roosevelt had cabled Churchill that the United States was at war with Japan. "Today all of us are in the same boat with you and the people of the Empire and it is a ship which will not and cannot be sunk."

Churchill responded the next day. "Now that we are, as you say, 'in the same boat,' would it not be wise for us to have another conference?"

Roosevelt thought it wise, and Churchill arrived by air in total secrecy and moved into the White House on December 22, his presence announced only after he was safely inside and the gates closed. A figure almost none in Washington had ever seen, but who had enchanted Americans with his leadership, his oratory, his appetite for food, cigars and whiskey, his wit. He was there, and he would speak beside the Christmas tree.

Twenty thousand people came to stand in the cold inside and outside the black iron fence. Guards at the gates intoned, "No cameras, no packages." Those carrying Christmas packages from a day's shopping on F Street simply piled them on the grass outside the fence, trusting they would find them when they returned, a lingering aspect of Washington's small-townishness. The prime minister of Great Britain came out with Franklin and Eleanor Roosevelt, Harry Hopkins and Crown Prince Olaf and Crown Princess Marthe of Norway, who were refugees and house guests. Roosevelt pressed a button and a huge evergreen down at the lower end of the lawn sprang to light. Applause.

Joseph Corrigan, rector of Catholic University in Northeast Washington, delivered the invocation. "All the material resources with which Thou hast blessed our native land we consecrate to the dread tasks of war."

Roosevelt spoke. "It is in the spirit of peace and good will, and with particular thoughtfulness of those, our sons and brothers, who serve in our armed forces on land and sea, near and far—those who serve and endure for us—that we light our Christmas candles now across this continent from one coast to the other on this Christmas evening."

Now, he said, our visitor, Prime Minister Churchill, wanted to speak to Washington and the world. Churchill stepped forward and spoke in the voice everyone—everyone—knew:

> This is a strange Christmas eve. Almost the whole world is locked in deadly struggle, and with the most terrible weapons which science can devise, the nations advance upon each other. Ill would it be for us this Christmastide if we were not sure that no greed for the land or wealth of any other people, no vulgar ambition, no morbid lust for material gain at the expense of others has led us to the field. Here, in the midst of war, raging and roaring over all the lands and seas, creeping nearer to our hearts and our homes, here, amid all the tumult, we have tonight the peace of the spirit in each cottage home and in each generous heart. Therefore, we may cast aside for this night at least the cares and dangers which beset us, and make for our children an evening of happiness in a world of storm. Here, then, for one night only, each home throughout the English-speaking world should be a brightly lighted island of happiness and peace.

Let the children have their night of fun and laughter. Let the gifts of Father Christmas delight their play. Let us grown-ups share to the full in their unstinted pleasures before we turn again to the stern task and the formidable years that lie before us, resolved that by our sacrifice and daring, these same children shall not be robbed of their inheritance or denied their right to live in a free and decent world.

In God's mercy, a happy Christmas to you all.

Now it was dark. The crowd was silent. They picked up their Christmas packages and moved out through the gates into the street. It was lined with trolley cars, many of them recently brought out of retirement and returned to the streets to meet the needs of a city now desperately overcrowded. Some were nineteenth-century double-ended wooden cars with clerestory windows around the roofs, and when they rolled away through the dark with their pale yellow interior lights they looked like swaying Japanese lanterns lit with candles.

V

Boom Town

Most Americans were unaware that Franklin Roosevelt had no use of his legs. To stand, he needed to wear heavy metal braces. To walk, he clung to a railing or someone's arm. Poliomyelitis had crippled him in 1921, and he had never really recovered. But he had worked out numerous little stratagems for concealing all that from the public. When he made a speech he entered the auditorium before the audience arrived; they would find him already seated behind the dais. When he traveled by car, he was lifted in and out of the back seat away from public view. News photographers understood that they were not to photograph the president sitting in his wheelchair or being carried, and when anyone violated that rule the Secret Service confiscated the film. Of the several hundred thousand photographs of Franklin Roosevelt in archives today, only a handful show him in his wheelchair.

Roosevelt seemed generally to bear his handicap with grace and good spirit, but it forced him to live what was in many ways a vicarious life. His mobility restricted by both his handicap and the duties of his office, he had no real sense of the momentous changes occurring in the city outside. And at times he seized on the random complaints of those around him to express what were, perhaps, his own frustrations. That, at least, seemed to be the case a few months after Pearl Harbor when he began complaining that the city of Washington hardly knew there was a war on, that there was "less realization of the actual war effort in Washington, D.C., than anywhere else."

He was wrong, of course. Washingtonians probably had more reminders of the war effort than people in any other American city. But the president could not see them and imagined them carrying on in their usual drab, lifeless manner. The cheerleaders were asleep under the grandstand.

What about bands and flags and parades? That might do it. So the president ordered a mammoth patriotic ceremony on Memorial Day 1942. He was infuriated to discover that the District commissioners had banned all parades, saying the crowds might become dangerous and unmanageable. A few words from the White House and the city government changed its rule. And on Memorial Day, there were bands and flags and soldiers and sailors, marines, tanks with sirens, army planes overhead. Sitting in the reviewing stand were representatives of all twenty-six Allied nations. With them was the president, wearing a seersucker suit, Panama hat and black armband, watching one of his favorite art forms: a pounding, roaring, flag-and-trumpet parade.

Roosevelt was so pleased that he called next for a tremendous Fourth-of-July fireworks display on the grounds of the Washington Monument, with flags, rockets, bands and red, white and blue flashes of fire across the sky. But the city government had banned fireworks too. The sparks might set fire to the new, wooden temporary buildings going up along the mall. The president was not deterred. The hell with the fools in the District Building! Shoot the rockets up from a barge in the Potomac and let the sparks fall in the water. Put the Marine Band in its scarlet coats and brass trumpets on another barge. Tell the army to light them with searchlights so people could see them from the Washington and Virginia shores. Tell them to play "The Stars and Stripes Forever" while the rockets burst overhead. It was another wonderful show, and it revealed a quality in Roosevelt that many of his friends had never seen before. Beneath the statesman and politician was a P. T. Barnum.

Gorgeous as they were, there was no need for Roosevelt's spectacles to wake up the city. Washington was already growing and changing more rapidly than any other city in the country. The population of the metropolitan area had mushroomed from 621,000 in 1930 to well over a million by the end of 1941. Seventy thousand new people arrived in the first year after Pearl Harbor alone. Government employment had more than doubled since the beginning of 1940, and more than five thousand new federal workers were pouring into Washington every month, often bringing their families with them. The District government was issuing over fifteen hundred building permits a month and still could not keep up with the demand. The transportation system was staggering under its new burdens. The city's antiquated trolleys could handle only about a third of the government workers trying to get to their offices; the others had to drive downtown, where parking spaces were almost impossible to find. Traffic moved at a snail's pace at nearly every hour of the day; during rush hours it was often completely paralyzed. Visitors arriving at Union Station had to fight through crowds that made the enormous concourse nearly impassable. Cabs were so scarce that government workers took to using their own cars as taxis during off hours. "Washington needs a subway," Alden Stevens wrote in 1941, "and needs it as quickly as it can be built. . . . It has been shown to offer a relatively simple engineering problem. It would not be inordinately expensive."

Residents of Washington, accustomed to bumping along in an easy rut, listening to "Amos 'n Andy," and driving Chevrolets to Ocean City, Maryland, for summer vacations, were not altogether ready for this. Their placid, comfortable town was becoming a noisy, crowded, expensive city—a place that newcomers liked to joke combined the charm of the North with the efficiency of the South.

A young man new to the city in the first years of the war set out for lunch one day carrying his shirts, planning to drop them off at a laundry on his way to Fan and Bill's Restaurant. No, they told him, the laundry was accepting no more customers. With all these people moving to town, they were swamped with work, were weeks behind already and simply could not take on any more. What could he do? He would look silly walking into a restaurant with an armload of dirty shirts and socks. They told him others had found it best to wrap their laundry in brown paper, take it to the post office, and mail it home to be washed.

Chaos was bearing down on Washington. Its form was already easy to see when Arthur S. Flemming of the Civil Service Commission told a House committee in 1942 that still another five hundred thousand government employees would be needed in the coming year, probably more than that.

They came. They came on every train and bus, nearly all of them women, wearing dyed-to-match sweaters and skirts and carrying suitcases tied shut with white cotton clothesline, or cardboard boxes printed with the names of the sewing machines and hair dryers that had come in them. They carried department-store shopping bags already splitting up the sides. They came in response to recruiting advertisements in local newspapers across the country. One of the advertisements trying to entice typists to work in Washington said, "It takes twenty-five girls behind typewriters to put one man behind the trigger in this war." If that figure had been right, when the army grew to 7.5 million men, as it did, it would have required 187 million "girls behind typewriters"—more than the total population of the United States.

Formal civil service exams had been dropped for the war. Too slow. The government could not wait months for the forms to be mailed, graded and classified. If you could type and had a high school diploma, you were hired. $1,440 a year.

The women were told to go from the trains and buses to a mass receiving station, a huge loft above a five-and-dime store, a scene of noise, crowding, confusion. They milled about, still in the clothes they had worn on the trains, carefully studying each other to see if dresses and hair styles and lipstick colors just off the train from Alabama were unacceptably different from those just off the train from Minnesota. They lined up at desks hauled over from government warehouses and staffed with women slightly older than the new arrivals, women trying to conceal their fatigue from answering the same questions a hundred or more times since that morning. Where will I work? Can I work for some famous general or admiral? How do I get there? How do I find a place to live? Things moved so fast that many of the young women found themselves working at desks and typewriters and on the government payroll before they had even found a place to leave their bags.

New workers kept arriving, but they were never enough. The Veterans Administration could never find typists. It dealt with the problem by having its staff dictate through a mouthpiece and a flexible tube into a machine that recorded their words on cylinders. They shipped the cylinders in cardboard boxes to New York City where typists were available to transcribe them and ship the typewritten letters back to Washington to be signed and mailed. Slow and cumbersome, yes, but that was Washington's paper war.

The FBI was badly in need of clerks to work in its fingerprint files that rose clear up to the ceilings, and for these jobs it would only hire men. Why couldn't it use women now that so many young men were going into uniform? No, the FBI said, when women worked up on these high ladders, those below could look up their dresses. Why can't they wear slacks? No. Mr. Hoover did not like his female employees in slacks. Hoover was Hoover and that was that.

Six months into the war, there were so many new agencies, all known by their initials, nobody could keep them straight. The OPC was the Office of Petroleum Coordination. Its director was Harold Ickes, also the secretary of the interior. At a press conference he was asked about a new OPC ruling and he said, testily, "I can't speak for the OPC." There was a pause, stirrings of surprise and confusion among the reporters, until an aide whispered in Ickes's ear that he was the *director* of the OPC. "I'm all balled up on all these initials," Ickes explained. So were many others. By now there were the WPB, OPA, WMC, BEW, NWLB, ODT, WSA, OCD, OEM and many others. One office, issuing wartime regulations for plumbers, was the PWPGSJSISIACWPB. Did any single person in Washington, at any level, know what all these initials meant? Certainly no one person knew what each of them did.

All the new agencies, talking to each other, so overloaded the telephones that the Chesapeake and Potomac's system nearly collapsed, causing the company to run ads asking people to use the phones only when necessary. They also put out rules, forms and regulations in language that was almost incomprehensible. Maury Maverick of Texas, the head of a war agency, said he had just come out of a meeting where the chairman spoke at length about "maladjustments co-extensive with problem areas . . . alternative but nevertheless meaningful minimae . . . utilization of factors which in a dynamic democracy can be channelized into both quantitative and qualitative phases. . . . " Maverick coined a word that was to last beyond the war. He called it "gobbledygook."

White House staffer Jonathan Daniels said, "I never saw Babel, but I've seen Washington."

New typists were pouring into town, but new typewriters were not. By mid-1942, the government claimed to be six hundred thousand typewriters short. The typewriter industry had been ordered to shut down and turn to war production. No one explained why, if typewriters were as essential to the war as the government advertising said, their manufacture was stopped. But it was, and so the next Washington crunch, one in a continuing series, was the famous "typewriter crisis." With no new ones being made, the only solution was to buy used ones wherever they could be found. So the Office of War Information, the government's official propaganda agency, organized a campaign, one of the most intensive of the war, around the slogan, "Send your typewriter to war." Radio stations played a jingle, "An idle typewriter is a help to Hitler." Movie stars and military heroes toured the country posing for photographs. Maureen O'Hara posed smiling beside a table piled with twenty typewriters, each tagged, "For Uncle Sam." Posters were sent across the country.

A staff of eleven people ran the campaign, but with only modest success. Not many people with typewriters were willing to hand them over, knowing they could not be replaced. Not only that, most typewriters the campaign did bring in had twelve-inch carriages, and the new agencies, oblivious to all this, were using new forms, huge, elaborate and tedious, up to eighteen inches wide.

Chester Bowles later tried a more imaginative solution in the Office of Price Administration. He had men with pushcarts sweep through the empty offices at night and haul away one out of every seven typewriters. Then he waited to see who complained. Often no one did. He tried a similar trick with file cabinets, also scarce. In the barnlike government offices everyone working within two hundred feet of a file cabinet was asked what was in it. If no one knew, and often no one did, the cabinet was moved to another office.

Predictably, with all these typists pounding all day every day, the next crisis was paper. The U.S. Government entered the war owning $650,000 worth of printing and reproducing equipment. After less than a year, it had $50 million worth. There was not enough paper to feed all these new machines and there was not enough space to store what they spewed out. The federal government created more records in the four years of the war than in its entire previous history. The national archivist, Solon J. Buck, charged with storing retired government records, warned Congress that all this paper would soon fill an acre of ground to the height of the Washington Monument, or fill eight buildings the size of the only building he had. OPA alone was producing more paper than the entire government had generated before the war.

What to do with it all? The bureaucracy, reacting like the rabbitlike reproductive organism it was, gave birth to a new title, "records managers." They were charged with eliminating useless paper, but only after they had established that it actually was useless. A Washington story, perhaps true, was that one of the new records managers, complaining of being "engulfed in a tidal wave of paper," needed the approval of eleven different superiors to destroy a pile of old records. Finally, he was told yes, he could destroy them, but only if he made copies of all of them first.

A small new addition to Washington's thickening "alphabet soup" was the CAS—Central Administrative Services. This was the agency in charge of office supplies and equipment, messengers, car pools, mail collection and delivery, trash collection and maintenance. Its hapless director, Dallas Dort, complained constantly that his agency was so unglamorous and so remote from the patriotic fervor of war that he never could get enough money or enough staff or enough of anything. The CAS bungled, dropped, spilled, lost or stole almost everything it touched. Its deliveries of mail between government offices were slow and unreliable. Mail arrived at the wrong offices or did not arrive at all. A lend-lease official once walked past the CAS mail room and saw bundles he had sent out weeks before still lying untouched on the floor. CAS messengers, mostly teenaged boys too young for the draft, roared through the streets on motorcycles, leaving clouds of mail blowing out of their shoulder sacks and scattered in the streets behind them. In early 1943, a pedestrian discovered bundles of confidential mail sent out by the Office of War Information lying in a gutter at Nineteenth and H streets. CAS chauffeurs were caught using government limousines for joyrides or weekend visits to their mistresses.

The CAS's duties also included the disposing of "secret and confidential trash." It bungled this, too, mixing "safe" trash with "classified" trash and strewing both kinds all over town. Some agencies chose to burn their own discarded secret papers. A State Department officer proudly told a Senate committee that State had its papers burned in its own furnace by a trustworthy black janitor who did the job carefully and was paid only $1,800 a year. Senator McClellan of Arkansas pointed a trembling finger at the witness and bellowed, "You mean to tell this committee the CAS is so incompetent you have to entrust your secret papers to an eighteen-hundred-dollar nigra?"

The catalogue of CAS's sins and failures was a long document of laziness, carelessness, stupidity, delays, errors and, not least, simple theft. One investigation revealed that during gasoline rationing when government automobiles were left in the CAS repair shop, mechanics routinely drained their tanks and stole the gasoline for their own use. Chauffeurs reported that, time after time, when they drove away from the CAS shop, their engines stalled and died in traffic.

The dollar-a-year men had to confront, in their own agencies, confusion and inefficiency on a scale such as they had never seen in their private businesses. They were appalled at the lack of accountability. Even after a monumental blunder it was impossible to find out who was responsible. They also found that, without Civil Service protection, some bunglers could be fired, but others—with friends in Congress—could not.

Jerry Kluttz, the civil service columnist in the *Post,* reported that a vice president of a New York City bank heard of a Washington job opening in the Office of Economic Warfare, applied for it and awaited an answer. While he waited, Leo Crowley, director of the OEW, dropped into the same New York bank and asked its president to recommend somebody for the job he had open in Washington. The bank president recommended the same vice president who had already applied for the job. The vice president was hired on the spot and moved to Washington. Weeks later, at work in his new office, he got a letter from the OEW that had been sent to his old New York address and forwarded to him in Washington. The letter said he had been rejected because he was not considered qualified for the job. Looking again, he found he had signed the letter himself.

Kluttz, an expert in government employment policies, also reported that within six months of Pearl Harbor, more than half the young women hired as stenographers and typists had quit in disgust and returned home. One government secretary wrote to Kluttz,

If I did not exist, $1,620 a year could be spent for the war instead of my salary. I am one of a huge number of government employees who spend their days killing time. I should be useful here, but I'm an utter waste. My hardest task is standing in line to cash my pay check. Clerks who are criticized for spending too much time at the water cooler will agree there is nothing else for us to do. Our fervent plea is for someone to put us to work.

That column brought Kluttz hundreds of letters making the same complaint—people had been hired and paid and given nothing to do. "You want to help fight this war by working with all your energy, but all you do is sit all day and waste time," one wrote. "Who in the world is responsible for this crazy system?"

Nobody was responsible. It was simply the way the government worked, in both war and peace, although in wartime it was worse. The single fact most clearly differentiating government employers from private employers was, always, that government agencies did not have to earn their money. Congress simply handed it over every year and almost always more than the year before, so it was there to be spent and it was unthinkable not to spend it. Nobody in government ever benefitted in any way from saving money. Whatever was not spent had to be handed back to the Treasury, and if an agency had money left over at the end of one year, how could it ask Congress for more money the next year? If it had money left, Congress might even cut, not increase, its budget the next year, an event regarded as one step short of suicide. So agencies all hired people they did not need, people for whom they had no work, because the money was there, and it absolutely, positively had to be spent. War or peace, this basic principle of government never changed.

The dollar-a-year men trying to deal with the waste and inefficiency did what came naturally to them—they called in management consultants, sneeringly described by the office force as "efficiency experts." OPA hired a management firm to help clear up at least some of the confusion and waste in its offices. One result was OPA Memorandum 9808-1, entitled DESK PROCEDURE, instructing the employees how to use their desk drawers more efficiently. It explained that typists were to have desks with three drawers, numbered 1, 2 and 3, while executives were to have six drawers, affixed with paper stickers numbered 1 through 6. Number 1 was to be the "pull drawer," not further described; 2 was to be the "work drawer"; 3, the "file drawer"; 4, the "middle drawer"; 5, the "dictate drawer." And 6, the "miscellaneous drawer," presumably to hold aspirin tablets, galoshes, tobacco, dry socks, unpaid bills and other accoutrements of the executive life. This was followed by meticulous instructions on how to lock a desk without locking the keys inside, and, for example, how number 5, the "dictate drawer," was to be used: "Compartment one should contain material which has been analyzed and the executive is ready to dictate on. The second compartment is for forms and papers the executive deems necessary to keep in his drawer instead of the typist's." Memorandum 9808-1 was soon given a decent burial in the bulging, sagging files.

The military bureaucracy was little better. Architect Alan Dickey was given the job of furnishing the Pentagon when it was finished. He recalled that "if you gave a general an itty bitty desk you'd be out of a job the next day. . . . If anyone needed five desks they would requisition ten, making a shrewd and cunning calculation that if their request was cut in half they would be making a patriotic sacrifice while still getting all they wanted. A general got an executive desk with dentil mouldings around the edge in some kind of hardwood. His secretary got a five-foot desk, or if she was only a typist she got one four and a half feet wide, fifty-four inches. A file clerk just got a tiny flat-top desk. There was a good deal of ass-kissing by those who didn't get desks as big as they wanted. . . . The personnel section was the biggest clump of people in one room with no partitions so they could watch and see who was working. If we'd put in a lot of little cubbyholes they couldn't see them and some would be working and some asleep.

"The military's files right away got to be a mess. They sent urgent messages to units in the field to stop sending carbon copies on onion skin paper. It was so thin and flimsy it sagged down in the file folders. If the copying machines that came along later had been here during the war I'm not sure the Allies would have won. We'd all have drowned in paper."

Captain Frank C. Owens, inspector in the army Medical Corps, found his office overrun with ants. He asked the Quartermaster Supply Office for help. The answer was that the quartermaster supplied ant poison only for ants found nesting inside army buildings; if they had come in from outside, his request should be directed to Engineering. He wrote back: "It is rather difficult to determine which ant comes from within and which from without . . . and this could result in a Quartermaster ant being exterminated by Engineering poison . . . and lead to lengthy letters of explanation." The resolution of this problem is lost to history.

Among the thousands of people loaded onto the government payroll were the hacks and misfits ordered hired by members of Congress who never saw the war as any reason to change their old habit of loading the federal payroll with their friends, hangers-on, unsatisfactory sons-in-law, unemployable cousins, courthouse idlers, maiden aunts fallen into straitened circumstances and relatives addicted to the bottle. Jonathan Daniels heard an agency head say of an employee forced on him by a powerful congressman, "He's a half-wit, but he's good enough for what he's doing." And newspaper reporter George Dixon came across a pretty young woman, the niece of a Southern senator, newly appointed to the Department of Commerce as "an adviser on heavy industry." He politely inquired into her qualifications for the job and she responded, "I guess you didn't understand me. I said my uncle was a senator."

Until they learned better, the dollar-a-year men in the war agencies resented seeing their payrolls loaded with incompetents sent over by members of the Senate and the House. But they soon learned there was no fury so deep as that of a member of Congress denied patronage jobs, a personal slight never to be forgotten until revenge in some form was achieved. The nastiest and most tireless practitioner of both patronage and revenge was Senator Kenneth McKellar of Tennessee. For nearly ten years he had carried on an abusive, vindictive campaign against David Lilienthal, chairman of the Tennessee Valley Authority, whose offices were in McKellar's state. Lilienthal's crime was that he refused to hire McKellar's relatives. Already, one of McKellar's two brothers was the Memphis postmaster and the other worked for the Senate Post Office Committee, but the senator could never get enough. Year after year, in speech after speech, he had forced the Senate to listen to his long, ugly attacks. In one, he accused Lilienthal of "denying Christians the right to practice their religion." His basis for this was the belief—

wrong—that Lilienthal had refused to allow a Bible salesman to sell on TVA property.

The war did nothing to change McKellar's ways. On May 5, 1942, he stood on the Senate floor in his black suit, white shirt, black bow tie, red face, gold-rimmed glasses and well-tended paunch, and ranted at "that goddamned Lilienthal and his eely, oily ways. . . . " He liked the alliteration so much he said it four times—"that goddamned Lilienthal and his eely, oily ways"—each time stretching "ways" out into a long, slow, descending glissando of vowel sound, "waaaaaaays." His hatred of Lilienthal became an obsession for a politician *Time* called "the premier spoilsman of the Senate." Even in McKellar's dotage, when he occasionally wandered off the Senate floor and urinated against the marble columns in the reception rooms, his attacks continued. Some thought this consuming rage was what kept him alive.

At OPA, Leon Henderson, described by Roosevelt as "the toughest bastard in town," tried for a time to hold out against the demand for patronage. He had set up his agency to work through local offices staffed with local people, and Congress quickly took notice. Ernest K. Lindley, columnist in the Washington *Post,* wrote:

> Here is a lot of patronage . . . and naturally they want it; perhaps even more they fear the appointments will be used by governors or other potential opponents to strengthen their own positions. In some cases, OPA asked Senators and senior Congressmen to suggest appointees . . . and it was offered nothing but the riff-raff of ward-heeling politics. It has refused to hire them.

Congress's reaction to this refusal was so bitter that some members demanded complete control of Henderson's hiring. The Senate voted to require its approval of any OPA appointee paid more than four thousand dollars. Then Henderson realized what he had to do: he added a new office in each state to serve no purpose whatever but political patronage. But by resisting for so long the congressional bloodlust for patronage, he had already wounded himself critically. His sins were not forgiven or forgotten. They would eventually cost him his own job.

Two weeks after Pearl Harbor, surveyors with transit levels and red and white-striped rods appeared, unannounced, on the twenty-acre campus

of Mount Vernon Seminary, a girls' school at Massachusetts and Nebraska
avenues. Elmer Kaiser, chairman of the school's executive committee,
came outside and asked what they were doing. Staking out the property
for the U.S. Navy, they said.

What? The navy taking over the school without notice and without
discussion? Just like that? Yes. Just like that. That was the transaction,
and that was the extent of the formalities. The navy decided it wanted
the school and its Georgian brick buildings, classrooms, dormitories, its
land, its chapel, everything; and while the girls were home for the
Christmas holidays, the navy just took it. It offered $800,000 for property
easily worth $5 million and finally agreed to pay $1.1 million. That left
Kaiser and the school administration wondering what to do with the
students when they came back to school in January. The navy offered
no help. The school officials, in haste, scoured the neighborhood in
upper Northwest looking for a temporary place for classrooms. They
found that Garfinckel's department store a mile down Massachusetts
had just finished a branch store and was not yet using the second
floor. That floor became Mount Vernon Seminary. The girls returning
from Christmas vacation were housed in private homes in the neighborhood, while the navy began erecting a six-foot chain-link fence and
turning their old campus into a military intelligence station for monitor-
ing radio signals and breaking diplomatic codes, an operation that
became permanent and after the war was called the Office of Naval
Intelligence.

The high-handed seizure of the Mount Vernon campus came at a
time of maximum military hubris. What the armed services wanted they
took. The navy did not need the campus. These security operations
were mainly based at Fort Meade in nearby Maryland where there were
miles of empty land for unlimited expansion without seizing and closing
down established civilian institutions in the city. But the U.S. military,
like others through history, knew that war gave them a pretext to seize
what they would want later in peacetime but would be unable to get.
The Mount Vernon campus was in one of the most attractive areas of
Washington, acres of trees and grass and red brick Georgian buildings,
including a stylish residence quickly taken over for the new naval
station's commanding officer. The navy liked it, and the navy took it.

Washington's planning commission asked the navy to explain its
seizure of Mount Vernon, since it was "located in an [architecturally]
restricted neighborhood," which it was the commission's job to protect.

The navy responded only that it was immune to all zoning regulations and that the communications station at Mount Vernon was "vital to the war effort and its nature should not be publicized." Besides, the navy was Franklin Roosevelt's favorite military service, a fact it never forgot.

The new Pentagon was the world's largest building, but the military services filled it to the rafters while still combing the city and seizing any other buildings they fancied. The army alone took over thirty-five buildings and searched constantly for more. It was said around town that if the military could seize and occupy enemy lands as quickly as it seized Washington's, the war would be won in a week.

The Gridiron Club, whose members were the senior newspapermen in Washington, held its annual dinners at the Willard Hotel. A guest at one of them not long before Pearl Harbor was Arthur Douglas, president of the Statler hotel chain and brother of William O. Douglas of the Supreme Court. Seated beside him, Gridiron dinners being for males only, was Jesse Jones, the Texas multimillionaire now running the Reconstruction Finance Corporation and charged with lending money to stimulate business growth in the Depression. He ran the RFC as if it were his own private business. "It's getting hard for people to find hotel rooms in Washington," he said to Douglas. "Why don't you folks build us a new hotel?"

"I hadn't thought about it," Douglas said.

"You build a hotel and I'll finance it for you. Five million dollars."

The deal was made there at the table, and the Statler chain bought and demolished a block of old Victorian residences on Sixteenth Street between K and L for a new hotel. Desperate as Washington was for hotel rooms, the Statler did not have an easy time of it. The plans called for aluminum window frames. Newspaper columnist Drew Pearson put on one of his little campaigns, insisting that the aluminum could be better used in warplanes. To shut him up, the hotel substituted steel frames, which needed constant painting. They left the aluminum frames in a warehouse, where they stayed throughout the war, and eventually sold them for scrap. An order for pillows was cancelled because the military was taking all the feathers.

But that was not the worst. When the hotel was nearly finished, the navy began sending men over to examine it with an eye to seizing it for officers' housing. By now, the navy's acquisitive habits were well known and the Statler's manager, Fred Kenney, was afraid he would lose his hotel the minute it was opened. He suspected that when the last bed was made, the last bathroom mirror hung, the lobby carpeting installed and the last potted plant in place and an opening date announced, the navy would march in. So he carefully avoided announcing an opening date. Instead he opened the hotel quietly and gradually, a few rooms at a time, with no announcement and no advertising, aiming to get it filled and running before it could be seized. It worked. Before the navy caught on, he had every room filled with business people and lobbyists. Mrs. Roosevelt was coming in frequently for lunch. Dumping her and all the other guests out into Sixteenth Street would have brought screams of anger and protests too loud for even the navy to ignore. The Statler Hotel survived.

It opened not an hour too soon. The demand for rooms was so great that virtually all the hotels in Washington announced that nobody could have a room for more than three days. But Herbert Blunck (who had replaced Kenney as manager of the Statler) discovered that some business people were staying on for month after month in the same suites. How, he wondered, were they managing it? The answer, easily predictable, was money. When the mandatory check-out time came, they slipped cash to room clerks, who then rigged the records to show that the occupants had checked out and then checked back in.

Some visitors found other ways to deal with the room shortage. Members of Congress called hotel managers to demand rooms for friends, relatives and important constituents; some hinted at dark reprisals for any hotel operator who refused. At the Mayflower, there was an "Interim Club," a lounge on the mezzanine where businessmen without rooms could pay for access to showers, lockers, writing tables and telephone booths. For some the solution was to find a room in Baltimore, fifty miles away, and take the train into town early in the morning. At times the demand was too great even for Baltimore, and the overflow spread north to Philadelphia.

Within months after Pearl Harbor, the government had spread like a pool of warm axle grease, oozing outward over the city and into 358 buildings that had previously served other purposes. Government offices spilled into skating rinks, where the ice was melted and the floors covered with sawhorses and plywood desks. They poured into basketball arenas, theaters and auditoriums with the seats ripped out, into a concert hall once used for organ recitals, even into stables and tents. They took over old homes and new apartment buildings. OPA for a while had a kitchen and bath for every suite of offices; secretaries could be seen sitting in front of bathroom sinks, their typewriters perched on boards laid across the basins, their steno pads propped on the toilet seats.

And of course, there were the "tempos"—the cheap, drab buildings whose design Roosevelt had so carefully supervised. They appeared almost overnight—the record was thirty-eight days from start of construction to completion. The typical temporary building consisted of a main structure, about half a city block long, with five wings jutting out from one side. Foundations were of concrete, walls of neutral gray cemento-asbestos board, which after a few rainstorms became streaked with grime. The buildings were hideous. And they were everywhere. They lined both sides of the Reflecting Pool east of the Lincoln Memorial; two covered bridges spanned the pool to connect the various complexes. They nearly surrounded the Washington Monument. They lined Constitution Avenue, row after row of dreary office block covering acres of what had once been attractive parkland.

Washingtonians wondered what the fate of these buildings would be after the war. Tempos built for World War I were still standing and in use. Would the new structures survive a generation beyond the war as well? The answer was yes. Most of them stood until the mid-1960s.

Even crowded to suffocation (as it very nearly was), Washington could not handle the bulging military and civilian bureaucracies. New construction would take too long, and there simply were not enough existing buildings, including the temporaries, to hold this crowd and all their desks, typewriters and filing cabinets, not to speak of buildings to house them at night.

That realization produced a new solution—decentralization. Move the civilian agencies to other cities, the Bureau of the Budget said; this would open space for those working for the war. Roosevelt liked the idea. The agencies to be moved did not. It was unpleasant to transfer a whole office with all its staff and their families to another city on short notice. None wanted to go, particularly when a husband worked in a government agency that was leaving and his wife worked in one that was staying. But Roosevelt forced the issue. The Securities and Exchange Commission moved to Philadelphia; the Patent Office to Richmond; the Farm Credit Administration to Kansas City; Fish and Wildlife, Indian Affairs and National Parks to Chicago. The lieutenant governor of New York wrote to Roosevelt urging that Social Security be moved to New York City, where "we have plenty of apartments." Former New York governor Al Smith, now president of the Empire State Building, badgered officials in Washington constantly about installing whole agencies on his vacant floors.

In all, eleven agencies and 21,401 employees moved out, opening up two million square feet of office space for those who remained. The result was barely noticeable. Enough new people arrived in a few weeks to fill all the newly created space. Decentralization was not the answer either.

There was no answer. When too many laboratory mice are confined in one cage, they turn on each other, driven by the primal need for space and air. The bureaucrats reacted the same way, turning on each other with guile and cunning to compete for space in which to array themselves and their staffs and desks, resorting to lies, trickery, deceptions and anguished appeals for help seldom forthcoming.

Lewis W. Douglas of the War Shipping Administration wrote in piteous tones to the budget director: "For eighteen months we have been treated like an orphan child insofar as space is concerned. . . . I insist that we should be adequately treated at least once in our experience." The Budget Bureau did try to help. It urged other agencies to give up some space for Douglas and War Shipping. The reaction was as if Mad King Ludwig had been asked to give up his castles. Almost without exception, they replied that they had too little room as it was and that giving up even one desk, one water cooler, one rest room would certainly prolong the war and probably even lose it. Out of the question; we can't give up space for Douglas. He should give up some for us. Our work obviously is more important than his, and beyond that we have another thousand people coming in next Tuesday.

The Budget Bureau turned to an agency that seemed of less than critical importance to winning the war—the Commerce Department's Coordinator of Inter-American Affairs, run by Nelson Rockefeller. He was asked to give up seventy thousand square feet. After a good deal of stalling and evasion and exchanges of notes, all of them filled with gross exaggerations, Rockefeller reluctantly—as if offering up his blood and vital organs—agreed to surrender twelve thousand feet. The budget director, trying to preside over a battle less bloody but no less fierce than any in Europe or the Pacific, wrote to Roosevelt: "Any further squeeze on these agencies naturally will be resisted by the Secretary of Commerce and Mr. Rockefeller, and can be accomplished only by a directive from the President." Roosevelt wrote back, "You straighten it out."

It never was straightened out. None of it. The complaints never stopped. Some desks had to be used in three eight-hour shifts, and as each shift came in there were bitter complaints that the previous shift had left the desk in such a mess it was difficult to get any work done.

There was a pathetic note from the Office of Emergency Management: "This is to call your attention to the unsanitary, unhealthy, unattractive, unpleasant, distracting, noisy atmosphere under which we of the liaison staff are attempting to perform our arduous duties. To mention a few unpleasant difficulties, may I call your attention to the lack of drinking water, the lack of fresh air, the noisy heater, the about-to-burst boiler, the poor lighting and the horrible toilet facilities."

The liaison staff got no help. The FBI did. When Roosevelt returned to Washington in 1943 from his meeting with Winston Churchill in Casablanca, he read a letter from James Rowe, assistant attorney general: "While you were taking care of a few minor details at Casablanca, I regret to inform you that a problem of really major importance has become completely insoluble except in your hands." The FBI needed more space in the National Guard Armory, a building so enormous that it later housed the Ringling Brothers–Barnum and Bailey Circus. The FBI could put one hundred employees into an area the national guard was using for five officers. But the national guard was refusing to give it up.

> For the past six months, the Department of Justice has begged, badgered, threatened and pleaded to get [reserve Brigadier General Albert L.] Cox out of the Armory. We have even found another place for him in the Municipal Center.... The War Department tells us it has no control of General Cox ... because, although the Guard is federalized ... the War Department "unfederalized" Cox some months ago on grounds of incompetence.

For your information General Cox is the brass hat who leads
local parades on a white horse. . . . His competence is attested to
by the fact the War Department removed him as Provost Marshal
of the District. His mulishness can be attested to by me, by J.
Edgar Hoover and the entire FBI.

Rowe added a postscript: "I suggest you send this memorandum to the
Hyde Park Library so future generations will know what kinds of problems a wartime President has." Roosevelt ordered Cox out.

Late in 1940, the Bureau of the Budget sent Roosevelt an urgent memorandum he did not welcome:

Bold and concerted action is required. Inflation cannot be
stopped so long as wage increases, as well as government expendi-
tures, create additional purchasing power. Wage increases cannot be stopped as long as prices rise. The price rise cannot be
stopped unless part of the rapidly increasing purchasing power is
absorbed by fiscal measures. Fiscal measures cannot be effective
as long as businessmen, wage earners and farmers can make up
for their taxes by increasing income. Only simultaneous action
on all fronts can stop the inflationary spiral.

Roosevelt understood perfectly well that coping with all this would
be a horrible, bruising task that could easily do him great political
damage. Besides, he was already under assault in Congress by Senator
Taft and his friends, who were accusing him of trying to use the war to
entrench himself in office forever.

But Roosevelt also believed, at least at first, that the coercive measures the Budget Bureau had suggested were unnecessary. He clung to
the comfortable liberal view that people were fundamentally decent and
that when a problem was explained to them they would act voluntarily
to solve it. And so, throughout the first years of the war, he tried
repeatedly to avoid coercion and rely on voluntarism, to appeal to the
unselfish, patriotic spirit of a people at war, a spirit he was certain
existed. Out of that faith came a series of grand experiments known as
the "war drives."

The administration's first great effort was a tremendous voluntary program to reduce the deficit, encourage saving, trim spending and thus curb inflation—the sale of war bonds. The campaign would not only raise money, Roosevelt believed. It would give the public a sense of involvement in a war being fought thousands of miles away, a war so distant many Americans had difficulty at times remembering it was there at all. The government asked employers to urge their employees to buy war bonds through payroll deductions, and it asked celebrities, civic organizations and local governments to help promote the drive.

Washington, naturally, received particular attention. Movie stars, sports figures and military heroes came to town to appear at bond rallies. Military bands played in parks and in theaters. The Elks clubs marched down Pennsylvania Avenue. Babe Ruth, now long retired, appeared at an exhibition game at Griffith Stadium, trotted once around the base paths, and gave autographs to bond buyers. Bing Crosby stood on the pitcher's mound and crooned "White Christmas." Thirty thousand people gathered at the Treasury Plaza next door to the White House to see Hedy Lamarr, Abbott and Costello, Larry Adler, James Cagney and Dinah Shore. Costello told the crowd, "Money don't mean a thing if you ain't got the swing, and we'll swing by the necks if Hitler comes over here." Some people laughed. Others wondered what was funny. Kate Smith presided over a twenty-four-hour radiothon to sell bonds and sang "God Bless America," a song Irving Berlin had written for World War I but that got little attention until Smith revived it and turned it into the jukebox national anthem. An all-soldier musical extravaganza, *This Is the Army,* played at the National Theater; only bond buyers could purchase tickets.

The bond drive was an artistic success but a financial disappointment. Treasury Secretary Henry Morgenthau had predicted bond sales would finance two-thirds of the cost of the war, but they never raised as much as 10 percent. In the first nine months of 1942, bond sales raised $10 billion while the government was spending $160 billion. Still, people responded enthusiastically and purchased bonds. America's schoolchildren loyally brought nickels, dimes and quarters to class to buy stamps to paste in books that when filled could be turned in for $25 bonds. But it was simply impossible for the American people to support themselves, pay their taxes and have enough money left to buy bonds in the stratospheric amounts needed to finance the war.

It had never been realistic to expect them to hand over that much money.

The results were equally discouraging for government's attempts to meet other wartime needs with voluntarism. In one appeal after another, the public was asked to conserve this and donate that and volunteer for something else. There were press releases, magazine ads, and announcements on the radio about every twelve minutes. At NBC's radio station WRC in Washington, the announcer's booth had a bulging bin labeled "SX," meaning free public service announcements to be read on the air in systematic rotation between the commercials and the pop records. Dozens of them were aired every day. A writer in the newsroom, wondering if anyone was listening, wrote a meaningless SX announcement of his own and slipped it into the announcer's bin. It read in its entirety:

There is an urgent need and you can help. The war has created the problem and only the voluntary cooperation of the American people can solve it. It will take only a few moments of your time and when peace comes you and your family can remember with pride that you did your part and helped shorten the war. But there is no time to lose. Please do your part today.

It was read on the radio for two months, and neither the announcers nor anyone in the listening audience ever seemed to notice. The government's cajolings and importunings had become as constant as rain drumming on the roof. The public had ceased to listen.

Almost no shortage was too mundane to inspire a drive. One campaign collected kitchen drippings and scarce vegetable fats. Another brought in lead from empty toothpaste tubes and metal foil (or "silver paper," as it was called). A scrap metals drive brought in the entire Tacoma Narrows Bridge, which had collapsed, a rowing machine that had belonged to Governor Saltonstall of Massachusetts, a hundred-year-old slave chain from Mississippi, fourteen tons of copper stills seized from moonshiners in West Virginia, two iron deer from Walt Disney's front lawn, and—from the Brooks Costume Company in New York City—suits of armor once used in a Broadway production of *The Vagabond King*. But none of these drives ever produced enough of anything.

Gradually, Roosevelt and his advisers were forced to concede that voluntarism had been given a fair chance and had failed. The war would have to be financed with taxation. Scarce goods would have to be rationed. Inflation would have to be held down with wage and price controls. Compulsion began replacing voluntarism, and the Office of Price Administration pushed its way further and further into areas of American life where no government agency had ever pushed before.

None of the wartime agencies earned any great affection among the American people or in Congress, since in most cases their only reason for existing was to force people to do what they would not have done without being forced. In time the American public did come to tolerate most of it, but they never came to like it. And in Washington, the OPA was loved least of all. From its first day to its last, in trying to hold down prices and wages and prevent gouging and profiteering, the OPA was engaged in trench warfare with Congress. The assault was led by two Republican senators, Robert A. Taft of Ohio, earlier a leader of the isolationists, and Kenneth Wherry of Nebraska, who liked to boast that he was an embalmer licensed in not one but three Midwestern states. They waged a campaign of abuse and insult. The OPA and its director, Leon Henderson, they called "derelicts from the war" and "leeches on the body politic."

When Henderson asked authority to control prices and wages, the congressional committees lazed through five weeks of hearings, about four and a half weeks longer than it took Henderson to explain the urgency to anyone able and willing to understand. But numerous members of Congress, under pressure from some of their voters at home, did not want to understand. What they did realize was that wartime was a time to make money. Unions, farmers and business had been forced since the early thirties to scratch for a dollar here and a dollar there, finding few. Now, the wartime boom was a chance to make up for ten years of poverty. Farmers had struggled through the thirties, surviving only with the help of the New Deal, and now they wanted to produce all they could and sell it for as much as they could get. The unions were fearful that now, as their members were going back to work, the Washington bureaucrats would find a way to hold down their wages. Businessmen who had hated the New Deal all along believed that once such bureaucratic power as the OPA's was established it would never go away.

The history of wartime profiteering started long before Henderson and his OPA. The Rothschild riches had begun during the Napoleonic wars. American fortunes were made in the Civil War, one from the sale of spoiled meat to the Union army. More armaments millionaires were created in World War I. And just five years before Pearl Harbor, the Senate had received a formal committee report saying armies in wartime could never be supported "without the evils of profiteering, mountainous debt and inflation. Whatever attempts are made to eliminate these evils will be in direct conflict with the efforts to stimulate war production." Congress, and the lobbyists now swarming in to protect their employers' interests, smelled money. And as Senator Taft put it, "No goddamned bureaucrats are going to deny it to them."

Numerous members of Congress—Senator Prentiss Brown of Michigan, for one—did see the need and did work courageously for an effective wage and price control program. But through it all, OPA's support in Congress was grudging, cantankerous, little and late. When Henderson asked for $210 million to start up his operation, Congress— after much haggling and abuse—gave him $75 million and, along with the money, a list of complaints about OPA's "snooping" and "Gestapo methods."

Henderson was paying the price for his sins. He was a believer in modern administrative methods. He had to deal with a Congress that was still essentially a nineteenth-century institution deeply skeptical of the "professors" and "left-wing theorists" he had assembled—particularly since he had managed to hire them only by refusing to open the OPA payroll to political patronage. But hobbled as he was, Henderson forged ahead.

In May 1942, the United Press, in the zippy language it used in trying to compete with the more powerful AP, ran a lead story: "OPA administrator Leon Henderson announced today he was yanking the nation's sweet tooth for the duration." Sugar rationing introduced the American people to the first ration books they had ever seen—thin covers of light tan cardboard with pages of tiny stamps, about half the size of normal postage stamps, stapled inside. They were distributed through the public schools by teachers and volunteers seated behind folding tables. The volunteers often failed to show up, and so the teachers had to do the work and take the abuse alone, of which there was more than enough. One teacher wrote to the Washington *Post* asking why they had to do this job when there were "plenty of people in Washington who don't have to work for a living." Another teacher's letter complained of a woman so infuriated at being questioned that she poured a bottle of ink across the table. "The public," she wrote, "shows little consideration for the teacher-volunteers, such as the woman who waited until late in the day to come in and register for a family of sixteen."

When gasoline rationing came, it was worse.

German submarines lay off the Atlantic coast watching the American ships go by—fat, slow tankers and freighters. It was a shooting gallery, where the Germans could lie quietly and wait for the most inviting targets. Ships riding high in the water, empty of cargo, were allowed to pass; they were not worth a torpedo. The submarine captains waited instead for tankers wallowing deep in the water under heavy loads of gasoline coming up to the east coast from refineries around the Gulf of Mexico. They were slow, defenseless, easy to find and easy to hit. So easy that people stood on beaches from Florida to New Jersey and watched in horror as the tankers turned into white-hot torches sinking into the Atlantic. In the mornings, sunbathers would see the bodies of seamen washing ashore in the surf.

There never was any shortage of gasoline. There was only a shortage of tankers to transport it. And so, beginning in May 1942, Leon Henderson announced gasoline rationing in the seventeen Eastern states. Deliveries elsewhere—by train, truck, pipeline and tankers up the Pacific coast—were normal.

It was one of the great fiascos of the war. Once again, the unhonored heroes and heroines of the hometown war, the teachers, were called on to issue ration cards—"A" cards good for three gallons a week, "B" cards good for a few more gallons to those having greater needs, and "X" cards for unlimited gasoline to those whose driving was essential to the war.

While Henderson and Eleanor Roosevelt publicly and conspicuously applied for A cards, other Washington residents were strikingly more generous in assessing their own importance to the war. In the first round of registration, three-fourths of the drivers in the city swore their driving was of such extreme urgency that they needed far more than the A card's three gallons a week. The OPA had estimated about 1 percent of the driving population would need X cards. In Washington, they were claimed by 12 percent. Henderson was so irritated he made public the names of all X cardholders, whereupon several hundred people reassessed their needs and returned their X cards.

But not Congress. Its members not only declined to stand in line at

Crowd listening to Marian Anderson sing at the Lincoln Memorial, April 7, 1939. (*Acme*)

LEFT: Eleanor (Cissy) Patterson. (*UPI/Bettmann*)

BELOW: Evalyn Walsh McLean (wearing the Hope Diamond) with Senator Joseph Guffey, January 31, 1939. (*AP*)

Slum area. (*Library of Congress*)

National defense exhibit on Commerce Square. (*Library of Congress*)

Connecticut Avenue storefronts. (*Martin Luther King, Jr. Library*)

ABOVE: Japanese diplomats Saburo Kurusu
(in front) and Kichisaburo Nomura leaving
the State Department on December 7, 1941.
(*UPI/Bettmann*)

RIGHT: Listening to FDR's call for a
declaration of war, December 8, 1941.
(*UPI/Bettmann*)

Air raid wardens wearing gas masks in training school at the D.C. fire department. (*Martin Luther King, Jr. Library*)

Leaving the White House for Christmas services, December 25, 1941. *Left to right:* Lord Beaverbrook, Eleanor Roosevelt, Winston Churchill, Franklin Roosevelt, General Edwin Watson, Mrs. J. Roosevelt Roosevelt. (*UPI/Bettmann*)

ABOVE: War Production Board training class.
(*Library of Congress*)

RIGHT: Office of Price Administration
Director Leon Henderson. (*AP*)

BELOW: OPA window display.
(*Library of Congress*)

The Gayety Burlesque theatre. (*Library of Congress*)

Rubber scrap drive. (*Martin Luther King, Jr. Library*)

ABOVE: Government girls sharing
a room (sleeping in shifts) in a D.C.
home. (*UPI/Bettmann*)

RIGHT: "That's the night shift."
(Parade *magazine*)

BELOW: Entertaining guests at
a government women's residence.
(*Library of Congress*)

'That's the night shift. Rooms are mighty scarce around here."

Car pooling in a "Sedanbus." (*Martin Luther King, Jr. Library*)

Trailer park for defense workers on U.S. 1 near Alexandria, Virginia. (*Martin Luther King, Jr. Library*)

Staff evacuates French embassy, November 17, 1942. (*UPI/Bettmann*)

View of the Pentagon from across the parking lot, December 22, 1942. (*National Archives*)

Before a session of the Senate Investigating Committee, May 3, 1943.
Left to right: Senator Harry S Truman, Interior Secretary Harold Ickes,
Senator Bennett Champ Clark. (*UPI/Bettmann*)

Churchill and Roosevelt with their military chiefs of staff, May 24, 1943. (*UPI/Bettmann*)

Colonel reviewing a detachment of women marines. (*Library of Congress*)

Fleet of army trucks passing the National Archives. (*National Archives*)

Roosevelt delivering a radio address, November 8, 1943. (*Library of Congress*)

Anti-aircraft gun on the roof of the main post office. (*National Archives*)

ABOVE: Chester Bowles, seated in front of a graph of living costs. (*Library of Congress*)

RIGHT: WPB chief Donald Nelson leaving the White House. (*AP*)

Navy Department temporary office buildings around the Mall. (*National Archives*)

Roosevelt returning to Washington, November 10, 1944, in a car with Harry Truman and Henry Wallace. (*Library of Congress*)

Roosevelt's coffin being loaded onto a caisson at Union Station, April 14, 1945. (*Martin Luther King, Jr. Library*)

Crowd on F Street on V-J Day, August 14, 1945. (*Martin Luther King, Jr. Library*)

Sailors and girls riding on top of a car on V-J night. (*National Archives*)

the schools. They had their own rationing office installed in the Capitol, where two hundred members asked for and got X cards. There was an outcry—angry mail from the voters and headlines in the newspapers. A few members rushed to return their X cards with the limp excuse that they had not understood the rules. Others remained defiant, rising on the Senate and House floors to attack the press for destroying public confidence in their elected leaders and again attacking "Henderson's Gestapo."

They were infuriated first at having the names of those taking X cards made public, and second at remarks by an OPA official on what were and were not a congressman's official duties. The official was asked if congressmen using gasoline to visit government agencies on errands for the voters at home were doing official business. He replied, "Decidedly not." Here, as Congress saw it, the kitchen help and the stable boys had come up the back stairs and were lecturing the lords of the manor on their duties.

Representative Charles Faddis of Pennsylvania offered the opinion that when a congressman goes home and drives around "to talk to the man on the street corner, the man in the grocery store, the man behind the plow, the man in the office, that is part of his official duties. . . . It is also a part of his official duties to attend to the business of his constituents by doing their errands downtown, the opinion of any nitwitted bureaucrat to the contrary." His audience was so attentive, even appreciative, that Faddis was emboldened to go on: "One of the reasons for the fall of France was that the press of the nation made a practice of holding the officials of that nation up as objects of contempt and ridicule until they destroyed the faith of the people in their own form of government. Is our press trying to do the same to this nation?" Representative Leland Ford of California offered these solemn thoughts for the consideration of his colleagues: "Every congressman knows there is a positive and determined effort to undermine and discredit Congress in the eyes of our people and to destroy it through propaganda. I offer as evidence of this the present attempt to fix the duties of Congress by these bureaucracies."

Leon Henderson, for publicity and in support of his gasoline rationing, had himself photographed riding a bicycle to work and riding his secretary on the handlebars to show that even bicycle rides could be pooled. Congress contemplated this picture in the newspapers and two members,

Leland Ford and Clare Hoffman of Michigan, held the following exchange in the style of two vaudevillians:

Hoffman: "Do you recall that picture in the Washington papers showing Mr. Henderson riding his secretary around on the handlebars of his bicycle?"

Ford: "I certainly do."

Hoffman: "In your conversations with him, did he suggest that a congressman, regardless of his age or physical condition, should get his secretary to work that way, or to transact errands on a bicycle, or did he not say anything about that?"

Ford (missing his cue): "Well, I did not give as much thought to it then as I do now. I did not realize the incompetence and inefficiency of that department."

Hoffman (detecting a change of subject): "You mean as the operator of a bicycle, or what?"

"Well, even as the operator of a bicycle."

"He seemed to be getting along all right."

"Not to me. I don't think he can even ride a bicycle properly."

Hoffman continued: "Now . . . we cannot even get bicycles."

Ford: "That is right, and perhaps we cannot get secretaries either if the bureaucrats decide we do not need them in our official duties."

Ford stood at his seat and waited for more straight lines, while Hoffman plowed on: "It would seem that if the folks sent us here and paid us ten thousand dollars a year we should be trusted with cards for gasoline."

This time Ford was ready. "You are using the old-fashioned idea that this is still an American constitutional form of government, the same as I have, but under the European philosophies of these new bureaucrats and these crackpots they do not accept your theory of government, of the American form of government. . . . "

In the Senate, Sheridan Downey of California thought that in these difficult and embarrassing circumstances, it would be helpful for the Senate to place itself on record as devoutly in favor of rectitude and self-sacrifice. He introduced a resolution saying the senators would refuse "any special rights, privileges or exemptions they may be accorded under the terms of any gasoline rationing order, and shall consider themselves bound by honor to the acceptance of rationing restrictions which are of general application."

But Senator Alben Barkley of Kentucky, the Democratic majority leader, felt senatorial rectitude should be assumed and no resolution was necessary. "I am not one of those senators who feel it is necessary for the Senate to pass a resolution binding the membership to be honorable men. If I thought it necessary to pass a resolution to make us honorable, I would not want to be a member of this body. I have not yet registered. I shall register before the day is over, and I do not know what sort of gasoline card I will take, but I shall take whatever I am entitled to, without any apologies to anyone in Washington or outside of Washington." [Loud, sustained applause.]

Senator John Bankhead of Alabama thought it "might be a good idea, and a valid exercise of his duty, for the attorney general to ask a federal grand jury to investigate newspapers, columnists and others who are trying to destroy the confidence of the people . . . on grounds that it is seditious conduct."

Other senators agreed, but nothing came of it.

Finally, when the Senate had exhausted itself in attacks on Henderson, the OPA and the press, it voted on Downey's resolution to promise senatorial rectitude. It was defeated by 66 to 2. Only Downey himself and Claude Pepper of Florida supported it.

But public resentment had reduced the value of X cards. Gasoline stations began demanding proof that X cardholders were entitled to them and often refused to sell them any fuel at all. After only two months, a new system was introduced. There were A, B, and C cards only. Nobody was allowed unlimited gasoline. And so once again, in the heat of July 1942, the teachers went back to the tables and to still more unpleasant scenes with cranky and quarrelsome people tired of being pushed around and forced to stand in lines.

If gasoline had to make the dangerous passage through the wolf packs of German submarines along the East Coast, most rubber for automobile tires had to come all the way from Southeast Asia, now under Japanese control. Harold Ickes believed that there was enough scrap rubber lying around in attics and basements to get the country through the war, and the president agreed to let him run one more campaign with one more set of slogans and SX announcements and one more tour of movie stars pursued by photographers carrying Speed Graphics.

Ickes launched the drive by announcing he would donate the rubber doormats from the entrances to his Interior Department. But the Public Buildings Administration objected, saying without the mats people would slip on the wet marble. It locked them away to keep them from Ickes's grasp. (How the mats locked away would prevent people from slipping on the marble was not explained.) Ickes simply looked elsewhere. Leaving a White House meeting, he picked up a rubber doormat outside the entrance to the president's office wing and had his chauffeur throw it into his limousine's trunk. The rubber drive asked for used tires, tubes, heels, boots, shoes, girdles, hot water bottles, baby bottle nipples, garden hoses. The White House announced that the president's dog, Fala, was donating his rubber bones. Gasoline stations were to be the collection stations. The Amoco station at Massachusetts and Wisconsin avenues posted a small sign: WE ACCEPT ANYTHING MADE OF RUBBER EXCEPT CONDOMS. Ickes predicted that his drive would collect a million tons, but he got less than half of that. In Washington, the government asked for ten pounds per person. It received less than ten ounces. The result was that on December 1, 1942, OPA announced nationwide gasoline rationing—no longer just in the Eastern states and no longer to save gasoline, but to save rubber. But there was more. Under the old card rationing system, there was no way to check on the gasoline stations. Some sold their favored customers as much as they wanted, with or without ration tickets. Now, there was to be a new system, with books of tickets that had to be handed over with each purchase.

Patrolman James Powell of the District Police Department was assigned to work undercover with the OPA to help enforce the rationing. Soon he estimated 25 percent of the gasoline stations in town were cheating. On Kenilworth Avenue he found a gang of thirty-five counterfeiters turning out fake stamps. In the post office in the suburb of Falls Church, Virginia, time after time mail bags filled with ration stamps were stolen. Powell discovered a gasoline station on Thirteenth Street more than eager to pay $1,250 for fake gasoline tickets. While Powell stood watching the money being counted, the telephone rang. The station manager ran in and said, "You've got to be careful. I just got a call from a friend in the Police Department. He said a couple of OPA investigators are watching us through binoculars."

"I sweated a little," Powell said. "He wanted to put the tickets in his safe. I knew if he did we'd have to haul away the safe, and it looked heavy. I told him that was the first place the OPA would look, so he hid them under a pile of seat covers. Then I went outside and gave the signal, taking off my hat. The OPA moved in and arrested them."

A few months later OPA learned that in Detroit the Mafia's infamous Purple Gang had set up a counterfeiting shop so expert it came near to breaking down the whole system. The OPA and the U.S. Secret Service worked out a way to examine the tickets under infrared lights, detecting counterfeits and refusing to accept them. That saved the whole rationing system, just in time.

But by now nothing could save Leon Henderson. He was sick. He was battered. He was tired. He was warmly despised by every lobbying group sent to Washington to explain over and over why its members needed special exemptions from regulations and to explain why they had no objection to price controls on their competitors but wanted none for themselves. People who had spent the Depression years struggling to survive, some on little more than cat food, now saw an eight-course banquet but were told by Henderson they could not sit at the table. Taft, Wherry, and more than half the members of Congress were bitter that under the pressure of war—no other pressure could have done it—they had been forced to surrender to Henderson and his OPA more power than any Congress had ever granted any executive agency of government, an agency run by a man they despised. Henderson did nothing to make it easier for them. He was not one of the boys. He was never known to have slapped a back at a Rotary Club luncheon. He was merely a brilliant public servant who took nothing for himself. When the price and wage controls began to work, and they did work, those who ran the OPA owed much of their success to him, for having already done the pick-and-shovel work and taken the abuse.

On December 17, 1942, citing back pains and eye trouble, Henderson resigned. His critics called it a "victory for Congress." They were right.

Henderson's successor was Prentiss R. Brown, a recently defeated liberal Democratic senator from Michigan and one of Congress's few enthusiastic supporters of price controls. Having watched conservatives destroy Henderson, Brown attempted to placate them. He announced on taking office that prices could not "be held at a flat level." He delegated an increasing amount of authority to his deputy, Lou R.

Maxon, a conservative advertising director from Detroit and an embittered enemy of the New Deal.

By early summer 1943, Brown was even more beleaguered than Henderson had been. Nothing he did could satisfy the congressional enemies of OPA; but his futile efforts to please them had won him the enmity of the New Dealers. "We in the OPA are in the frontline trenches on the domestic front," he said. "I know of no group or class that we do not reach—and we please none." Desperate to save himself, Brown fired Maxon—who left behind a five-page memo charging that OPA was filled with "indecision, compromise, miles of legalistic red tape" and "Left Wingers," "New Thinkers," and "Tugwellites" trying to "force radical and dangerous concepts on the public under the excuse of wartime needs." To replace Maxon, he brought in Chester Bowles, who three years before had left his $250,000-a-year job as president of the Benton and Bowles advertising agency for a $7,000-a-year position as rationing and price control director in Connecticut. He was generally considered to run the most successful such program in the country. "No sensible person would seek a job of this kind," Bowles told reporters when he arrived in Washington.

Three months later, Prentiss Brown resigned, and the Coast Guard was dispatched to search for Bowles, who was sailing off the coast of Maine, and tell him that the president had named him the new director of the OPA. "And the familiar Washington pattern begins again," one reporter wrote.

Bowles, however, managed to defy the pattern, or at least to bend it. He was helped in doing so by his experience in Connecticut. The state's Commissioner of Motor Vehicles, John T. McCartney, was the governor's man for patronage. When Bowles was first appointed state OPA administrator, McCartney invited him to lunch and said he assumed that when Bowles began hiring salaried people for his rationing offices around the state, he would "consult the local Democratic party leaders and ask for their suggestions." Bowles responded that when the rationing rules were fully in effect the public would so despise the boards that the Democrats ought to think about placing their political enemies on them. The American people simply could not believe the United States could ever run out of anything because they had always lived with surpluses, and when the rationing rules began to deny them what they wanted, they would instantly assume the bureaucrats had blundered again. Did

McCartney's Democrats really want their people mixed up in a mess like that?

In each city and town, Bowles created a board of unpaid volunteers assisted by a few paid people doing the clerical work. He insisted that a board include one businessman, one teacher, one union officer, one storekeeper, in rural areas one farmer, and one respected person from no special category, usually a clergyman. He wanted to avoid the public's usual contempt for boards filled with politicians and retired rich people. It worked, he said, because the public now understood that the rules issued by the rationing boards were made by local folks they all knew.

When he arrived in Washington to join the national OPA, his first complaint was one that Leon Henderson would have understood. In the 1942 election, a number of Democratic congressmen had been defeated and had then been sent over to the OPA with instructions that they be hired immediately, displacing Republicans where necessary. Bowles argued that the OPA could not earn the public's support if it was seen as a graveyard for defeated politicians. But he soon conceded, as Henderson never had, that nothing could be done. The tradition of jobs for defeated congressmen was so ancient, so hallowed, so taken for granted, it could not even be discussed. This was Washington.

Bowles did what he had to do while introducing Washington to Madison Avenue's black arts of promotion and persuasion. He was particularly adept at handling groups of businessmen who came to Washington to complain that they should be allowed higher prices. Bowles first brought in experts from the Treasury to draw a frightening picture of the growing inflation that government was frantically trying to control; the success of this effort, they said, was in extreme doubt. Then a man from the War Labor Board came in to report that the unions were demanding enormous wage increases; only with the most heroic effort could this dam be kept from bursting. Then military officers back from the battle fronts delivered horrible, hair-raising descriptions of young Americans facing dirt and blood and dismemberment and death. And, finally, an officer from the Pentagon described the military's system for sending out telegrams to American families saying, "We regret to inform you that your son/husband/father has been killed in battle. . . . " The hard-nosed businessmen who had come to Washington looking for price increases went back home with tears in their eyes — and no money.

Bowles also used these skills in dealing with Congress. He showed a committee, probably for the first time in Washington, how a complicated issue could be explained with an easel, a pointer and a series of cards lettered in color with bar graphs and charts, in the manner of an ad agency's presentation to a client trying to sell shampoo. His charts, he admitted later, were deliberately made a little crudely. He did not want his presentation to be so slick as to look like professional salesmanship. It usually worked.

Another Bowles trick: When he was in the witness chair before a committee of Congress, as he often was, he noticed occasionally that somebody from outside Congress, usually an industry lobbyist, would hand a committee member a card with a tough, nasty question written by one of OPA's many critics. The committee member would look at the card, read the question, and wait for the answer. Bowles' trick was to say, "The question is not entirely clear to me. Could you please . . . explain it a little further?" The embarrassed congressman, unable to elaborate because he knew nothing about the question, would simply drop it.

Bowles later said that in his years at the OPA, he found that 2 to 3 percent of the American people were inherently dishonest and would cheat on any OPA rule, 20 percent would obey the rules regardless of what anyone else did, and the other 75 percent were willing to be honest but not willing to be suckers if they thought they were being deceived by the bureaucrats. John Kenneth Galbraith, then a young economist from Princeton running some of the price control programs, took a similarly jaundiced view. The big retailers with big reputations and hopes for public acceptance after the war did not dare defy the OPA ceilings; the publicity of a prosecution would ruin them. Others, however, were less careful. "The cattlemen were the worst," he recalled. The only truly substantial and persistent black market was in meat.

Bowles had a smoother ride at the OPA than Henderson or Brown, partly because he did not have Henderson's reputation as a "pinkly partisan" economist, and partly because he was not as abrasive and was more easily able to persuade Congress to come through with the power and support he needed. He had, after all, spent a highly successful business career in advertising, persuading people to buy what he was selling even if they did not want it.

He presided over the OPA to the end of its days after the war, and with reasonable success dealt with the lobbyists for farmers, labor and business. He also dealt with such members of the public as a woman who wrote that she had always fed her fourteen cats on pork kidneys, but could no longer do so because the kidneys were rationed. One of her cats was a sixteen-pound stud, and without his pork kidneys, she claimed, he grew nasty and dangerous. She was fifty-five, living alone and frightened. An earnest OPA administrator wrote a sympathetic reply: There was nothing in the rules to permit exceptions for cats. Had she tried unrationed fish?

Through it all, Chester Bowles had at least one steadfast supporter: Franklin Roosevelt. The president challenged him only once. He called one summer day to say his neighbors in Warm Springs, Georgia, who grew a lot of peaches, felt the prices OPA had allowed them were too low. What was the explanation? Bowles told him. Roosevelt sighed and hung up.

"Parties for a Purpose"

Washington's Sunday *Times-Herald* arrived with its clean typography and printing, and eight full pages of spicy detail on public and private social affairs in the city along with more of its unrelenting attacks on Roosevelt and his New Dealers running in a purple stream across the editorial page and on over into the cartoons and news columns. Its anti-Roosevelt prose read as if its writers sat at their typewriters red in the face, the veins standing out and throbbing in their necks while they sweated through their underwear. One of its writers explained his political views: "I am not a conservative. I am a *royalist.*"

On this Sunday morning in 1943, the *Times-Herald*'s owner, Mrs. Eleanor Patterson, known to all as "Cissy," lolled on her pale-green silk sheets in her marble mansion at 15 DuPont Circle, the breakfast-in-bed tray removed, the crumbs brushed away and the pillows fluffed. She read through her own newspaper, paying special attention to the entire section devoted to news of society. This was her own creation, her own special interest. She devoted huge staff and resources to it and it was one reason her paper had the city's largest circulation. A rival publisher, observing Cissy's success while his own paper with its heavyweight political commentary had fallen behind, said, "People in this town don't care about a goddamned thing but sports, comics and society."

Cissy leafed through her paper and made notes of comments, complaints and suggestions to be telephoned to her editors. Then she laid the paper aside and picked up a book of eight-by-ten photographs. In a few hours she was to leave for another dinner at Evalyn Walsh McLean's house in Georgetown. What to wear? In her loose-leaf book was a color photograph of every item in her clothes closets—every dress, skirt, blouse, hat, shoe, scarf, belt, each of them catalogued and numbered. As she turned the pages, a maid in a dove-gray and white lace uniform stood with pad and pencil awaiting instructions. Mrs. Patterson studied her pictures and said tonight she would wear something like dress number 76, belt 48, scarf 39 and shoes 105. No hat. The maid disappeared into clothes closets as big as small department stores and collected each item from a green silk-padded hanger numbered as in a restaurant checkroom, made certain each was pressed and immaculate, and delivered Mrs. Patterson's evening ensemble to her dressing room. By eight o'clock, Cissy was ready for another of Evalyn's famous Sunday night dinners with dance orchestras, movies and caterers for a hundred or more Washingtonians rich, famous or powerful or all three.

Not many huge fortunes were ever made in Washington, but a great many made elsewhere were spent there. Mrs. Patterson's came from her family in Chicago, Mrs. McLean's from her father's gold mine in Ouray, Colorado. They and others with money had moved to Washington beginning in the mid-nineteenth century when they decided the town was becoming interesting. There was an active social life centered around the White House, Congress, the Supreme Court and the foreign embassies that often were able to produce genuine, as opposed to spurious, European nobility who might be, and sometimes were, enticed into marrying their daughters. The caterers were adequate, the servants cheap, plentiful and obsequious, the Chevy Chase Club was convenient and suitably restricted, there were not so many of the tiresome immigrants then pouring into New York, and Washington was on the railroads' main line between New York and Southampton and Palm Beach.

Some who lived there were rich men originally invited to serve in various presidents' cabinets or who had bought themselves seats in the United States Senate and had decided—or their wives had decided—to stay on. They had made money and in those tax-free days had kept it all. They had no need to work, and thought it might be amusing to serve for a time in some suitable government post, and if the salary was not even enough to pay the maids and chauffeurs, no one cared. Maybe even a couple of years as United States ambassador to some pleasant country with a good climate—some nice place placid enough to cause no diplomatic problems and no work—might be a pleasing social medallion for a man who until now had spent all his time making money in the manufacture of steam boilers or railroad cars, or gold mining in the west.

One attraction in serving the government was that in these late-nineteenth-century years it seldom did much. Congress adjourned and left Washington in May or June to escape the heat. Not a great deal was happening in the world that seemed worth Washington's attention, and American foreign policy essentially was to avoid having any. The rich families came and built themselves marble, mahogany and stained-glass-and-pipe-organ mansions on the good streets in northwest Washington, mainly Massachusetts Avenue. When World War II began, they or their descendants were still there.

At a press conference in January 1942, President Roosevelt went into an irritable, rambling discourse about the city's social figures who were hanging around Washington and taking up space while contributing nothing to the war.

"I suppose," he said to the reporters standing around his desk in the Oval Office, "if we made it very uncomfortable for the—what shall I call them? Parasites? in Washington, the parasites would leave. There are a good many parasites in Washington today. we all know that."

The reporters wanted to know how he would move the parasites out.

"Well, I know what I would do. I would write a story with a headline, a large headline, in the Washington papers. The headline, very simple, would go right in a box, right across the front page: ARE YOU A PARASITE? —now a lot of people in this town are going to say, 'I wonder if I am a parasite or not?' "

He was having a good time with his little sermon about people he detested, and most of whom detested him, and went on with it: "Those people now living here not essential to the war effort should be asked to move out . . . that class of people who live in Washington for social reasons . . . people who live in twenty-room mansions on Massachusetts Avenue, for instance, occupying homes there rather than government or business."

Then he made vague threats about taking over their big houses and converting them into government offices. As the press conference ended he turned with an aside to his press secretary, Steve Early. "I hope," he said, "Cissy won't take that personally," referring to Cissy Patterson. Then, after a moment's hesitation, "I hope she will."

She did. Even though she fit Roosevelt's description of a "parasite," living as she did in a mansion of more than twenty rooms a few feet off Massachusetts Avenue, she was delighted to have new material for her paper's attacks on Roosevelt. The real Washington parasites, her *Times-Herald* said, were "the New Deal bureaucrats and bubble-headed social engineers intent on bringing socialism to America." The New York *Herald Tribune* said the first parasites to leave should be the government's 2,895 press agents. The *Post* quoted the anonymous taxi driver reporters seem always to find when they need a juicy comment: "As I get it, they want more room for more clerks to do the work the clerks they've got ain't doing." The *Post* also said, satirically, that it was "happy to report the discovery of two more persons willing to give up their space in Washington, making a total of three." Hope Ridings Miller on the society page of the *Post* rose bravely to confront this grave issue. It was true, she wrote, that "quite a sizeable number of purely pleasure-seeking out-of-towners are still coming to Washington for the express purpose of settling down for the season." She quoted one as saying to her, " . . . so much more amusing than Florida this year. Palm Beach, you know, is cold and dreary and horribly dull." Miss Miller concluded, "No doubt about it—wartime Washington is the most thrilling city that ever was."

Roosevelt's attack on the socialites became the subject of jokes and banter at Washington dinner tables. A host said in his after-dinner toast, "I want to welcome my fellow parasites." Even so, there were strains in social Washington: How could they go on with their nonstop revelry when the wounded from Pearl Harbor were being brought into the city's military hospitals and flag-draped coffins were being shipped back from overseas every day? When General George C. Marshall, the army's chief of staff, had had to abandon his practice of sending his own hand-written note to the family of every man killed in battle because now there were too many and his notes had to be replaced with Western Union telegrams? Well, they could and did accept the rationale some-body thought up—that the dollar-a-year-men running the war agencies often lived in hotel rooms and often alone, and after their daytime labors with copper allocations and price controls they deserved a little relaxa-tion at night such as only a hostess with a proper house and kitchen could provide.

Miss Miller in the *Post* printed a letter from a reader in Chicago saying, "Less tea-partying and more defense bond buying around Wash-ington might speed up the war effort more than anything else." She responded with some heat: "It's about time somebody cleared up this Great Misconception. It's about time, in other words, that the country at large gets wise to what makes the Washington party wheels go around. Society for society's sake died a natural death on the banks of the Potomac when the first bomb burst over Pearl Harbor." Now, she said, Washington had "parties for a purpose, where influential people gather to transact business, make contacts and otherwise advance the war effort." Thus anointed with a patriotic purpose, the parties went on and throughout the war they never stopped. After government, the papers said, socializing was Washington's second largest industry.

Among the informational bulletins offered those trying socially to be upwardly mobile was one from another society writer in the *Post* whose column said, "If Mrs. X (she knows who she is) hopes to make it socially, she had better stop serving canned soup and desserts of canned peaches and vanilla ice cream." No doubt, but food was not the real dinnertime attraction; it was difficult to serve food of any consequence during the wartime rationing and the meals were mostly unrationed chicken. No, it was not the food that people came for, but big-name guests. One guest with a resounding name and title could easily fill a table with other names exalted enough to gratify the hostess. An acceptance from the first name with suitable title attached was crucial, since that allowed her to send out invitations saying, "In honor of . . . " That would work if the guest to be honored was a wielder of government power whose name was in the paper at least twice a week, a famous show business personal-ity such as Clark Gable, who was in town occasionally, an author of books not too left-wing, or an ambassador from some country not known primarily for tropical disease.

These were the requirements for the dinnertime stars. Once a star agreed to come, the other chairs could be filled with people who were merely presentable. It was not unusual for a hostess to fill the secondary chairs at her table by inviting people she had not even met and knew only by repute. Nor was it unusual for them to accept, leading to conversations like this: "Are you having dinner at Mrs. Brown's tonight?" And the response, "Yes, I am. Who *is* she?"

The other requirement now was that a party somehow be given some flavor, however faint, of being related to the war. A number of guests in uniform would do, or a woman wearing a badge saying "USO Hostess," or a few women in Red Cross uniforms looking as if they had just come from a day of rolling bandages.

And the Washington socialites took it all so seriously! Mrs. Walter Tuckerman, to her middle age and beyond, meticulously saved the place card from every lunch, tea and dinner she had been invited to for forty years and mounted them all in a shelf of leather-bound books, noting for each affair the date, place, who sat on either side of her and who said what, back to and including a dinner in 1907 when she sat beside William Jennings Bryan.

Why such frenzy to fill a dinner table with people who might be famous or hold great power but who might also be insufferably dull? Archduke Otto of Austria, the pretender to the nonexistent Austro-Hungarian throne of the Hapsburgs, continued to be sought after even when he was found to be a bore who ate like a timber wolf and then sat lumpishly and groggily in the living room refusing to leave until pushed. Why did the hostesses pursue this?

In the forties in Washington it was still unusual for a rich and socially well-connected married woman to work. If she did, her husband was assumed by his peers to be unable to support a household on his own and somehow to be inadequate. A woman active in the Washington social frenzy must, as a condition of entry, have money. And so there were servants to do the housework and to leave her to wonder, day after day, what to do with herself. Taking any job other than charity work was considered to be unsuitable.

Allowed to do nothing else, denied a chance to compete with the men during the day, they joined in competing with the other women at

night in the only game open to them—competing for the grandest guests
and for the most flattering publicity.

Social competition and social climbing were not invented in Washington in World War II, but they did seem in that time and place to have
been raised—or lowered—to the level of trench warfare. For the ambitious hostesses, no effort, no expense, was too great in their campaign to
conquer the society pages, to entice celebrities to their tables, seemingly
in the belief that the next best thing to being a celebrity was to feed one.
In this contest, if a hostess fed enough famous people and her feats were
reported in the papers in sufficiently flattering detail, she could become
as important at night as her husband was during the day, and perhaps
more so. Even a degree of rudeness was acceptable in this dinnertime
competition. When the Senate was about to vote on Dean Acheson's
nomination for assistant secretary of state, a woman called him and said,
"If you're confirmed, will you come for dinner? If not, will you come
after dinner for dancing?"

Margaret Case Harriman, a skilled observer of Washington's social
climbing, reported in *Harper's* that one hostess simply went to pieces
and panicked when most of the heavyweight guests she had invited failed
to appear. Around midnight, when one of the guests who had come to
dinner was trying to say good night, the hostess stared wildly at her and
screamed, "Don't *speak* to me! Not a single soul I *wanted* has showed up!"

The war itself had some effect on all this, one effect being that
people of this social and financial class had little else to do. Those
accustomed to traveling had to stay home. Almost all the world was
closed to tourists. Cruise ships had disappeared from the seas. Travel by
airplane and train was difficult, since the military and the war agencies
had travel priorities entitling them to seize any seat on any train or plane
at any time, and they never were reluctant to use them. A family of five
could arrive at the airport with piles of baggage and find they had been
"bumped" off the plane and their seats taken by army officers going on
leave and OPA clerks delivering a new set of orders to the Kansas City
regional office. There was not enough gasoline for automobile trips.
Resort hotels had been seized to house the military or interned enemy
diplomats. Most Washington restaurants had been uninteresting even in
peacetime, specializing as they did in overcooked vegetables and everything else deep-fried in the same fat, and now with rationing and food
shortages they had even less to offer. On one night's menu, the Willard

Hotel offered tongue and oxtail and nothing in between. So, there was little else to do but have parties at home and eat a few more chickens.

Then, again, nearly all the businessmen running the war agencies were from out of town, since industrialists were not to be found in Washington, where there never was any industry. Most of them planned at the war's end to return home and they and their wives saw this as their big chance to make social conquests good for points in the future. Who else, back in Indiana, could talk entertainingly of having sat at dinner with a hand-kissing Russian prince who but for the Bolsheviks would now be living in regal splendor in the Winter Palace in Saint Petersburg? The Washington society columns were syndicated to other papers across the country, and social triumphs in the capital would soon be known everywhere.

Still another reason for the hyperactive night life was common in peacetime but more so during the war. A prominent senator or the head of a war agency was totally unreachable during the day but accessible across a dinner table at night, and a rough estimate was that a fourth to a half of those at these parties were, in one way or another, on the make, using an evening at somebody's dinner table as a chance to lobby, to promote a cause, to find jobs for themselves, to establish business relationships or to find law clients for the postwar years.

For all these reasons, and because America was the only major nation whose capital was far removed from the battlefields, wartime Washington, in the view of those experienced in the field, was socially the most aggressive and most tireless city in the western world. European visitors studied the scene and proclaimed that Washington actually was a court, but while Louis XIV had entertained his courtiers at Versailles, the Roosevelts had withdrawn from the race and left the courtiers to entertain each other.

They did, at dinners, luncheons, Sunday breakfasts, hunt breakfasts, dance breakfasts, teas and tea dances, receptions and balls in ballrooms at home for those who had them and at the Mayflower and Willard for those who did not, and—most common of all—cocktail parties. Often there were fifty to a hundred on one night, and from the mezzanine floor of the Statler Hotel downtown on across town through Northwest into the suburbs there was the rattle of ice and glass, the drone of conversation and the loud shriek of alcoholic laughter.

If it was called a cocktail party, that meant in the standardized social codes that drinks and salted peanuts would be served. If it was more ambitious and was garnished with boiled shrimp lying around a bowl of red sauce, it was called a reception. British visitors found the cocktail party baffling, since they had seen nothing like it at home and the dynamics of it escaped them. But it was popular simply because it was easy and inexpensive to give and easy to attend. An energetic member of the circuit could fit in two or three within the five-to-seven-thirty hours— the guests were not seated and so many more could be squeezed in. Since cocktail parties were formless and unstructured, with no exact beginning and no clear ending, guests could arrive and leave as they pleased, and display their dexterity at holding a drink and a cigarette and shaking hands all at the same time. And for as much or as little time as they liked they could join the crowd in milling around the room— counterclockwise, it was said, because of the same Coriolis effect that caused water in the Northern Hemisphere to swirl counterclockwise out of a bathtub.

Winter cocktail parties were the worst. With the crowds and the smoke, the closed-in overheated rooms, the oxygen was soon depleted and the noise rose to the level of the Washington zoo's small-mammal house. In the spring, they were more bearable if staged outdoors when the ornamental trees were in flower. The air was cleaner, the noise could float down the street rather than bouncing off the ceiling and a woman could stand prettily holding a glass beneath the cool, quiet fireworks of a cherry tree in blossom.

The city's newspapers, the *Post, Times-Herald, Evening Star* and *Daily News,* carefully chronicled the doings of the wartime social figures with three-dot items revealing the oddities and peculiarities of Washington's frenzied partying. Here follows a random composite:

Gene Tierney of film fame, arriving with Oleg Cassini, charmed quite a circle of guests before she had to go on to another party Natalie Phillips was giving in her honor . . . Dorothy Thompson was a center of attention herself, saying "To the Russian front, may it advance!" . . . Dr. Serge Voronoff, of ape gland and rejuvenation fame, down from New York with his beautiful wife (the former Gertrude Schwaetz, cousin of Mme. Magda Lupescu, who is the traveling companion of King Carol of Rumania) . . . a center of attention was Governor Alf Landon

of Kansas, in town for the Republican dinner tomorrow night . . .
"I thought you'd ride in on a bicycle," someone said to Leon
Henderson . . . Mrs. Cordell Hull patiently explaining over and
over that her husband would come along later if he could possibly get away from the state department . . . only trouble about
the party was getting in. Time and again, the foyer was so
crowded the embassy officials decreed that the front door must
be closed . . . the drawing room has red brocaded walls. Mrs.
Truxtun Beale and Mrs. Nicholas Longworth, both wearing red
frocks looking as if they had picked them to wear in this room
. . . everybody at the party made at least one trip upstairs in the
Peruvian Embassy to see the lavish array of wedding gifts that
filled two rooms—a chased silver tea set, a punch bowl and cups,
a gold flat table service, an electric sewing machine, a silver fox
coat, candlesticks, vases and goblets, and half a dozen sizeable
checks displayed in a glass case . . . coasting in late were the
Coordinator of Inter-American Affairs and Mrs. Nelson Rockefeller
. . . a goodbye-to-a-yacht party given by Colonel and Mrs. Robert
Guggenheim. The Firenze, their floating palace, is to be turned
over to the Navy for wartime use. Gene Tierney shaking hands
on the foredeck . . . wartime tension manifests itself in many ways
and not wanting to be alone is the most obvious. A Senator's wife
stopped me to exclaim, "I've simply got to get on to three more
parties in the next hour" . . . a popular man-about-Washington
was talking, not boasting, just stating a fact and saying that in
forty years in this city, "I never, my dear, *never,* have seen
anything like the number of parties going on now. Do you know,
I've dined out for ten nights straight, and at least two cocktail
parties every night for the last month."

Yes, there were social gatherings staged not for the edification of
society writers but for the ordinary pleasures of food, drink and
conversation. For one, Senator Lister Hill of Alabama lived on 49th
Street in the Spring Valley neighborhood and on summer evenings he
liked to have small groups for dinner served on a back porch he called
"the piazza" and overlooking a vegetable or Victory Garden. His wife,
Henrietta, the classic southern woman dressed in crisp, stylish cottons,
was all beauty and charm and soft, gentle speech and cast iron, offering

no deference to any politician's vanity. "I take care of the garden while Lister plays his political games." After dinner on the porch, as Jonathan Daniels, one of the guests, described it, she did not ask but instructed the Majority Leader of the United States Senate, Alben Barkley of Kentucky, to stand and sing "Wagon Wheels." He did. She then ordered him to tell the joke he had told a thousand times and Washington had laughed at for forty years and whose punchline had entered the language. Barkley told, yet again, about asking a Kentucky resident for his vote in the next election and reminding him that over the years he had done him numerous favors—got his brother a job in the post office, got his son out of jail and arranged a federal loan to save his farm. The voter responded, "Yes, but what have you done for me lately?"

At the White House, once the center around which Washington's high society swirled and danced, but now withdrawn from the game, the Roosevelts seldom did more than invite small groups to quiet, informal family dinners, including far more social workers than socialites. Still, invitations to these small dinners were coveted, even though the Roosevelts' housekeeper, Henrietta Nesbitt, probably served the worst food in the history of the White House, bringing snide remarks from the guests, once they were out the door, about the seemingly unvarying menu of turkey and candied yams, and even though at times the dinner table conversation could be awkward when Eleanor and Franklin began snapping at each other.

Early in the war, when the White House withdrew, the field was clear for the rich, the ambitious, the climbers, the embassies. They seized the moment, even with all its problems, and, indeed, in wartime the problems were awesome. There was, for example, the difficulty in finding servants. Men and women of modest skills now could make far more money in the war industries and at the same time escape being told at six o'clock that twenty people were arriving for dinner at eight. Hostesses traded heartbreaking stories of servants who advertised for jobs with the stipulation that they would not come for interviews; prospective employers must come to them. And servants were known to commit the high crime of simply disappearing without notice. The folklore after the war had it that this was the watershed in American history when if a new house-keeper did agree to come to work, her first announcement was "I don't do windows."

The Roosevelt-haters among the rich socialites, which was most of them, blamed their servant problems on Eleanor Roosevelt and accused her of encouraging the servants, mainly black women, to be more assertive. They were right. She did. Shortly after Pearl Harbor she infuriated Massachusetts Avenue by suggesting that domestic servants form a union to bargain about wages and working hours. Nothing came of it, but she was never forgiven.

There were other problems. The dinner guests now most ardently desired were not always the old-line officers of government in Congress and the cabinet agencies and the courts, all of whose precedence and order of seating at the table was long established by the rules of protocol everyone understood and accepted. The coveted guests now included those running the war agencies, like Donald Nelson at the War Production Board and Leon Henderson at the Office of Price Administration. When the Congress of Vienna in 1814 set the rules of protocol and established an agreed set of diplomatic niceties, people like Nelson and Henderson were not even imagined, no provision had ever been made for them, and now a hostess could never be sure who outranked whom. A Washington story often told but hard to confirm was that the ambassador of France, seated at dinner in a place he felt inappropriate to his rank, reacted in cold fury and walked out. The State Department would offer advice on the seating of diplomats, but when it came to civilians in the war agencies, it refused any help. Often, the solution was to serve the food from a buffet and to seat people at separate round tables. That eliminated seating problems and also reduced the need for servants.

Then there were the difficult questions about dress. In the 1930s an invitation saying "informal" meant black tie rather than white, but now in wartime no man wanted to be seen in evening clothes. By far the preferred dress for those of fighting age was a military uniform, preferably one deftly and artfully made by Lewis and Thomas Saltz in their men's store on G Street. Women owning neither a Red Cross uniform nor a USO Hostess button simply had to bear up.

The Washington newspapers watched over wartime society with some ambivalence. They continued full and even fulsome coverage in the society pages, but the news pages were often critical and scolding—although in the *Times-Herald,* whose owner, Cissy Patterson, was a socialite herself, it did appear that the tone of the coverage depended on who was being covered. As when, in late 1942, Bernard Baruch gave a party for Harry Hopkins and his new bride, Louise Macy, inviting ranking New Dealers to a dinner and dance at the Carlton Hotel. Next morning, the *Times-Herald* printed a report by Walter Trohan saying, "Forty dollars a plate—a sum which would provide 1,180 cartridges for Marine rifles in the jungles of Guadalcanal—was the cost of the party at which 60 New Deal officials feasted, drank and danced." The party cost Baruch three thousand dollars. "This sum," Trohan noted, "went for a menu which listed 35 items from caviar to champagne, flowers, an orchestra and bottles of imported French perfume which went as favors to the women." Leon Henderson, he wrote, skipped about the dance floor with every woman who attended the party and was one of the last to leave. Henderson read the story and said, "About what I'd expect of Cissy, that goddamn bitch."

Despite all the agonizing difficulties, the partying went on with such force and persistence that word of it reached around the world and foreign visitors to Washington asked to be taken to observe it.

A woman in Ohio wrote to a Washington journalist she had heard on the radio and said she and her husband were coming to the city for a week or two while he did business with a war agency. They knew no one, would like to see more than the monuments and memorials, and wondered if there was any way strangers in town could get a glimpse of the partying they had read so much about? The journalist responded that it was remarkably easy:

Put on a silk dress and tell your husband to wear a dark suit and a shoeshine. Ride out Massachusetts Avenue any afternoon around five o'clock. When you see an embassy with people and cars entering and leaving the driveway, there will be a reception in progress. Walk in. You will be greeted at the door by a functionary who will not know who you are because he does not know who anyone is. Say something vague to him, like "Senator Brown is coming along in a few minutes." There is no Senator Brown, but he won't know it. He will assume you are somehow associated with a Senator and he will say his country is delighted you came to the party. Inside, you will find a bar, a string orchestra, a buffet with foods including the country's native specialities, and a crowd of people mainly from other embassies. None of them will know who you are, but it will not matter because most of them don't know each other. Eat and drink as much as you like, make polite but non-committal small talk, mention "the Senator" occasionally, stay until about seven, thank them and leave.

She followed these instructions and later wrote that she and her husband had been to three embassy parties and had a wonderful time.

When Henri Bonnet arrived in 1945 as ambassador of France after his country was liberated from the Germans, he was invited to excessive and fatiguing numbers of embassy receptions. He found them to be a tiresome waste of time, but some he had to attend out of diplomatic duty, and he described how he dealt with them:

> If it is winter, leave your coat in your car to avoid a wait in the checkroom line. Go through the receiving line and when you shake hands with your host say your name at least twice to be sure he knows who you are and to assure that you get credit for being there. Immediately look around the room for a back or side exit. Move slowly and steadily toward it. Along the way, allow a butler to place a glass of champagne in your hand. Do not drink it, since on some nights you will have to do this two or three times. Give the appearance of being intent on moving across the room for some important reason. You are, after all, the ambassador of France and people will always assume you are doing something important. Move through the room, smile, shake a few hands, but do not stop. If you stop, someone will start a conversation difficult to end. Keep moving this way until you reach the exit. Set your champagne glass on a table if there is one. If not, pour it into a potted palm. Then leave. My best time was in and out in eight minutes.

Before the war, the Latin American embassies had been of little interest to Washington socialites, but with so many European countries occupied by the Germans and their embassies suffering, the South and Central American embassies assumed with a new seriousness the task of keeping social Washington amused at night. When President Fulgencio Batista of Cuba visited, the embassy flew in a planeload of tropical flowers, set up eight bars, hired one dance orchestra for the first floor and another for the second, and at dawn the party was still going with guests upstairs dancing to Glenn Miller's version of "In the Mood," and downstairs to "Little Brown Jug."

When Mexico invited two hundred people to a party, five hundred came and nobody seemed to notice or care. The guests were whatever officials of government could be induced to dance one more night away, diplomats from friendly countries, socialites from Washington and others who took the Pennsylvania Railroad's Congressional down from New York. But not many members of Congress. Most of them, living on their ten-thousand-dollar salaries, could not appropriately dress themselves or their wives, some were young and tied down with children, and there was always the danger of political damage if their names appeared in society columns reprinted across the country and the voters at home read about their elected representatives out drinking and dancing all night rather than doing something to help win the war. One exception was Representative Edith Nourse Rogers of Massachusetts, a wealthy widow with high social connections. At a British embassy lawn party celebrating the Queen's birthday with champagne, wine punch and strawberries with clotted cream, the society writers carefully studied the scene and agreed that Mrs. Rogers was the only woman there perfectly dressed for the occasion—a flower-printed silk chiffon dress and a wide-brimmed straw hat.

Adolf Berle, assistant secretary of state, wrote in his diary, "More kings are expected." Too bad, he thought, because "they take so much time." For dethroned and exiled European royalty and their courtiers, Washington was one of the few places left to them. London was being bombed. Paris was Hitler's. Rome was Mussolini's. Madrid was a Nazi outpost. The rest of Europe was either occupied or inaccessible, and they trooped to Washington where—they had been told—the hostesses would fall on them like hounds on soup bones. Some, like Crown Princess Marthe of Norway, were invited by the Roosevelts to stay in the White House and spend weekends in Hyde Park. Queen Wilhelmina of the Netherlands also was a guest in the White House, where the house-keeper recalled an engaging picture of the Queen having breakfast on the White House south portico while being serenaded by a military band standing out on the lawn in the rain.

The Japanese carrier fleet was only a few hours away from Pearl Harbor when the new ambassador from the Soviet Union flew in across the Pacific and took up his duties in the embassy in the old Pullman mansion on Sixteenth Street—Maxim Litvinov and his English wife, Ivy. He arrived wearing a gray denim suit similar to those issued by prison wardens to highway work gangs. It looked to Thomas Saltz "as if he'd slept in it for twenty-five years and was so grubby it would have stood up by itself." Litvinov's first stop in town was in Saltz's store, where he asked to be outfitted from head to foot in clothes suitable for an ambassador in a western country. Saltz put him into traditional clothes, shortening the collars to hug the back of his neck, cutting the sleeves short enough to display a half-inch of shirtsleeve, cuffing the trousers to barely graze his shoetops and cunningly shaping the vests to accommodate and minimize a substantially protruding stomach. A few days later, when Litvinov called at the White House to present his ambassador's credentials. Roosevelt's first words to him were "You get that suit in Moscow?"

In czarist Russia he had been a gunrunner for Lenin and Stalin and seen the insides of a dozen jails until the czar's Cossacks exiled him to England, where he went about London pamphleteering and speaking and promoting the new Marxist theories, and in this work he met an English woman named Ivy Low. She was busily involved with the Fabian Society and Sidney Webb at the London School of Economics and she was attracted to Marxism. They were married and when Moscow again was accessible to him they moved there, he to join the government and she to set up classes teaching English. Now he was settled into an official respectability and had no further need for the aliases he had used as a gunrunner: Litvinov Harrison, alias Papasha, alias David Mordecai, David Finklestein, alias Gustav Graf. He had survived a life of poverty, intrigue and danger to be sent as ambassador to the only country Stalin thought would be of any help to him in defeating Hitler.

In Washington, the Litvinovs discovered the eager socialites had caught the scent of a new diplomatic-political celebrity in town. They now saw Russia as an ally, an enemy of the enemy and therefore a friend, and the Litvinovs as new and important and exotic and good for social points in the drawing room. The invitations piled up in a snowfall at the embassy's front door.

But the prize went to Marjorie Merriwether Post Close Hutton Davies, the heiress to the Post-Toasties cereal millions, and her husband, Joseph E. Davies, former ambassador to Moscow. Through her life, Mrs. Davies had held to a stance of queenly majesty and presence, though still on occasion displaying a taste for holding social hippodromes that looked less like the work of a queen than of Sigmund Romberg in an operetta. She and Davies were married in 1935 in her Manhattan apartment on East 92nd Street equipped with forty rooms, two ballrooms and twenty-five servants. There was a pink wedding cake five feet wide, forty musicians, a choir and four thousand dollars' worth of pink flowers dyed a slightly darker shade to match her pink velvet wedding gown with white fox fur trimming and a train ten feet long.

Now in Washington, his ambassadorship to the Soviet Union behind him, the Davieses announced that the first reception for the Litvinovs would be held in their residence at 1801 Foxhall Road, where a tree-lined driveway curved down through a hilly, wooded glade to a mansion expensively decorated with Russian art and such rarities as an autographed photograph of Joseph Stalin displayed in a silver frame ornamented with a lacquered red star. There were other Russian treasures Stalin had given to Davies during his service in Moscow and others he had been allowed to buy at bargain prices.

On a cold and rainy January 19, 1942, while the Russian army was pushing the Germans back to Mozhaisk, sixty miles west of Moscow, there was a half-mile traffic jam on Foxhall Road as the entire Washington establishment turned out, along with photographers from *Life* magazine for a "Life Goes to a Party" spread, and Washington's newspaper society writers—all of them. *Life* called it "Washington's biggest blowout since the war began," and Hope Ridings Miller in the *Post* said there were "more celebrities than I have seen under one roof." The guests were received and then guided by Ridgewell, the butler, to a room where Mrs. Cordell Hull alternated with the wives of Supreme Court justices in pouring tea from a golden pot into gold-rimmed white teacups made in czarist Russia and brought home when Davies's ambassadorship ended. The table was spread with a lace cloth and piled with tiny sandwiches and petits fours in Mrs. Davies's favorite colors, green and pink. A string quartet on a balcony played Russian music over the heads of most of the Supreme Court, most of the Roosevelt cabinet, Vice President Henry Wallace and society writers taking notes for these column items:

Judged by any standard, the Soviet envoy is a success in Washington, but one look at the list of guests on hand to greet him and his wife yesterday is proof enough that socially the two have already run away with the town . . . even cave-dwelling Washingtonians, seldom seen these days in official society, were numerous in the flower-filled rooms that were crowded to the walls from shortly after five o'clock . . . Mr. and Mrs. M. Lincoln Schuster (he's the New York publisher who recently brought out Mr. Davies's best-seller, *Mission to Moscow*) . . . Mrs. Woodrow Wilson, a popular center of attention . . . receiving in the music room, the host and hostess greeted a line of guests that was still moving in as late as seven o'clock . . . the Soviet ambassador smartly turned out in striped trousers and cutaway . . . Mme Litvinov had chosen a floor-length dress of purple crepe with a narrow band of varicolored beads adorning the bodice . . . an atmosphere of all-out gaiety I have noticed very infrequently in Washington this season . . . Vice President Henry Wallace, not among those present at the usual afternoon party, was on hand for well over an hour.

When the receiving line finally dissolved, Mrs. Davies circulated among her guests and in passing Richard Harkness, an NBC news broadcaster, she asked, "What time do you have?"

He said, "It's seven twenty-five."

"Thank you. They forgot to wind my watch."

The *Post* reported in its news columns, "The representatives of the proletariat are 'going over' in Washington. And society's spotlight, not entirely blacked out by the war, is beaming on Ivy Litvinov and her spouse."

Ivy Litvinov's social success even survived a speech she made to a Women's National Democratic Club luncheon where she made some remarks years ahead of their time and poorly received in 1942. She said that in the Soviet Union women did not pride themselves on merely being the wives of prominent men. "I notice," she said, "that at this meeting all the women are introduced as 'the charming wife of Mr. So-and-So,' even me! We don't have that in Russia. We have no so-called 'charming people.' Nobody would go to hear me speak because I am the wife of an official. A Soviet woman is an individual personality, standing on her own achievements—not a shadow of her husband's importance." The women Democrats were polite, many of them hating every word of it and agreeing that if she could survive that, she could survive anything.

She did, until two years later when Stalin, hearing the reports from Washington, decided the Litvinovs were too pro-American and ordered them home to Moscow, to be replaced by an embassy functionary named Andrei Gromyko, who had spent two years working in the embassy as counselor, living in a remote suburb and refusing to speak to his American neighbors.

Cissy Patterson, having chosen her costume from her book of photographs, put on dress number 76, belt 48, scarf 39, shoes 105 and told her chauffeur to drive her to Evalyn Walsh McLean's.

Mrs. McLean was almost ready for another party at Friendship, her house at Wisconsin Avenue and R Street in Georgetown. The mansion had been feather-dusted and festooned with flowers, round dining tables had been set up in four rooms, the dance orchestra was setting up its music stands and the trombone players were taking their horns out of cases lined with purple velvet, and out back the caterers were arranging the food—chicken, again—they had trucked in and were wondering among themselves how long they would have to wait this time to get paid. For the inconvenient fact was that despite Mrs. McLean's taste for free spending and despite her flashing decor of silver and silk and oils and ormolu, she was running out of money, even though she was still able to wear the forty-seven-carat Hope diamond dangling down the front of a Hattie Carnegie dress as she was tonight. She was dressed and ready for the party and so were the males in the house, but for one last-minute detail now to be attended to. Thomas Saltz drove out from his men's store downtown to do for the McLeans what they were unable or unwilling to do for themselves: he drove out to tie the men's neckties. As he finished this and left, the first guests were arriving—John L. Lewis and J. Edgar Hoover.

Among the rich and socially ambitious families moving into Washington in the late decades of the nineteenth century were two that were destined, between them, to make a little history of sorts. One was that of a pick-and-shovel miner named Thomas F. Walsh who roamed the American west looking for gold and not finding much until he paid a few dollars for a mine in Colorado thought to be played out. When he hacked through into a previously unknown shaft, he found ore by the ton and found himself rich. His wife, Carrie Bell, quickly turned to dreaming of palaces and princes and Paris gowns and cotillions under crystal chandeliers and she pronounced the crude and boisterous frontier life of Leadville and Denver inadequate to her newly inflamed social ambitions. News had reached the west that people of wealth and fashion were moving to Washington—so many that the New York *Times* asked, "Is Washington monopolizing our millionaires?" The Walshes moved in to pursue a higher degree of refinement.

The other family, that of Edward Roll McLean, was better placed socially in Cincinnati, where he owned the Cincinnati *Enquirer* and was involved with a Democratic political machine seemingly intent on draining the city treasury dry. When the investigations and prosecutorial questions began, he thought it was time to hook his private railroad car, the *Ohio,* to a train leaving for Washington and eventually to buy the Washington *Post,* then a paper of modest consequence. Washington was the hometown of his wife, Emily Beale, whose father was General Edward F. Beale, another gold mine millionaire.

The Walshes produced a daughter, Evalyn, and the McLeans a son, Edward Beale, whom they called Ned, and from the first day of his life they spoiled him to the squishiest degree of rottenness. Ned never went to school, any school, a day in his life. School was brought to him. Tutors tried vainly to teach him something, anything, until he found they could be bribed with cash to demand of him no work and no effort, while still producing reports pleasing to his parents. His mother even paid his young friends to let him win at baseball and Parcheesi—to build his confidence, she said. Before he was twenty, he had learned little more than how to shift the gears and work the clutch pedal of a car and so immediately was rewarded with a sporty racer called the Pope-Toledo. His other skill was drinking whiskey, and he pursued it with such devotion that by his twenty-first birthday he had to rig a handkerchief sling around his neck to keep his right hand steady enough to hold a glass of whiskey without spilling it.

Thomas Walsh by now had built at 2020 Massachusetts Avenue Washington's most formidable mansion—sixty rooms, gold doorknobs, a French-Italianate design in stone, an entrance hall copied from an ocean liner's grand saloon and rising clear and open a full four stories to a stained-glass ceiling throwing softly filtered light down onto a carved and sinuously curving art nouveau stairway. A pipe organ, the essential symbol of wealth, was built into a separate room of its own. Evalyn grew up at 2020. She, too, was totally spoiled. When she complained to Daddy Walsh that walking to school was "a little trying to my dignity," he produced for her a blue victoria coach drawn by two prancing sorrels and driven by a coachman in silk hat and gloves. Said Evalyn, "My own preference, generally, is for show."

When they were both eleven, she and Ned found each other in dancing school, found they were equally spoiled and in time found they shared a taste for frivolous spending. When they were both twenty-two, she agreed to marry him on condition he stop drinking, a promise he kept perhaps fifty times.

The Walshes planned a wedding on a scale to equal or surpass a staging of Verdi's *Aida* with elephants and spear carriers in the Roman Colosseum. They engaged the services of clergymen, florists, caterers, organists, orchestras, composers, seamstresses, tailors, the Pennsylvania Railroad and limousine drivers up and down the east coast from Richmond to Philadelphia. Washington's socialites waited in awe and wonder to see just what could be done with all that gold mine money, a tremendous mansion, a taste for extravagant display and two richly spoiled brats. Nothing, as it turned out. Evalyn and Ned, eager to get away and be alone, eloped to Colorado and were married in private. But the Walshes were forgiving at being denied their day as impresarios, and the two families settled on each of the newlyweds the round sum of one hundred thousand dollars to pay for a suitable honeymoon.

It was not enough. The two of them, along with Evalyn's personal maid, a chauffeur and a yellow and red Packard, set off for Europe and the Middle East, scattering money as they went, returning to Paris on their way home flat broke, only to find waiting there a letter from Daddy Walsh offering love, affection and more money. Newly enriched, Evalyn felt the need for a wedding present and bought it—the first piece of what eventually came to be her legendary collection of jewels, the 92½-carat diamond Star of the East, for one-hundred-and-fifty thousand dollars. Back in the U.S., she evaded customs duty by hiding it in her underwear. Daddy Walsh, on hearing this, laughed and dispatched his lawyer to square it with U.S. customs, while Ned and Evalyn moved onto Daddy

Walsh's huge country estate, Friendship, then on the fringe of the city out on Wisconsin Avenue. Now Evalyn and Ned took over the place the Walshes called their "country house." It was seventy-five acres of mansion, lawns, greenhouses, swimming pool, golf course, stables, gardens, fountains, winding walks, statuary and a collection of wildlife—ducks, donkeys, goats, geese, ponies, cattle, a llama on the front lawn, a children's coach painted in circus colors that once had belonged to P. T. Barnum's midget General Tom Thumb, a parrot screaming profanities in a hallway and, in Evalyn's bathroom, a monkey often out of his cage and hanging by his tail from the towel racks. "A mad place, truly," she said.

It was there, in her father's second house, that she began her luxurious entertainments on Sunday nights, attended by Washington politicians, socialites, journalists, diplomats, and visiting celebrities invited for drinking, eating, dancing, looking at movies, laughing and gossiping and admiring each other's clothes.

It was all wonderful until Ned died the year of Pearl Harbor, leaving their finances in such a mess that Evalyn was forced to sell the Friendship mansion to the U.S. Government. It became McLean Gardens, a housing project for government war workers. She moved down the street to another house, smaller but still grand, and moved the name Friendship to the new house.

In his last years of life, Ned's drinking had destroyed whatever stability he had ever had. His drunken mismanagement of the *Post* forced Evalyn to sell it at auction to Eugene Meyer for a fraction of its value. Ned was so far gone toward the end that he was forced to travel around the city with a thick-necked bodyguard. Capitol policeman Edward T. Driscoll reported that on the grounds outside the U.S. Senate Ned encountered a man he disliked and ordered his bodyguard to throw him to the pavement and hold him down while Ned urinated on him. On other occasions he urinated into the fireplace in the East Room of the White House and down the trouser leg of the ambassador of Belgium. These and other unattractive acts caused a jury to declare him insane and to send him to a mental hospital, where in 1941 he came to the end of a short life that had started with everything and ended with nothing.

There had been years of foolish spending and waste. There had been such entertainments as his stag parties with whiskey, cigar smoke, dice, cards and whores brought in to dance in the nude. There was the will of

Ned's father, who saw before he died that his son could not manage his own affairs and certainly could not manage the *Post*. The will put Ned on an allowance, denied him any role in running the *Post* and appointed American Security and Trust to manage his estate. It took a long legal battle to modify the will and to give Ned the chance to lose the newspaper exactly as his father had known he would. Of the money left by Ned's parents and Evalyn's, now dead, much of it was in real estate and not cash; the wartime tax rates, as Evalyn constantly complained, were as high as 94 percent and by her standards she was strapped. Her children refused to spend their own inheritance to finance her extravagance even when she threatened to take them to court. She had to pawn and later redeem the Hope diamond several times to pay the debts Ned left— three hundred thousand dollars—and it came to the embarrassing point of caterers refusing to unload their trucks of food unless they were paid first.

Frank Waldrop, a friend of Evalyn's, wrote the anti-Roosevelt, anti-New Deal and hard-line isolationist editorials in Cissy Patterson's *Times-Herald*. One Sunday night at Evalyn's, he was seated across from a Commander Dahl of Britain's Royal Air Force, who carefully waited for a pause in the conversation to say, "Mr. Waldrop, do you realize that if you were to go to England today there are men in your U.S. Eighth Air Force who would tear you limb from limb for the things you write?"

Waldrop asked himself, "How do I handle this? Do I get up and walk away from the table?" But by then, he said, he had learned not to fight over every insult thrown at him and responded, "Well, I guess I won't go to England."

Nasty little scenes were not unusual at Evalyn's on those Sunday nights. She thought it dull and unproductive of social excitement to have a table of guests who always agreed with each other, and instead preferred to seat at the same table an isolationist reactionary senator and a liberal interventionist and then to stand back and wait for the screaming arguments. They came, and she was amused to create a social-political cockpit where the British ambassador might be seated with Walter Winchell, the retailer of titillating gossip and Broadway wisecracks in his newspaper columns and radio programs. Or John L. Lewis of the United Mine Workers' Union beside a notorious labor-baiter. And so at times, to Evalyn's pleasure, a guest would rise from the table red in the face, fling down his napkin and stalk out. But those who stalked out usually came again if invited. As Waldrop saw it, "Everybody's nerves were on edge. Everybody had somebody killed in the war or about to be killed or could be killed. You sat there and started out talking abstractions and wound up talking personalities. That sort of thing happened every day, people who wanted to be reasonable and accessible but wartime passions didn't work that way."

Franklin Roosevelt sat in the White House and read that Evalyn's guests included Cissy Patterson, Waldrop, Martin Dies, son-in-law Reynolds, and what seemed to him an inordinate number of appeasers, apologists for Hitler, isolationists, America Firsters and right-wing Republicans who detested Roosevelt. He privately compared this social circle to Britain's "Cliveden set"—upper-class people who were perceived as anti-Semitic appeasers of Hitler and had been accustomed before the war to gather at Nancy Astor's house, Cliveden, in Buckinghamshire. Roosevelt speculated that Cissy's newspaper might be cunningly playing up Evalyn as the leader of Washington's Cliveden set in order to conceal her, Cissy's, own responsibility. And the more he ruminated about this parallel he found between the parties at Friendship and Astor's prewar gatherings, the more it irritated him. At a press conference in 1942 he said in public what he thought.

A reporter asked about the fears that war loans to the Soviet Union would strengthen it so much that after the war it could challenge the United States.

"I think that is about on a par with the other arguments that are set up by the Cliveden set in Washington."

The Cliveden set in Washington? Who were they?

He refused to give any names. "You know the names. I am awfully polite."

That set them off again. Most of those in Washington's social life did not quite know what Cliveden was. One, at a party, asked the British ambassador if it was pronounced to rhyme with "give" or with "hive"? He said, "We call it to rhyme with 'give,' but in fact we don't call it at all."

Hope Ridings Miller rode to the rescue, explaining what Cliveden was, how it was pronounced, and reported that people who previously had asked each other if they were parasites now asked, "Are you a Clivedener?"

Frank Waldrop said, "Mrs. McLean was no appeaser. It was the people around her Roosevelt hated—Cissy Patterson, Mrs. Longworth, who was always shooting her mouth off, and Mrs. McLean was found guilty of associating with people like us."

The Communist party's magazine *New Masses* insisted there was more to it than that. In a 1942 article by Bruce Minton, it said,

> Friendship has become the general headquarters of fifth columnists, the clearing house of those who "justify" Hitler, who gloat over Pearl Harbor, who blame Japanese aggression not on policies advocated and often instituted by their own group, but on the administration which refused to capitulate to Tokyo. There are the men and women who eagerly supported Franco, who cheered Munich, who applauded the Nazi invasion of the Soviet Union, now complain about lend-lease, urge negotiated peace with the Axis.

Minton's article was accompanied by a drawing of overdressed, overweight and overly bejeweled people at dinner being served by a waiter with a napkin over his arm embroidered with the label "A. Hitler, caterer."

New Masses did not enjoy wide readership among Evalyn's friends, but they all managed to find this issue and to react in outrage. Both Evalyn and Cissy demanded a criminal indictment of Minton, but the courts refused. They and others named in his article promised they would put *New Masses* out of business by driving it into bankruptcy with lawsuits. They never did that either. They wrote angry letters to the newspapers and that was about it.

Minton's attack was excessive and unfair and in some respects false, but some of what he wrote was true. Evalyn herself was about as politically sophisticated as the monkey that chattered in her bathroom. When Roosevelt first complained that she presided over what amounted to an American Cliveden set, an assistant, William D. Hassett, told him she did not have brains enough to lead or conviction enough to espouse a cause or adopt a principle. She lived for her own pleasure, to surround herself with ostentatious luxury and people she found amusing, well dressed and socially adept. If they had opinions of any substance, she seldom knew what they were and would not have understood them if she had. She had grown up in a family whose interests seldom ranged beyond clothes, parties and social success, all of which were theirs without effort or thought. And she was married to Ned, who was at least as vague as she was—Ned, who was happiest in a duck blind with a shotgun and a bottle of whiskey and, as Evalyn put it, when he was occupied with "booze and blondes." No jury would ever have convicted either of them of holding a serious thought. If she ran a Cliveden, she could hardly have been aware of it.

And a number of decent and honest people joined in the frolics at Friendship, among them Lord Halifax, the British ambassador, who said he was indebted to Evalyn for enabling him to meet and talk with people he could not otherwise have met. But there were appeasers there, and blatant anti-Semites. One was a society gossip columnist in the *Times-Herald* who was confused by one of the new Russian ambassador's former aliases and leeringly asked if his readers were aware that his name was not Litvinov but Finklestein. There were guests who argued that Hitler merely intended to rectify the excesses of the Versailles Treaty from World War I and deserved credit for saving Europe from Bolshevism, who admired Generalissimo Franco for bringing "stability" to Spain, and who were confident Roosevelt would use the stresses of the war to make himself a dictator.

In her last years, the Washington Evalyn had known all her life was disappearing under the pressures of war. Her fortune was dwindling. Her health was failing. Toward the end she turned to small displays of generosity, perhaps out of guilt at the excesses of two families' frivolous self-indulgence. She placed a bench and water cooler and paper cups at the bus stop in front of Friendship and had her butler keep it filled. She asked military units around Washington to choose by lot a number of enlisted men to be invited to her house on Sunday nights. She went to the USO club bearing gifts by the hundreds and passing around the Hope diamond to be fondled and admired by the soldiers and their women friends and to have their pictures taken with it hanging around their necks. Since the death of her parents, 2020 Massachusetts was empty, and she gave it to the Red Cross rent-free even when a buyer appeared offering cash. She had the mansion's carriage house converted to a recreation center with jukebox, food and drink for young women doing war work. She invited young people in uniform to come to Friendship any day for lunch and a swim in her pool. "But don't expect to see me. I sleep all day."

Cissy Patterson watched Evalyn's decline in health and fortune with some uneasiness. Through her society pages in the *Times-Herald,* she was, after all, the keeper of the flame for Washington's social world. Evalyn was tired, she told friends, and the town needed a new hostess, a woman with beauty, money, energy, and a house grand enough for large-scale entertaining, plus the willingness to take it on. She discussed the problem with friends, running through the names of several women, discarding some for one reason or another. The choice was Cissy's to make because she did, indeed, have the power to make any woman who could meet her requirements the queen of Washington society.

She settled on Gwendolyn Cafritz, the wife of Morris Cafritz, who had made a fortune in Washington real estate. Gwen Cafritz had black hair, brown eyes and a tawny beauty from her Hungarian parentage. Cissy called her and asked to visit. Gwen was eager. Come anytime, she said. The same afternoon would be fine. Cissy arrived to examine her and her new house on Foxhall Road, built in the late 1930s in some vague version of art moderne—straight lines, curved white brick walls—and, with its iron railings, looking like a cruise ship beached in a green sea of lawns and gardens that rolled on for acres. To receive Cissy, Gwen wore a new, expensive silk tea gown and offered them champagne, caviar and a tour of the house. From a terrace, looking to the south, her view went all the way to the Washington Monument and the United States Capitol. One floor down was a ballroom with a transparent dance floor decorated and lighted from below.

It was an audition. Gwen knew she was being considered for a major role and since Cissy approved, she got the part. And shortly, Gwen was featured in Cissy's society section in a half-page portrait captioned "Beauty of the Week." She began having parties, inviting Congress, the Cabinet, the courts, the agencies, the Washington establishment. They all came. With Cissy's imprimatur, her house became the place to go. She steered her guests out to her huge terrace ringed with flaming oil-fired torches—a new touch in Washington—to her view of central Washington, and downstairs to a ballroom that looked like a nightclub. Each of her entertainments was chronicled in the *Times-Herald* in full and flattering detail.

Gwen was in. She was now the foremost Washington hostess and loving every minute of it. She and Morris picked up where Evalyn Walsh McLean was leaving off, staging social extravaganzas and helping Washington's social figures to go on dancing the war away.

VII

Press Lords and Reporters

On the morning of September 17, 1942, the telephone rang on the bedside table of an Associated Press reporter who spent every day covering the news at the White House. It was the U.S. Secret Service White House security detail calling to say, "We will pick you up at eleven o'clock tonight on the southwest corner of Fourteenth and New York." That was all. The message meant President Roosevelt would be traveling somewhere that night and the reporter was to go along, but under wartime secrecy the security people would not say in advance where he was going for fear of giving an enemy, foreign or domestic, a chance to plant a bomb or plant himself with a weapon. The caller gave no information on why the president was going or on how long he would be gone. The reporter was left to guess if he would be away for a day or a week and if he should pack clothes for a hot climate or cold.

At the stated hour, a Secret Service car picked him up and drove to an obscure railroad siding, a spur line running under Fourteenth Street into the basement of the Bureau of Engraving and Printing, built there to allow the bureau secretly to ship out its newly printed paper money. The reporter boarded a train parked there underground, its shades drawn. Just before midnight it moved out through a maze of tracks and switches to a remote railyard where lines of boxcars parked on both sides made the train nearly invisible. There was a wait until they heard the slam and felt the jolt of another car, a heavy one, being hooked on to the back end. Now the president in his private car, the *Ferdinand Magellan,* was attached to the rear and the train moved out. Only then would press secretary Steve Early say where they were going, why and for how long.

This time they were going, he said, on a long trip to "inspect the war plants." The president wanted to show their workers he was interested and to tell them the country was depending on them. This trip would take him to the west coast and back, would last two weeks, and only three reporters had been invited to go along—from United Press, Associated Press and International News Service. They had been chosen because every print and broadcast news agency in the country was served by one or more of them. Not invited were the radio networks or the reporters called "specials," those who wrote for individual newspapers such as the New York *Times* and the Washington *Post.* None of the newspaper columnists. None of the newsmagazines.

Why? Why, of the thirty or forty usually traveling with the president, had only three been invited this time?

"Because," Early said, "the boss says if they all came along the train would need more sleeping cars and it would be so long it would attract too much attention and it would be impossible to maintain any secrecy." Furthermore, he said, censorship was being invoked and not one word about the trip could be sent out until it was all over and the president was back in the White House. The news would be announced from there.

Secrecy? They asked in rising anger how the president could keep his trip secret when the itinerary showed he would be riding in his convertible with the top down through war plants in a dozen cities, waving to thousands of the workers who would then tell thousands of others they had seen him? What kind of secrecy was that? It didn't make any sense. Would Steve go back and talk to the president and see if he would change his mind?

Roosevelt sat alone back in his private car, built by the Association of American Railroads and sold to the White House for one dollar. It was equipped with two elevators to lift his wheelchair on and off, an office, a lounge, a bedroom and a galley. Beneath the floor were twelve inches of steel-reinforced concrete to protect him if a bomb were planted in the roadbed. The windows were bulletproof. The sides were of armor plate heavy enough to resist an artillery shell. There were three under-water escape hatches adapted from navy submarines to allow him to get out if the train derailed on a bridge and sank to the bottom of a river. His car was so heavy the locomotive engineers said pulling it was like pulling a fishing line with a lead sinker on the end.

The presidential train always carried at its front end, behind the locomotive, an oversized baggage car once owned by the Barnum and Bailey Circus and now used for four automobiles—two huge sedans and two convertibles for the President and his Secret Service escort. Along the way the automobiles were washed and filled with gasoline, ready for the next ride through the next city. The second railroad car carried communications gear. Then came an upper-and-lower-berth Pullman car for the radio operators and the railroad staff, a roomette car for the press, nearly empty this trip, a club car with a bar, card tables and armchairs in the classic dark green railroad plush, a diner, another roomette car for the Secret Service agents and the president's personal staff, and finally the *Ferdinand Magellan.*

As the train rolled along, always avoiding tracks near the east coast to make it impossible for a German warship to shell it from the Atlantic, Roosevelt never left his own car. Maneuvering his wheelchair through the watertight door, also adapted from a navy submarine, and across the swaying and lurching train platform was so difficult he had all his meals sent back from the diner and he occupied himself with watching the scenery—a special pleasure for a man physically immobile—dictating letters to Grace Tully, reading the newspapers put aboard at each stop and whatever messages came in from the communications car up front.

In earlier years, the railroads had demanded 125 first-class tickets to move a president's special train. Calvin Coolidge complained angrily at this outrageous expense, refused to pay, and rode across the country on a regular train. But it was awkward to have the president of the United States sitting in the same Pullman car with pajama salesmen and hardware drummers and strangers approaching him to ask for government jobs, and so reluctantly the railroads settled for charging each passenger, including the president, one first-class Pullman fare. The reporters' employers paid for theirs and the White House paid for everyone else. That left only the matter of tips for the Pullman porter. Roosevelt always thought that for a weekend trip to Hyde Park and back a five-dollar tip was sufficient. The porter assigned to his car, Sam C. Mitchell, thought otherwise and used his seniority in the Brotherhood of Sleeping Car Porters to have himself transferred to the press car, where on a weekend presidential trip he got two dollars from each reporter and wound up with forty to fifty dollars.

Steve Early did walk back and deliver the reporters' complaints—that thousands of people seeing the president in their cities and then, because of the censorship, finding no mention of his visit in their local papers, would lose faith in the papers and, indeed, in the government itself. Roosevelt listened impatiently and said no, the trip would go on as planned. He was determined to play out his role as a wartime leader involved with the war plants and military bases. He was convinced, probably correctly, that herds of reporters traveling with him and filing reports every day would make the trip appear to be a politically moti-vated stunt just before the congressional elections coming up in a few weeks. Instead, what he wanted on his return to Washington was a burst of publicity about the president, the commander-in-chief, just back from an inspiring visit to the defense plants, doing his duty and looking after the war.

While the press fumed, he traveled 8,754 miles, and as Robert Sherwood, one of his speechwriters, described it, "Roosevelt loved all this air of mystery. It was part of his nature to wear the mantle of military security like a small boy playing cops and robbers. Furthermore, he loved to irritate the press which had so often irritated him."

He visited Detroit and rode with Henry and Edsel Ford down a production line a half-mile long. In Portland, Oregon, he whispered into a microphone before fourteen thousand shipyard workers, "You know, I am not supposed to be here today. So you are the possessors of a secret that even the newspapers of the United States don't know. I hope you will keep the secret because I am under military and naval orders, and like the ship we have just seen launched today, my motions and move-ments are supposed to be secret." Yes. Here was Roosevelt, as Robert Sherwood said, behaving like a small boy playing games.

The talk in the train's club car was that censorship was being used capriciously as an arrogant exercise of White House power for no purpose but to punish the press for its sins. And when Roosevelt returned to Washington on October 1, expecting a splash of favorable publicity, there was unusual interest and unusual anger among the reporters at the press conference scheduled for the same day.

Before a press conference began, Roosevelt always talked with Steve Early about what questions could be expected that day and how he should deal with those he disliked. This time, Early told him he could expect angry questions about his trip. While they talked, the scheduled time for the press conference passed and the reporters waiting outside began pounding on his office door. A few British newsmen visiting that day were appalled. Who were these people pounding on the president's door? How could they possibly do that? In the British press tradition, reporters paid greater deference to government officials.

When finally the door was opened the press filed in, spilling cigarette ashes on the rug. One of their number was Earl Godwin, in his seventies, substantially overweight and breathing hard, but still able to do a folksy fifteen minutes each night on the Blue Network, which later became ABC. Because of his age and bulk, Roosevelt always let Godwin pull a chair and sit at the corner of his desk. The others stood in a semicircle around the desk littered with cigarettes, holders, ashtrays, framed photographs, paperweights, an array of miniature flags, pens, mementoes and souvenirs.

Standing behind Roosevelt were two or three staff members, including Steve Early, there to help him occasionally with the elusive fact. Once, when he was asked a question about one of the dozens of war agencies known by their initials, he turned to an aide behind him and asked in a stage whisper, "The SPCBM—what on God's earth is that?"

The October 1 press conference was hot, smoky and crowded. The President opened it by saying the arrangements for his trip had been made solely for the safety of the commander-in-chief himself. And a statement everyone present knew was false—that including more correspondents would have required one or more extra trains.

He then spent a good deal more time than seemed necessary responding to the criticism in Congress from Representative Charles Halleck of Indiana, who said it was obvious to him the trip was a political stunt pulled off just before the elections. It was even more obvious that Halleck, a tough, hard-drinking, red-nosed Republican politician, would have found something to criticize whatever Roosevelt did. But the president was trying to make it appear that guarding against this kind of political attack was his reason for keeping them off his train and keeping his travels out of the news.

Then, trying to turn the complaints away from himself, he quickly veered off into his constant complaint that some of the press and radio, primarily the columnists and commentators, were damaging the war effort by spreading Washington stories not based on fact. Elizabeth May Craig, correspondent for a group of small newspapers in Maine, a grandmotherly woman who always wore hats resembling abandoned birds' nests and who spoke in high, querulous, quavering tones, asked, "What is your complaint about the press?"

"May," he said, "ask the press. They know. You know as well as I do."

"Mr. President, I don't."

Roscoe Drummond of the *Christian Science Monitor* asked, "Could you give us any concrete examples, Mister President?"

"No. That would only inflate those I have in mind."

While these sessions usually were good-natured and convivial, this one turned sour and angry. Where Roosevelt usually was forthcoming with little jokes, he had none today. He was cold and formal and trying to turn the hostility away from himself by repeating his old, familiar and tiresome complaint about a group he detested—newspaper columnists and radio commentators. Once he had called them "excrescences." To which May Craig, referring to Mrs. Eleanor Roosevelt's newspaper column, "My Day," had said, "But Mr. President, you've got a columnist in your own family." That day he laughed. This day he did not.

Most of the White House reporters liked him, and Roosevelt liked most of them, but the press as an institution, a power center, and particularly its publishers, he seemed to detest. He claimed through all his years in office that 85 percent of the press opposed him, when in fact the opposition at worst was around 50 percent. He persisted in saying that he knew most of the reporters meant well, but said he also knew that they were forced by their publishers to write critically about him. With two or three exceptions, that was not true. But a phrase he used constantly was " . . . what you fellows are told to write."

He had won them over in his first days in office by setting a new standard of openness. He had, in fact, invented the modern press conference by accepting direct questions. Previous presidents had demanded that they be written and submitted in advance. Herbert Hoover, on being asked to accept questions directly, refused and said, "The President of the United States will not stand and be questioned like a chicken thief by men whose names he does not even know." Roosevelt took the questions as they came, turning aside those he did not want to answer by saying mildly, "There's no news on that today." But he usually had something to offer, if only some comments for the press about how its work should be done. A favorite phrase was "In other words, if I were writing the story, here is how I would say it." And he liked to say that so long as the news columns printed his words without coloration, he did not care what the editorial pages said, since he knew—as everyone knew—that most people never read them. But even while insisting he did not care, he did care. His hatred of editorial criticism never ceased. He fancied himself an expert on the ethics and cultural biases of journalism and always argued that the American people held the press in contempt. Occasionally, he even read their news reports aloud and criticized them like an angry teacher lecturing a particularly slow-witted class.

What he wanted, of course, was what every Washington politician has always wanted—to be presented to the public in the precise style and emphasis he chose, with nothing added or subtracted, without any comment or interpretation by news people he thought incompetent if not ignorant. "I am," he once said to a newspaper editors' group, "more closely in touch with public opinion in the United States than any individual in this room." Newspaper publishing, he said, was a local business and could not possibly have a national view. "There is not a newspaperman that comes into my office that understands the ramifications of national problems."

So, as he saw it, the obligation of the press simply was to report his words without changing a comma or a period and with no attempt at interpretation or analysis by those who knew little and understood less. The reporters were nice, pleasant fellows, yes, but essentially middle-class people out of red-brick colleges and ill equipped by knowledge or intellect to interpret or explain the words and deeds of the president of the United States. Even Walter Lippmann, among the most scholarly newspaper columnists of the time and better educated than Roosevelt, drew his scorn: "In spite of his brilliance, it is very clear that he has never let his mind travel west of the Hudson or north of the Harlem."

* * *

Graham J. White, in his study *FDR and the Press,* suggests that Roosevelt's dislike of the press could be discerned as early as 1925. In that year he wrote a newspaper review of Claude G. Bowers's book, *Jefferson and Hamilton,* and praised it as one of the greatest political studies of Jefferson's "mobilization of the masses against the autocracy of the few," as opposed to Hamilton's favoring " . . . the force of wealth, of birth, of commerce, of the press." And Roosevelt's book review concluded with " . . . as I lay down this book . . . I wonder if the same contending forces are again mobilizing. Hamiltons we have today. Is a Jefferson on the horizon?"

What Roosevelt did not mention in his book review was that he, himself, recently had written a letter to a thousand Democratic party leaders urging that Jefferson's political views become the philosophical foundation of their party. But then he had been wounded and infuriated by newspaper editorials sneering at his letter and calling it irrelevant. Roosevelt had complained then to party leaders about the arrogance of the press in some of the same phrases White House reporters were hearing now, years later. And one of his first acts as president had been to appoint the author, Claude G. Bowers, ambassador to Spain.

Roosevelt exercised more power for more years than any president in American history. He moved power and money from private hands to public. He forced industrialists to admit, if not to accept, that the country no longer held to Coolidge's view that "The business of government is business." He forced them to deal with the unions they despised. He taxed them at rates as high as 94 percent. He forced them in wartime to manufacture what the government wanted and not what they wanted.

An example of this came shortly after Pearl Harbor when Charles E. Wilson, president of General Motors, came to Washington with a group of automobile industry leaders bearing this message: They would build the weapons, yes, but they must also continue building passenger cars. The country, they said, was so addicted to cars it could not function without them. Public transit everywhere was inadequate. Without cars, people could not get to their jobs, farmers could not get to their fields. Businesses dependent on the automobile would collapse. Without cars, the country would be so demoralized it could not successfully wage a global war.

Wilson's well-rehearsed message was delivered in a conference room in the Social Security building on Independence Avenue, and there to listen and respond was William E. Knudsen of the Office of Production Management. The press was locked out of the meeting, but in the hallway outside was a small group of reporters, including I. F. Stone, who wore a hearing aid, then constructed with a separate receiver to be clipped to a coat pocket and a wire running up to an earpiece. Stone pressed his receiver flat against the conference room door, turned up the volume, and as the door vibrated from the sounds inside, he heard everything said in the meeting and repeated it to the others.

He heard Wilson's plea to go on building cars and heard him say Detroit had a seventy-five-million-dollar inventory of engines and bodies and drive shafts and chromium bumpers, and at least they should be allowed to assemble these existing parts into new cars.

Knudsen said, "Charley, there's no rubber. No tires for new cars."

"Then let us assemble them anyway and sell them to our dealers without tires."

But Knudsen knew that would only lead car dealers to apply horrendous political pressure on their local ration boards to release the few tires still available and held for emergencies.

"No, Charley."

With those two words, the Roosevelt administration shut down the largest industry in the world and forced it into other work.

Just after Pearl Harbor, Roosevelt invited business and union leaders to the White House. They were asked for a no-strike, no-lockout commitment for the duration of the war. They accepted that but disagreed angrily on whether business had to accept union shops. At this moment, Roosevelt came in, congratulated them on what they had agreed on, ignored what they had not agreed on, wished them a merry Christmas and sent them home. They left bewildered and angry. Roger Lapham, chairman of the American Hawaiian Steamship Company, said as he walked out the White House door, "I've been raped in Macy's window at high noon."

With business and labor in line, happy or not, his isolationist enemies in Congress silenced by the attack on Pearl Harbor, the American public behind him in support of the war, depression and unemployment ending and even a labor shortage beginning to appear, in early 1942 Roosevelt held all the reins but one. There remained only one major element in American society still beyond his control and still able to harass him every day—the newspaper publishers he despised.

Fat bundles of their papers were delivered to the White House every day and the president's morning habit was to lie in bed in an old gray bathrobe, stained and perforated with cigarette burns, drinking coffee, smoking, and reading one paper after another. He read them religiously even though some of them left him so infuriated he could not get them out of his mind. It was impossible to say how much they affected his presidency, how much he was influenced by what seemed to be the consuming, corrosive hatred of his public life. Some of those around him wondered, as Senate Majority Leader Alben Barkley asked him, "Why don't you just ignore those sons of bitches?" But he never could.

There were, indeed, some who could be disliked without great effort. And they were delighted to know they infuriated him. For one, Colonel Robert R. McCormick, whose Chicago *Tribune* he insisted on reading every morning, much as he detested it. Among much else, he read that McCormick believed and had his paper print the report that "Moscow has ordered the Reds in the United States to back Roosevelt. . . . " He read McCormick's pronouncements that "Tribuneland" was the center of civilization. And such bizarre items as a front-page report that New York actually was not an American city—"Its Millions Loyal to the Alien Lands They Fled."

McCormick's arrogance carried over into his procedure for receiving business callers in his vaulted, baronial office high in the Tribune Tower. If a man not personally known to the Colonel called and asked to see him for some business purpose presumably worthy of his attention, a secretary questioned him in detail about his business, his acquaintances, his club memberships, his residence, family and educational background, and then was told he would be called back. If, and only if, his business and social credentials were acceptable to the Colonel, he was called and told when he would be granted an appointment, or audience. When he arrived, a receptionist steered him to a chair in an anteroom, whereupon a photographer walked in with a large, black Speed Graphic camera with flashbulb, aimed it in his face and took his picture, offering the bewildered visitor no explanation. The procedure then was for the picture to be developed quickly, printed and delivered to the Colonel, who examined it critically to see if the visitor was sufficiently present-able to be received in his office. If he thought not, as was often the case, the receptionist went back into the anteroom and announced, "The Colonel will not see you."

McCormick's attacks on Roosevelt continued all the way to the end. His paper kept saying the president came from a "family stock which never fought for the country and now betrays it." He kept pointing out that in World War I, while McCormick was serving abroad in uniform, Roosevelt—then able-bodied—had spent a safe and comfortable war in Washington as assistant secretary of the navy. He had his paper explain over and over that Franklin's branch of the Roosevelts represented the socially inferior descendants of a Dutch immigrant family of Eastern parasites and idlers who enriched themselves early in the opium and slave trades, kept the profits entirely to themselves, created nothing of permanent substance, never distinguished themselves in war, that Frank-lin won political power with false campaign promises to reduce the size and cost of government, and on taking office quickly began using it to destroy the qualities of industry, entrepreneurship, thrift and righteousness that made America American, and since he had slid lightly through Harvard on his family's name, he had learned too little history to under-stand the folly of dragging the United States into Europe's endless wars.

These views in various forms and permutations appeared regularly in McCormick's news columns, editorials, features and Carey Orr's front-page political cartoons, and the whole acidic package arrived on the White House doorstep every morning.

Roosevelt could laugh at attacks from his political opponents and even turn them to his own benefit. But attacks in the *Tribune,* the Hearst press, the New York *Daily News* and the Washington *Times-Herald* always infuriated him. He complained about them in private and com-plained about them in public.

If he could not control his publisher-critics, he could go around them with his "fireside chats" on the radio. For here he could have what he always wanted and the press would never give him—a seamless pipeline running directly to the American people with nobody in between to turn the valves or to put in colorings, flavorings, or unwelcome additives of any kind. The networks' sole contribution to his radio talks was to supply an announcer who introduced him in the unvarying words, "Ladies and gentlemen, the president of the United States." And at the end, "Ladies and gentlemen, you have heard the president of the United States. We return you now to our studios." That was it and that was all.

The networks instantly made free time available whenever he wanted it. In fact, they gave free time to almost any political figure who asked, partly because in the thirties and forties they were a little afraid they would not be allowed to remain a private enterprise. There were still some New Deal theorists who thought radio should be taken over and put under government control. But by the war years, politically powerful interests, big newspapers and others, owned radio stations, and Congress was not eager to confront them or to buy out their huge investments in studios and transmitters. Then, too, the networks had developed enormously popular stars such as Jack Benny, Bob Hope, Amos n' Andy, Fred Allen, Edgar Bergen and Charley McCarthy, Eddie Cantor, Fibber McGee and Molly. Equally important, the networks had earned respect for their news coverage of the war with Edward R. Murrow of CBS, John MacVane and Robert McCormick of NBC, George Hicks of the Blue Network, Elmer Davis, Lowell Thomas, and H. V. Kaltenborn. These were all admired figures with public constituencies so vast it would have required a politician of uncommon courage to threaten them. None did.

Further, the networks put on wartime service programs such as one produced entirely in the War Department and called *Chaplain Jim, USA.* In free time on the Blue and without commercials, it was written by a soap opera producer and had an actor playing an army chaplain dealing with the problems of young soldiers away from home. NBC broadcast a weekly hour called *America United* which invited spokesmen for business, unions and agriculture to discuss their roles in the war and usually found them to be about as antagonistic as they ever were in peacetime. On one of these programs, William C. Dougherty, president of the Letter Carriers Union, shouted across the table, "How you ever gonna have world peace if the letter carriers don't get a pay raise?"

The big networks tried to ensure their survival as a private business by the most punctilious behavior. They refused advertising for beer, wine, liquor, deodorants, depilatories, undertakers, cemeteries or any financial schemes. NBC insisted that anyone appearing on its radio network after 6:00 p.m. wear evening clothes and black tie. Nothing whatever—not a sound effect, not a commercial, not the music or any other element in any program—could be recorded. Everything from sign-on to sign-off had to be live. With their generosity with free air time for politicians, their star entertainers, their war news coverage, their fastidiousness, they survived.

While Roosevelt fretted about his publisher-critics and their hostile newspapers, he did not realize that the day of the press lords was ending. The publishers who used their newspapers to promote their personal political biases were seeing their days of power coming to an end and they would last little longer than Roosevelt himself.

The press lords had thrived in the days when newspapers held a monopoly on the dissemination of news, before Henry Luce invented the weekly newsmagazine, when radio mostly offered only light entertainment, when the most popular magazines dealt in fiction and fashion, *Popular Mechanics* explained how to fix the brakes on a Ford, *The Nation* and *The New Republic* printed political commentary too left-wing for a mass audience and the *Saturday Evening Post* was full of fiction about Tugboat Annie and Scattergood Baines, plus occasional articles of a conservative tone. So the press lord, however irresponsible, abusive or even unhinged he might be, was free in those early years to do as he pleased.

But with the war, radio became a serious news medium. The newsmagazines had begun "Press" sections where, for the first time, newspapers were treated to tough and systematic criticism. *Time* was never so happy as when it was ridiculing Chicago's Colonel McCormick as a pompous buffoon. And there was the seminal work of A. J. Liebling in a series in *The New Yorker* called "The Wayward Press"—work of such wit, clarity, acerbity and truth that journalistic pomposity could not stand against it. It was published in book form and it was still being read a generation later. Journalism schools raised their standards. The union, the Newspaper Guild, forced salaries up and led editorial employees collectively and successfully to resist and refuse outrageous orders from their publishers. In time, it reached the point where a principal owner of the New York *Times,* the publisher's mother, was deeply annoyed at an item printed in her paper but decided the only response available to her was to write a letter to the editor, which she did. The *Times* printed her letter, but nothing more was said or done. The press lord's day was over.

Roosevelt did not live to see this tidal change. Even worse for him, during his second term Washington acquired a new newspaper publisher,

Cissy Patterson, a cousin of the *Tribune*'s McCormick, a sister of Captain Joseph Patterson of New York's *Daily News,* and a lifelong friend of William Randolph Hearst. She bought two money-losing Washington papers from Hearst, the *Times* and the *Herald* and combined them into a single paper published around the clock and called the *Times-Herald.* What might Roosevelt have expected of her? He might have expected exactly what he got—one more paper in the Hearst-McCormick-Patterson style eager to attack and ridicule and belittle Roosevelt and his New Deal and to support the America First isolationists. Now his principal enemies in publishing, along with all their biases and hatreds and most of their editorials and features were combined in one woman and one newspaper published three blocks from the White House.

Cissy Patterson had come to Washington from Chicago with her parents when they decided, like other millionaires moving in from the west, that they would more easily be accepted into society in Washington than in New York, Newport or Southampton. The Pattersons commissioned Stanford White to design a marble mansion of thirty rooms at 15 DuPont Circle with a huge library filled with books seldom to be read and a balcony for chamber music never to be heard. They moved into the house in 1903, into a setting of theatrical splendor done up in brocaded silk walls, Belgian tapestries, Italian marble, French furniture and Chicago money. Cissy's parents believed that in Washington she would be exposed to attractive and sophisticated people, perhaps even to a titled European with an intriguing accent and an eye for an American heiress moderately attractive and immoderately rich.

They were right on all counts. Cissy soon was entranced with a Count Joseph Gizycka who spoke dreamily of his vast estates in a Russian-dominated area of Poland, his palace, his legions of servants and his life of Graustarkian romance that one day would be shared with a wife who would, of course, be a countess. A countess! The word rang like a silver bell in the ears of the rich folks from Chicago. And soon there was talk of marriage.

Cissy's brother, Joseph Patterson, was opposed and said so. Weren't all these rich American girls marrying Europeans nobody knew anything about beyond what they said of themselves in evasive terms and uncertain English? Had it not turned out in many cases that they owned the titles and the clothes on their backs and not much else? These bejeweled medals he wore—had they been awarded to him or to his great-grandfather? Who could tell? Weren't most of those old European families living in crumbling castles and remembering the money they once had? If their lives were so glittering and grand in Poland and Rumania and the other fabled kingdoms of Europe, what in God's name were they doing in Washington? Although Joseph Patterson knew little of Gizycka, he believed him to be a classic fortune hunter. But Cissy, now nineteen years old, was carried away beyond recall. The wedding took place in the mansion on DuPont Circle, whose curving marble stairway must have been built for brides. The Count and Countess Gizycka left for Poland.

Joseph Patterson in his career as a newspaper publisher was not always clearly and thoroughly proved to be right. This time he was.

When Cissy arrived in Poland with her new title and new husband, she found that his lands near Narvosielica were scrubby, dry and unproductive. His description of his "castle" seemed to have gained something in the translation. It was a whitewashed house of moderate size that seemed to have been built not by artisans but by the farm help in their spare time, and might easily have been the home of an unsuccessful sausage merchant. The wallpaper was peeling, the floors sagging, the plumbing ranging from primitive to nonexistent. And the servants were two or three surly farmhands in rubber boots and several lumpish women in cotton stockings carrying buckets and smoking clay pipes. The count's relatives were patronizing, repeatedly explaining to Cissy that while American women might have money, they were uncivilized boors and the count had lowered himself by marrying her.

But there she was, the Chicago queen now a countess, and from there on the details of her marriage became a mixture of fact and fiction. Her stories were varied and conflicting. By one of her accounts, the wedding night was so rough and crude she described it as a rape. The count promised no marital fidelity and practiced none. When the mood was on him he beat her with his fists and then left without explanation to spend the night in a bordello. Another of Cissy's tales was that one night she slipped out ahead of him, made cash arrangements with the bordello management, and when the count arrived for an evening's entertainment he was ushered into a bedroom where he found not a prostitute but the countess from Chicago.

In time, a baby was born, named Felicia, beautiful as a baby and beautiful thereafter. But by now Cissy had had enough of the count and the drab, boring life on an ugly and primitive Polish farm. On a winter's night she hired a sleigh with two horses and a driver, bundled Felicia and herself in furs and set out through deep snow in wolf-infested country-side for the nearest railroad station, intent on returning to DuPont Circle. The count discovered that his dream of riches had disappeared into the snowy darkness, pursued them to London, kidnapped the baby he saw as his collateral, and placed her in a Russian convent. Cissy had to return to Washington alone, not to see Felicia again until months later when, at her father's request, President William Howard Taft sent a handwritten note to the Russian czar asking him to order Count Gizycka to return the baby. He explained that "Mr. and Mrs. Patterson are prominent residents of Washington, and Mr. Patterson is the proprietor of the Chicago *Tribune,* one of the greatest newspapers in the United States." The czar responded, the count was compelled to obey, and Felicia was handed over. There was talk of a payment of several hundred thousand dollars. Eventually, a divorce was granted after a hearing in a Chicago court where Cissy testified, "He married me for my money and didn't get it. That's the whole story."

Back in Washington, there was one more marriage, this time to a pleasant but unexciting Wall Street lawyer who commuted to his office by yacht, wearing not medals but pinstripes, white shirts, striped ties and black wingtip shoes. Bored again, in four years Cissy told him she wanted a divorce. While contemplating this, he dropped dead of a heart attack at the country club.

With all that out of the way, Cissy dropped all the names and titles acquired by her marriages, thereafter styled herself as Mrs. Eleanor Patterson, and prepared for a business career. Her father, her brother, her best friends including William Randolph Hearst, were all in the newspaper business. So why not? After all, for a rich, twice-married socialite now approaching middle age, what else was there to do?

At first, her *Times-Herald* was not entirely hostile to Roosevelt. Her brother Joseph, who flirted with socialism, had his *Daily News* support the New Deal, even if somewhat gingerly, and Cissy, who worshipped him, always tended to follow his lead. What turned both of them and both of their newspapers into enemies was Roosevelt's lend-lease program. They called it the act of a dictator, a sneaky and illegal device to trick the American people, before they realized what was being done to them, into another war to bail out the British. While that was what set them off, Cissy had never forgiven him for defeating and embarrassing her in the battle over the Jefferson Memorial and the cherry trees. The final, irrevocable break came just after Pearl Harbor when Joseph Patterson, a captain in World War I, came to the White House and offered himself to Roosevelt for any wartime assignment he might have for him now.

Yes, Roosevelt said, he did have an assignment for him. It was to go back to New York and read over again all the hostile editorials his paper had printed over the last year or two. That was the only assignment he would offer. Patterson left the White House in tears. He and Cissy saw this as a crushing insult never, ever to be forgiven. It never was.

Had Patterson accepted the assignment Roosevelt offered, he would have found in his paper's editorial file a good deal to read. As *The New Republic* described it, his paper "wanted to keep our strength all at home and opposed aid to the anti-Nazi powers. It refreshed our memories on old quarrels with England, incited distrust of Russia, justified Nazi crimes by citing our own land-grabbing . . . called the President a dictator, forecast the suspension of Congressional elections . . . cheered [Charles] Lindbergh and the appeasers . . . [said in a 1941 editorial] 'Come On, Let's Appease Japan' . . . [and expressed in another editorial] a suspicion that this administration expects to be running some sort of totalitarian government either before or after the end of the war and is prudently getting ready for same."

Cissy took up her duties as a Washington publisher in a manner that seemed at times to lack seriousness. Often at midnight, after leaving the social swirl, she would appear in the *Times-Herald* city room smoking a cigarette through an upwardly tilted holder encrusted with diamonds, her sable coat trailing off one shoulder and dragging the floor, and five or six poodles barking and frolicking at her feet. The night news staff tried not to let her see them staring. She maintained a private railroad car, the *Ranger,* equipped with seven sets of silk sheets and seven sets of slipcovers to allow a change of color each day while she traveled. The car was maintained by a traveling staff of five servants who brought fresh flowers aboard at every stop along the way. On one trip aboard the *Ranger* she offered a Hearst newspaper executive a ride from Chicago to Washington. Along the way he made a caustic remark about her living like a queen. She looked at him coldly for a few seconds and then slapped him so hard she knocked him to the floor. When the *Times-Herald* unions talked of a strike, she announced, "If there's a strike I will lock the front door and it will never be opened again." The employees met, agonized, wondered if she meant it, decided she did. There was no strike.

But Cissy as a publisher was serious. And successful. In competition with the Washington *Post,* the *Evening Star* and the Washington *Daily News,* she managed by 1943 to build a circulation larger than any of them and earn profits close to one million dollars a year.

Then Roosevelt was forced to contemplate the fact that each of his three most vicious enemies in newspaper publishing enjoyed the largest circulation in his city—the *Tribune* in Chicago, the *Daily News* in New York, and now the *Times-Herald* in Washington. His staff tried, without conviction, to explain this phenomenon by saying that each paper in its own city had the best sports or comics or society news.

Cissy's paper, in fact, was good in all three, and it had more. It had a publisher who, on a whim, would publish on the front page a personal attack on whatever public figure displeased her at the moment. Cissy not only gave her readers the sports and comics and society and about as much of the hard news as most people wanted, she also met what must be one of the more urgent needs of the human race—something to talk about—with her outrageous opinions and her feuds with, among others, columnist Drew Pearson. He had been married to and then divorced from Cissy's daughter, Felicia. As the war approached, Pearson's column offered opinions in direct conflict with Cissy's. She retaliated by throwing his column out of her paper and writing that since he was not in uniform in wartime he was a "yellow-bellied slacker." Walter Winchell's column, dropped for the same reason, led to another feud and Cissy's suggestion that Winchell, in the naval reserve, be assigned to a submarine certain to be sunk. In 1944, she was infuriated because Roosevelt opposed draft deferments for premedical students and responded in a way that by now surprised nobody: she filled a page with an editorial signed by her along with photographs of twenty young men of draft age on the State Department staff. She wrote, "If the Army really needs ALL the young men it can get, it can find in Secretary Hull's fold an assortment of rich, able-bodied unmarried boys of no particular use to anyone . . . it would really be good for the 'panty-waist brigade' (and isn't *that* vulgar?) to have a taste of the war." Secretary of State Hull responded that Cissy's attack was violent and unfair, that nearly all the young men she listed were serving overseas in jobs of direct assistance to the military.

Wrong, violent, unfair, yes. But something for Washington to talk about, even when Cissy's wrath took a turn for the bizarre, as when she wrote that she had visited an insane asylum and had spent a little of her time categorizing "the better known liberals" by the types of mentally ill people she had seen there:

Henry Wallace . . . crystal-gazing crackpot . . . a harmless kind of nut.

Walter Winchell: Hard to tell just what's biting this middle-aged ex-chorus boy. False shame of his race . . . may be at the front of it all.

Poor puppet-king Marshall Field rightly belongs in the 'harmless' ward, too . . . trailing his dirty sheet behind him.

Time called it " . . . some of the most vicious personal slander since the days when all journalism was yellow."

But the worst she saved for her ex-son-in-law, Drew Pearson. "Ah, Drew, rose-sniffing, child-loving, child-cheating, sentimental Drew . . . " He, Winchell "and other Quislings . . . manage to get paid big money for their treachery. . . . This filthy work of plotting, planning, sneaking, lying, spying, cheating, stealing, smearing in the mere HOPE of one day overthrowing our American form of government.

" . . . yes, they're nutty, all right, these 'liberals'—for they can't see further ahead than the first frenzied days of plunder, murder, fire, rape and prancing about with pale, fresh-cut human heads on bloody pikes . . . besotted in their lust for blood and carnage and dollars."

Pearson said in his next broadcast that this country needed "an organization for protection against ex-mothers-in-law. I would like to be a charter member." And Winchell said in his next broadcast, "Very special bulletin! The craziest woman in Washington, D.C., is not yet confined to Saint Elizabeth's hospital for the insane. She is, however, expected any edition."

It all recalled Franklin Roosevelt's words in a 1942 letter to Archibald MacLeish. "The trouble is that Bertie [McCormick], Joe Patterson and Cissy deserve neither hate nor praise—but only pity for their unbalanced mentalities." Yes, but Roosevelt held a less charitable view than he was urging on MacLeish. They may not have deserved to be hated, but hate them he did.

* * *

Most of the press and radio people in wartime Washington simply did their work without flaming outbursts or hysterical spectacles. Those who covered the White House every day were crowded into a tiny office just inside the entrance to the West Wing and a few feet from the president's office. The press room, or "press closet," as they called it, was cramped and cluttered with battered chairs and desks with drawers barely big enough to hold a pint of whiskey, every surface of every desk and most of the floor blackened with cigarette burns, the walls, ceiling and curtains smoke-stained into a color close to that of an egg yolk. The odors were of smoke, sweat, whiskey and dust that seemed to have floated in the air since Abraham Lincoln, or at least Woodrow Wilson. Less than a dozen reporters were there every day, but when Roosevelt had a press conference, usually twice a week, thirty or more others arrived to cover it and then to leave. The regulars saw them as unwelcome in- truders. When Merriman Smith of the United Press, a White House regular for twenty years, saw them walking up the driveway from Pennsylvania on a press conference day, he said, "Here come the twice-a-week geniuses."

On days without press conferences, there was little to do at the White House. Occasionally, Steve Early would wander over from his office across the foyer and thumbtack some routine news on the press room bulletin board. Or an announcement that Roosevelt was planning to go to Hyde Park for the weekend and those wishing to go with him should sign up no later than Thursday.

The Roosevelt White House was far from the best place in Washing- ton for journalistic enterprise, mainly because the presidential staff in the war years was still quite small. The exponential growth that came with later presidencies had not yet begun and the staff members dealing with policy never numbered many more than five or six. And the zeal for self-promotion seen among White House staff members in later years had not yet appeared. There were not yet a lot of staff lawyers busily pursuing prospective clients for their future in private practice, or nursing political ambitions of their own and cultivating the press with leaks, hoping the favor would be returned in the form of favorable publicity in the future. The staff members were intensely loyal to Roosevelt and honored to be working for him, and they did not talk to reporters behind his back. So, with nothing to report but Roosevelt's words on the days when there were any, and on other days nothing but Steve Early's thumbtacked notes, there were times when covering the White House could be a boring job.

A much larger group of reporters worked every day at a central office set up downtown on Independence Avenue and called the War Agencies Press Room. It had the look and the atmosphere of a wartime bus station—busy, crowded, noisy, bustling, littered. It was there solely for the distribution of press releases, or handouts as they were called, such as announcements of new rationing rules—how many pairs of shoes a person would be allowed to buy in the next quarter, how much butter a ration ticket would be worth next month, and hundreds of others. There was a press release from the OPA saying it desperately needed more typists. A reporter counted the typing errors in the release itself, found forty-six on one page, and concluded that the OPA's need was real. And there were others urging the public to support the war by doing this or that, buying more bonds, making fewer telephone calls, and a nice one from Chester Bowles of the OPA explaining why there were no cigarettes to be had in the stores. What Hershey bars and nylon stockings were said to be worth in the European war zones—almost anything—a pack of Chesterfields, Old Golds or Lucky Strikes was worth in the United States. Several congressional committees asked, where were the cigarettes? Bowles did not even try the familiar dodge of saying the armed services were taking them; nobody would have believed him. Instead, he said there were as many cigarettes as ever, enough for all who wanted them, but rumors of shortages had frightened smokers into buying more than they needed and hiding them in dresser drawers. It did seem that Bowles was right and that there were plenty of cigarettes, but the public no longer trusted Washington news like this, seeing the bureaucrats as forever seeking some advantage for themselves by appealing to the public's patriotism, and they continued to buy cigarettes wherever they could be found and hide them away in fear that if they did not hoard them, somebody else would.

The news of the fighting came in from overseas, not Washington, and always took priority in the newspapers and on the radio. What Washington reporters ground out and the press sent across the country for the edification of the public were Roosevelt's words and deeds, the war agencies' announcements about rationing, shortages, weapons production, news of the higher taxes needed to finance the war and which somehow remained in place a generation after it ended. Plus the wartime politicking in Congress, about as petty as usual.

The Washington press corps had expanded from a few hundred to about two thousand, including for the first time great numbers of women who were hired, often reluctantly, to replace the men gone into the military. But NBC, among others, still would not allow them to broadcast news on the air because it considered them "biologically incapable of total objectivity." Some of the older news correspondents had survived from presidencies long before Roosevelt's and regarded themselves, often rightly, as knowing more about the operations of government than those running it. Shortly after Henry Morgenthau became secretary of the treasury, he held a press conference and one of those attending was an older correspondent, Homer Dodge, in Washington since the Taft administration. He asked a series of questions so abstruse and technical that Morgenthau, more apple grower than financier, could not deal with them. He said to Dodge, "You must be new here."

Dodge said, "No, Mr. Secretary. You are."

A few of those surviving from Hoover, Coolidge and even earlier administrations were still affecting spats, canes, pince-nez glasses and Homburg hats. To the younger newsmen they looked like European foreign secretaries on their way to an international conference to sell out some innocent and unsuspecting country.

During their idle hours waiting for news from the White House and the war agencies, the reporters sat around nodding in heated agreement with the common wisdom that almost nobody ever got rich in journalism unless he owned the paper. Their incomes ranged from about three thousand dollars for a young reporter who was not a famous figure up to two hundred and fifty thousand dollars for one of the few who were: Drew Pearson, the highest-paid name in journalism and one of the highest-paid anywhere in the years when the president of the United States was paid one hundred thousand dollars.

Pearson's specialty was gossip and scandal. And he got plenty of it. A good deal of what he wrote was false and unfair, but he did produce the goods to send to prison several public figures long known to be crooks but Pearson proved it when no one else could. His method was to make it known he was receptive to leaks. When an embittered government employee, a jilted woman friend or an angry former wife had dirty and embarrassing information and wanted to settle a score, Pearson was the man to call. He promised and delivered anonymity. He took telephone calls in drugstores and sidewalk phone booths because, he said, "There are so many taps on my phone I could sell commercials." It made him famous, made him rich, and since he thought being attacked by politicians and publishers made him more credible to the reading public, he was delighted when Roosevelt at a press conference called him "a chronic liar," or when Cissy Patterson said of him, "I wish I were still in Chicago so I could have that son of a bitch rubbed out." And he was pleased when Representative Hamilton Fish of New York promised to horsewhip him and twenty other congressmen offered to help. When Senator Kenneth McKellar was not on the floor attacking David Lilienthal, he was on the floor attacking Pearson. In one monumental exercise in oratory, he called him, "an infamous liar, a revolving liar, a pusillanimous liar, a lying ass, a natural-born liar, a liar by profession, a liar for a living, a liar in the daytime and a liar in the night time." Pearson was so pleased he printed McKellar's entire speech in his column, believing that newspaper readers, always skeptical of the folkways of Congress, would believe a columnist called a liar in such encyclopedic depth must have been telling some inconvenient truth.

One of Pearson's discoveries he never printed. He learned that a member of his own profession, a Washington newspaper columnist, was making money with a crooked scheme of Byzantine complexity. Every month or so, the columnist wrote about previously unknown virtues he saw in Francisco Franco, Spain's Fascist dictator. Why was he writing this stuff? Nobody knew until Pearson discovered his scheme. It was this:

More than once, the columnist rummaged around in a junky antique shop and bought a scruffy oil painting for maybe fifty dollars, cleaned it up and hung it in his dining room. After a time, he invited the ambassador of Spain and several others to dinner. Along about the dessert course, the ambassador's eye chanced to fall on the painting.

"What an interesting oil! I have just the place for it in the embassy. Would you by chance be willing to sell it?"

The columnist, in front of witnesses, said he might consider selling and would discuss it later, and later sold for ten thousand dollars a painting he had bought for fifty.

Pearson never printed a line about this because he knew that in the inevitable libel suit, any wrongdoing would be difficult to prove; legally there had not been any. There was no law against selling a painting for a profit. And Pearson managed, somehow, to find out that the columnist had reported the sale, paid the taxes, and been careful to hold on to the painting long enough for the sale to qualify as a capital gain. The Spanish ambassador, as a diplomat, was immune to all American law and could not be questioned in any case. And proving a connection between columns praising Franco and the sale of the painting was impossible. It was a payoff but apparently it was legal. And so the columnist lived, prospered, died, and his nasty little secret was buried with him.

Very different from Pearson was another star: Elmer Davis, a former New York *Times* reporter, writer, and since the war began a commentator on CBS radio and among the best on the air. He spoke in tight sentences and a dry, nasal Indiana twang. When he offered to take speech lessons to eliminate it, CBS was wise enough to refuse.

A sample of his style: When the Senate was about to vote on a bill seen as beneficial to the war but economically harmful to the state of New Jersey, a senator from the state said he was "torn," and would, he said, examine his conscience to decide how to vote on the bill. He wound up voting against it.

On his broadcast that night, Davis reported: "Senator H. Alexander Smith of New Jersey spent the day wrestling with his conscience. He won."

There were Pearson and Davis and Lippmann and Murrow and the other stars. And there also was Gabriel Heatter doing fifteen minutes every night on the Mutual Broadcasting System and, when any excuse could be found, opening his broadcast with the line, "Ahhh, there's *good* news *tonight!*" While others reported the news and commented on it, Heatter did more. He lived it. Any attack on Americans anywhere was an attack on him. He reported the bad news, when it could not be avoided, in the mournful tones of a eulogy in a funeral chapel, sounding as if at any moment he might burst into tears and be unable to continue. But then, with only a brief pause to prepare his audience for a change of mood, he turned on a happy, chuckling voice to introduce a commercial for a laxative by saying, "If you're over thirty-five, as I am, may I recommend Serutan? It's 'nature's' spelled backward, you know. Here's your friend and mine, Len Sterling."

On the air and off, Heatter always referred to himself in the third person: "Heatter believes . . . Heatter has said." When Mussolini was overthrown and hanged in public, he said on the air, "Heatter hounded him like a dog night after night. Heatter called him a clown, a guttersnipe."

He had another distinction, no doubt unique in broadcasting. It was that he perspired so profusely he was always afraid his damp clothes would lead to a cold and sore throat. And after each broadcast he excused himself quickly and left the studio on a dead run to change his underwear.

On June 13, 1942, a little more than six months into the war, Franklin Roosevelt made another attempt, his fourth, to end what had become confusion approaching chaos in the management of war news and information. He formed a new agency called the Office of War Information and appointed Elmer Davis to run it. Now, Roosevelt said, a new office with a new name could do what everyone, himself included, was piously saying in public should be done—it should give the press and the public, quickly and accurately, all the war news that would not be helpful to the Germans and Japanese. Yes, nearly everyone agreed this should be done. Few believed it would be. Davis abandoned his CBS microphone and agreed to try, not realizing he was taking on a job that could only be done poorly if it could be done at all.

Even before Pearl Harbor, Roosevelt had tried to deal with this problem through an agency called the Office of Facts and Figures, the name carefully chosen to suggest that it would distribute dry facts and dry figures and nothing more. The reason for the name, at a time when isolationism was still in full cry in Congress and across the country, was to suggest that the new agency would create no interventionist propaganda and to head off Republican charges in Congress that here was Roosevelt sneakily setting up still another propaganda agency to promote himself and, in the view of his more dedicated enemies, to lead the country into war with himself in charge as dictator.

The Office of Facts and Figures was under the direction of Archibald MacLeish, the poet and Librarian of Congress. But the OFF seemed to know nothing about the heats and hatreds of Washington politics. And soon after Pearl Harbor, MacLeish was overseeing the production of mushy propaganda movies, the kind known in the trade as "church basement film," in a series called America at War.

His movies included such dialogue as "We Americans are affable enough. We've never made killing a career, although we happen to be pretty good with a gun . . . a sentimental people, a sympathetic people . . . we show it and we act it."

And in another film a young boy and girl are heard to say:

Boy: "That's one of the things this war's about."

Girl: "About us?"

Boy: "About all young people like us. About love and gettin' hitched and havin' some kids, and breathin' some fresh air out in the suburbs . . . about livin' and workin' decent like free people."

The Office of Facts and Figures quickly got into trouble with Congress and the press because it put out few figures and no facts but a lot of mawkishness. The OFF was a failure on all counts.

And so Elmer Davis moved in to set up the OWI and to cure all these problems. Oh, the White House announcement describing Davis's new powers read splendidly. His OWI would take over and consolidate the Office of Facts and Figures and three other agencies already dealing, more or less, with war news. Davis would have authority to order all agencies of government to follow news and information policies he prescribed. But the problem was that other agencies, particularly the army and navy, did not read Roosevelt's announcement or, having read it, resolved to ignore it, and did.

The army eventually put its own views on this question on paper, in a pamphlet called *Guide to the Use of Information Materials,* and the press was startled to read, "It should be recognized that news is not the sacred property of the press, but something in the public domain. In time of war the armed forces themselves are the creators of news and have therefore a vested interest in the way it is reported and edited. . . ." *Time* called this "a shocking product of brass-buttoned minds" and added, "Seldom in democratic countries had a servant of the people gone so far before."

During the war Davis had many fights with the armed services. He lost them all. He lost in trying to persuade them that in spite of their claim to a vested interest in the news, the American public's sons, brothers and husbands were doing the fighting and so whose news was it? The army's famous pamphlet said it was in the "public domain." If so, if the news was in the public domain like the Mississippi River and Yellowstone National Park, then it was owned by all and so owned by none. But the army and the navy felt they owned the news and behaved as if they owned it from the beginning of the war until the end. And they used it skillfully as the civilian agencies of government had always used it throughout history—to try to conceal their failures and blunders and to give out fulsome detail on their successes. Davis tried to get the news out quickly and accurately. He failed only because it never was in the basic nature of government agencies, military or civilian, to tell the full truth about themselves.

The navy, even more than the army, was intent on controlling and manipulating the news. The general belief in the Washington press was that Admiral Ernest J. King, chief of naval operations, given his preference, would have issued only one announcement during the entire war—that it was over and the United States had won.

Roosevelt himself continued to keep the reporters away whenever he could. When he met Winston Churchill at sea to draft the Atlantic Charter stating the Allies' postwar aims, British reporters were present. American ones were not. After his Casablanca conference, newsmen were herded like farm animals into a theatrically staged event called a press conference but they were not allowed to ask questions. Military secrecy had to be kept, they were told.

But in 1943, when the United Nations held a food conference at the Homestead Hotel in Hot Springs, Virginia, the question at hand was how to feed displaced and homeless people after the war. The conference had no military aspect whatever. But even there Roosevelt ordered newsmen barred from the conference. He simply did not want them around.

Raymond Clapper, the Scripps-Howard columnist, wrote:

This does his judgment no credit. He is persisting in it in the face of vigorous opposition from Elmer Davis of the OWI. . . .

This is not a military conference. There is no need for secrecy at all . . . except that Mr. Roosevelt wants it because at Casablanca he found it so much more pleasant not to have newspaper reporters around.

We newspaper workers are not, perhaps, the most likeable people in the world. We may not have the social graces that Groton and Harvard could have given us all had we been rich men's sons . . . [but we] try as best we can to keep the American people informed about their government.

* * *

It surely was true that the press was not always lovable, and in not loving it Roosevelt was at one with the vast majority of politicians through all of Washington's history. But for the American people there always remained the question: if their politicians behaved as poorly as many of them did with the press keeping some kind of eye on them, what would they be doing with nobody watching?

VIII

Congressional Blues

Summer, 1937: The senators perspired. Vandenberg of Michigan, trying to ignore the heat of a Washington summer and trying to ignore a boring speech, sat idly in the U.S. Senate chamber using a pocket knife to carve his name inside the drawer of his desk, the same desk and the same drawer where Daniel Webster had carved his name a century earlier. Flies droned in the heavy air. Visitors up in the balcony listened to the speaker and wondered who he was and what he was talking about, and tried to push the heat away by waving white cardboard fans stapled to wooden handles and imprinted with the message: "W. W. CHAMBERS, THE LARGEST UNDERTAKER IN THE WORLD. OUR FAMOUS SIXTY SERVICES FOR ONE PRICE." From the floor, with all the fans moving, the balconies looked like fields of white poppies blowing in a wind. Congress, concerned for its dignity and offended by the sight of sleazy commercialism, had banished the vendors of souvenirs, postcards, funny hats and mousetraps from the great rotunda of the United States Capitol. But the W. W. Chambers fans remained because in the summer, in a building without air conditioning, they offered all the help there was. The exhaust fans merely sucked the hot air out of the Senate chamber and drew in new hot air from the outside.

Until the late thirties, Congress usually retreated from the Washington summers by adjourning its sessions in May or June. Those facing elections went home to shake hands and make speeches over the fried chicken, mashed potatoes and green peas at the Rotary Clubs. Members whose seats were safe for another election or two often rented small houses in Maryland and Virginia around the shores of the Chesapeake Bay to take the breezes and await their next session, which was in the autumn if the times were busy or the following January if they were not. The annual sessions of Congress averaged a little over five months.

But by the late 1930s some members had discovered the comforts of the air conditioning in the Fox, the Capitol, the Earle and RKO Keith's movie theaters downtown. They asked to have cool air pumped into the House and Senate chambers and into their office buildings across the street. And so, in 1938, the United States Congress made a fateful decision that a few of the more cantankerous members said foretold the collapse of the Republic. It installed air conditioning. With its chambers and offices cool and pleasant, some predicted, Congress would stay in session all year and pass the additional time making even longer and more tiresome speeches, enacting more laws, spending more money and running the national debt still higher. Longer sessions, they said, would mean more government and more taxes, more forms for the people to fill out and more bureaucrats hired to read and file them.

As it turned out, the war demanded longer sessions anyway. And while the new air conditioning helped modernize the legislative process, little else did. Congress in 1939 was still carrying on in the leisurely and genteel manner of the days of McKinley, in a setting of marble stairways, horsehair sofas, polished brass spittoons, snuff boxes on the senators' desks, potted palms, Oriental rugs, leather chairs and Havana cigars. There were even a few members still affecting frock coats, wing collars and black string ties. It was a gentlemen's club with but one woman senator—Hattie Caraway of Arkansas, who sat in the chamber every day knitting, listening and saying nothing.

It was a club whose members had varying degrees of competence, intelligence and honesty. But each had one undeniable achievement worthy of his colleagues' respect—the ability to win an election. Sam Rayburn, speaker of the House, listened to committee testimony by a State Department official admired for his expertise and eloquence and said, "Yes, he's pretty smart, but I'd trust him more if he'd ever won an election for sheriff."

Members of the club were paid ten thousand dollars a year. Paid themselves, actually, since Congress set its own salaries and was ever fearful of giving itself so much that it would excite public complaint and criticism. But there were other benefits, all supplied free by the taxpayers—large offices and staffs; trips to and from their home states; free postage; ornamental green plants for their offices brought in from Congress's own greenhouse; inexpensive meals in the generously subsidized House and Senate restaurants; a so-called stationery store able to produce at wholesale prices any merchandise the members desired from jewelry to refrigerators to automobile tires; bowls of goldfish, fed and replaced as necessary by the Capitol staff; trips abroad with their wives when any excuse could be found; long-distance telephones; private elevators barred to the public; train and airline ticket offices kept solely for their convenience; parking in Congress's own private garages. And—not least—an office payroll totally under each member's control and available for the hiring of friends, relatives and mistresses, options all freely used. Senator McKellar of Tennessee, in his tireless pursuit of patronage, had his office so densely packed with relatives it looked like a family reunion every day.

These last prewar years were leisurely ones for the guardians of the Republic, with time for chatting and gossiping in the lounges and cloakrooms and telling such familiar anecdotes as the one about Nicholas Longworth, former speaker of the House, almost totally bald an at early age, lounging in a leather chair when another member ran his hand over Longworth's shiny scalp and said, "Nice and smooth. Feels just like my wife's bottom." Longworth then ran his own hand over his head and said, "Yes, so it does."

And they liked to recall Representative Phil Campbell, a Republican from Kansas, who thought his seat was so safe he no longer had to make the long and tiring train trips halfway across the country to speak and shake hands in his district. He bought a house across the Potomac in Virginia, moved into it and paid the property taxes. An opponent in

Kansas got the tax records, spread copies across the state and charged that Campbell had become a Virginian, not a Kansan. That was trouble enough. But then at a political rally he bribed Campbell's band to play "Carry Me Back to Old Virginny." That so stimulated the voters that Campbell was defeated, and years later they sat around in the House cloakroom and laughed about it. But the laughter was thin and chilly, because they all knew some equally nasty little surprise could at any time unseat any of them. And few were ready to leave. A staff member in a congressman's office told Jonathan Daniels that in the election coming up shortly, "They've got Bert licked. He knows it. But he's afraid to tell his wife. She just got a committee chairmanship in the Congressional Club, she likes Washington, she can't go back home. She'd be mortified. She can't take it."

The Congress took due notice of the war and did what it had to do, but it never was happy and seldom gracious about it. Franklin Roosevelt demanded vast powers it did not want him to have, but he got them. The War and Navy departments wanted money in stratospheric amounts and with no badgering and hectoring from Congress about how it was to be spent, and it was handed over. The wartime bureaucracies, which Congress always disliked, asked for authority over areas of American life formerly thought to be none of government's business, or powers Congress jealously had always held to itself, but they were granted. The liberals agonized that the war was being used as an excuse to wipe out social and welfare programs. The conservatives feared the war would set federal power so firmly in place that traditional American freedoms would never be seen again.

But the real cause of their anger was a fact they first denied but eventually had to accept—they were being stripped of their power because they could not run the war. Only a small, agile, centralized authority could run the war. Only the president could run the war. Congress with its slow and cumbersome procedures and with more than half a thousand individual and individualistic members could not run the war. They could stand on the sidelines and criticize, and they did. They could hand over money for others to spend, and they did. They could complain that Roosevelt was ignoring Congress, and they did. But there he was down Pennsylvania Avenue reveling in his role of world statesman and wartime commander in chief, hobnobbing with Winston

Churchill, dominating the headlines every day, mesmerizing the country with his fireside chats, making a public show of visiting war plants and military bases, meeting with his uniformed leaders to plan strategy, always in secrecy and with Congress excluded. The Senate and the House quibbled and cavilled and complained because they could do nothing else. But even their complaining brought complaints. Newspaper columnist Raymond Clapper wrote, "People don't give a damn what the average Senator or Congressman says. The reason they don't care is that they know what you hear in Congress is 99 per cent tripe, ignorance and demagoguery and not to be relied on."

That wounded them. One senator said to *Time,* "You take that damned column of Clapper's. What does he expect Congress to do? Go out and run the war? And if we start that, what will happen? The newspapers will be the first ones to jump on us and say we're bitching up the war effort, that we're mixing in stuff we have no business to, that we ought to shut up and let the army and the navy run the war."

Congress in its easy and relaxed ways had simply failed to keep up. The wartime bureaus and agencies downtown had stuffed their offices with economists, professors and specialists in such arcane fields as ammunition production and aircraft design. When they took the witness stand in committee hearings, the congressmen were simply overwhelmed— college freshmen knowing little sitting at the feet of famous experts who knew everything. Congressional committee staffs did have specialists in such legislative disciplines as tax policy, but most of them were hacks appointed for patronage reasons and no match for the fast-talking witnesses from downtown drawn up in battalion front and ready endlessly to debate every comma and period and every dime. At committee hearings supposedly held for the members to hear testimony and then decide for themselves what to do, there were times when at the end of a hearing they did not even know what questions to ask. And so they were reduced to waiting for ideas and suggestions from the president and, while bewailing their ineffectuality, rubber stamping their approval.

Senator Ellison D. ("Cotton Ed") Smith of South Carolina took the floor to complain, "The other day I went to a department and found the officials in profound conference. I could hardly get a hearing from the head of the bureau. I knew then that the officials were cooking up an order for the rubber stamps [in Congress] to say 'Yes, sir' to. That is all we are doing."

"This Congress," wrote Richard L. Strout in the *New Republic* in the second year of the war, "is almost wholly negative; it has shown no leadership for constructive planning in world crisis." Yes. Because it was a slow and deliberate nineteenth-century institution dragged ill prepared and against its will into the boiling and explosive wartime twentieth.

As much as some members might have liked to, Congress could not obstruct or appear to obstruct Roosevelt's running of the war. The public would not stand for it. So it busied itself with what little business was left to it. It filibustered successfully against repealing the poll tax. It fought against and made a soggy mess of Roosevelt's proposal to send federal ballots to servicemen and -women around the world for the 1944 elections. And with the enthusiasm of bloodhounds pursuing an escaped convict through the Georgia swamps by moonlight, it chased communists.

Martin Dies of Orange, Texas, seemed always to have his six-foot-three frame stretched out on a sofa in the House cloakroom while he offered wisecracks and smoked cigars. He had lived in Washington for ten years while his father served in Congress during Woodrow Wilson's time. He had observed that ordinary, routine congressional work was not the way to fame and glory and so he did little of it. The only effort he ever made was in trying to get Congress to start an investigation of something—anything—with him at the head of it. He pushed one suggestion after another—to investigate Roosevelt's restrictions on the freedom of the press and radio, to reduce unemployment by deporting all aliens, to investigate the charge that sixty wealthy families controlled the United States. A newspaper columnist wrote, "He made no secret of the fact he was looking for a safe political horse to ride to headlines and glory."

He found his horse in 1938. Representative Samuel Dickstein of New York, frightened at seeing Fritz Kuhn's German-American Bund arrogantly marching with Nazi flags in the streets of New York City, supported a Dies proposal to investigate fascism in America. Thus was born the Committee to Investigate Un-American Activities with Dies as its chairman and a budget of twenty-five thousand dollars. He made a few brief passes at Kuhn's Nazis and discovered that was not where the headlines lay. But when the American Federation of Labor published an attack on American communists, the Dies committee was swamped with mail and telegrams from people saying they had information on the crimes of card-carrying Bolsheviks and offering to come to Washington at their own expense to testify. Then Dies knew which way to rein his horse.

He turned to Hollywood and discovered what looked to him like a communist cell—a group of movie people who had sent greetings to the left-wing French newspaper *Ce Soir.* Among them was Shirley Temple, then ten years old. A red-faced Harold Ickes shouted, "They've gone to Hollywood and there discovered a great Red plot. They have found dangerous radicals there, led by little Shirley Temple. Imagine the great committee raiding her nursery and seizing her dolls as evidence."

Dies moved on, looking for communists in the Department of Labor, the WPA Federal Theater and Writers Projects, the National Labor Relations Board. The truth was that communists of one variety or another could easily be found here and there, but Dies was less interested in finding them than in producing headlines for himself.

Franklin Roosevelt said, "The Dies Committee made no effort to get at the truth, either by calling for facts to support mere personal opinion or by allowing facts and personal opinion on the other side." But Dies, now so excited he was smoking eight cigars a day, offered this advice to Roosevelt: "The president surely must realize by this time that his left-wing followers are the fountainhead of subversive activities."

On the floor of the House, bulging and beaming with self-importance, Dies rose and described for the edification of his colleagues

a new philosophy which in one country is communism, in another country fascism, in another country Naziism and in another country bureaucracy. But the underlying principles of all these philosophies is essentially the same. Stripped of their verbiage and viewed in the naked truth, we find similar phrases and expressions as well as similar philosophies and programs. . . . There is a united front of communists, crackpots and socialists [who were inciting racial hatred] and constantly the Negroes are told that now is the time for them to achieve that degree of social equality to which they are entitled.

He saved his hardest pitch for last, the charge that "Adam Clayton Powell, a Negro communist, advocates that I be assassinated—that my death would be preferable to Hitler's."

While Dies was happiest with communist targets, he would take anything he could find, including in one sensational case, a nudist. He announced his discovery that an economist in Henry Wallace's Board of Economic Warfare had spent several years in European nudist camps and was the author of a book, *Nudism in American Life,* advocating nudity "wherever feasible in home, office, workshop and factory." A public outcry forced the vice president to fire the man. Wallace accused Dies of having an "itch for publicity." He did—an itch that would not stay scratched.

The war years had started out better. The day after Pearl Harbor the Associated Press lead dispatch from Washington reported a "wave of unity" sweeping the United States. A New York *Times* editorial said:

> Gone is every sign of partisanship in the Capitol of the United States. Gone is every trace of hesitancy and indecision. There are no party lines today in Congress. There are no blocs, no cliques, no factions. The house divided against itself has ceased to exist in Washington. In its place there arises an assembly of American patriots whose single thought and passionate concern are the safety of our people.

House minority leader Joseph W. Martin of Massachusetts, after a meeting with Roosevelt on December 7, 1941, came out of the White House saying, "In the hour of danger there is no partisanship. In that hour we all stand as one people in support of America." Republican Senator Vandenberg wrote in his diary, "Now we are in it. Nothing matters except victory. The arguments must be postponed."

But unity meant different things to different people. Edward J. Flynn, long-time Democratic boss of the Bronx and now chairman of the Democratic National Committee, was an admirer of political "unity"—as long as the unity was on his own terms. "In the face of war," he announced, "politics are adjourned." To Flynn, that adjournment meant that the Republicans should suspend operations for the duration and leave the Democrats in charge. The worst thing that could happen to the country, short of military defeat, would be the election of a Republican majority in Congress. Republican criticism of the Democrats, he claimed, could only help Tokyo, Rome and Berlin, because "the Republicans were not as much interested in winning the war as in controlling the House." They were, he said, "peanut politicians." Flynn and his cronies, when they met in Democratic clubrooms upstairs over candy stores in the Bronx, had always liked to talk about eliminating the Republican party in New York City. Now, in wartime, it was possible to contemplate the same thing in the nation at large. Joe Martin was outraged. "Flynn wants to liquidate the Republican party and squelch all opposition," he complained.

The president, who often viewed Capitol Hill with the same contempt he felt for the press, seemed at times to believe that the most patriotic thing Congress could do was to adjourn for the duration. "I would say," he told reporters in his office early in 1942, "it is about time for a large number of people—several of whom are in this room—to forget politics. It's about time. We read altogether too much politics in our papers. . . . They haven't waked up to the fact that this is war. Same thing is true in Congress." Perhaps, he suggested, the two parties' political organizations should disband for the duration of the war. Perhaps the Republican and Democratic campaign offices could devote themselves to some useful public service, such as civil defense.

Anti-Roosevelt newspapers charged that the president was planning to cancel the 1942 elections. Martin sent him a telegram saying that "while we will support the war measures, the Republican Party also will retain its identity and will enter candidates in the 1942 elections and campaign on their behalf." Roosevelt answered back, "When a country is at war we want congressmen, regardless of party—get that—to back up the Government of the United States."

So much for unity. "As might have been expected," Martin said, "the perfect truce did not last long." Vandenberg wrote in his diary, "The worst of it is that there is still a substantial New Deal sector in high places which will constantly think of the war in terms of new opportunities for further New Deal experiments. . . . We are now living under government by executive decree." And Alf Landon, the defeated 1936 Republican candidate for president, complained, "It's a hell of a situation . . . when you want to support the administration one hundred percent to be confronted with the evident build-up for a fourth term and an increasing destruction of state functions." The age of cooperation had lasted about six weeks.

And so it was to continue: Throughout the war, Republicans in

Congress found themselves under constant pressure, in the name of patriotism, to support the commander-in-chief unquestioningly, to cease behaving as a party of opposition, even to get out of politics entirely and spend the war doing civil defense work.

Naturally, they refused. Senator Taft of Ohio snapped at reporters, "I'll be goddamned if I'll bow to Roosevelt and stand on a street corner as an air raid warden with a tin hat, flashlight and a bucket of sand." To Herbert Hoover, the Republicans' father confessor, he complained, "The administration is still busy asking for every power they can get, whether they need it or not, and I am making myself unpopular for objecting." On the Senate floor, he announced, "Criticism in time of war is essential to the maintenance of any kind of democratic government."

If they had to support the war, the Republicans did not have to support the New Deal; and with the eager backing of conservative Southern Democrats, some New Deal agencies were dismantled—including the Works Progress Administration, the National Youth Administration and the Civilian Conservation Corps. The CCC had sent unemployed men into the woods and parks to clear, clean and build roads and bridges and drainage canals. It had been one of the most popular and productive of the New Deal agencies. When it was abolished, Roosevelt did manage to salvage a little something out of it: He had a woodsy CCC camp near Thurmont, Maryland, converted into a secret retreat for his use on weekends. He called it Shangri La. It would later be renamed Camp David.

By the middle of 1942, the rules had been set. Members of Congress had to support the war. They had to defer to the president, the war agencies and the military on matters relating to the fighting. But they did not have to like it. Nor did they have to put aside any of their traditional interests and prejudices when it came to domestic matters, as they made clear in 1943 when Representative Vito Marcantonio, a member of the American Labor Party who represented New York City's Upper East Side, introduced a bill.

It was a proposal to eliminate the poll tax. Several Southern states, as part of their long effort to circumvent the Fifteenth Amendment, required everyone who wished to vote to pay a tax first. Anyone too poor to pay the tax was effectively disenfranchised. That was most blacks and many poor whites. Marcantonio's bill would prohibit the states from denying anyone a vote in federal elections for failing to pay.

This time it was the Southern Democrats who rose up in outrage. They detested Marcantonio anyway. He was coarse, loud, uncivilized— unfit company for gentlemen. He looked, talked and acted like the communists who haunted their dreams, even if most had never actually seen one. But even without Marcantonio's name attached to it, the poll tax bill was anathema. Without the poll tax, they feared, black voters might begin turning out en masse, electing sheriffs, mayors, governors— even senators and congressmen. Besides, they argued, it was unconstitutional. The Constitution, they claimed, gave the states the power to set qualifications for voters. Many conservatives outside the South agreed.

But Republicans in the House were more than happy to join with liberal Democrats in passing Marcantonio's bill. Many of these Republicans did not in fact favor it, but they knew that when it reached the Senate it would create an ugly public spectacle that might divide and embarrass the Democrats. For in the Senate, unlike in the House, there was the filibuster. Southern Democrats could delay a vote on the bill as long as they could stand and talk (or even mumble and gurgle). House Republicans were eager to watch the fireworks.

They were not disappointed. Long before the Marcantonio bill came before the Senate, Senators James O. Eastland of Mississippi and John McClellan of Arkansas had already announced that they would offer several hundred amendments, each of them subject to debate. When the measure reached the floor, in May 1944, the number of amendments had grown to more than a thousand. And so the Senate of the United States, which liked to describe itself as "the greatest deliberative body in the world," prepared for a charade, a political carnival: a contrived, tedious, often odious discussion of a bill that every member realized would ultimately be defeated.

They knew how it would lose, and they knew when it would lose. A deal had already been struck. Southerners would have a week to rail against the bill and wave the bloody shirt of white supremacy. Then there would be a vote on cloture—a vote to cut off debate, which required a two-thirds majority. The cloture motion would lose. The debate would end. The poll tax would survive.

While four thousand American bombers attacked Germany, while the Russians recaptured Sevastopol from the Germans, while Allied troops in Italy opened a spring offensive, and while Americans in New

Guinea fought their way onto two Japanese-held islands, the Senate played through its scripted and choreographed performance.

Tom Connally of Texas was first. He strode the aisle, the tails of his frock coat swinging behind him as he waved his arms and shouted. "Certain individuals urged on by the necessity for gathering in each scurvy vote, each scurrrrvy vote . . . Sir Galahads leaping on their steeds to come down and reform us . . . an outrageous assault on the Constitution!"

John Bankhead of Alabama warned that the Ku Klux Klan in its white sheets would ride again "if you force this on us. . . . If you treat the nigras right [out of delicacy, the word always appeared in the *Congressional Record* capitalized and spelled "Negro"], treat them good, give them justice, they'll stand by you." He thought so highly of the black servants who had worked in his household for thirty years he would, out of love and affection, do anything for them—except allow them to vote.

There were demonstrations from up in the visitors' galleries. Connally demanded that the demonstrators be thrown out. McKellar of Tennessee, taking a brief respite from his attacks on David Lilienthal, asked that they be allowed to stay because he intended to read the names of the communists behind the bill, and he expected that some of them would be in the gallery to hear their names called out. The Republican senators sat quietly, enjoying the spectacle.

McClellan in measured phrases assured the Senate the issue was not race and not the poll tax; the issue was the Constitution, the right of states to set their own standards. "There are some things we intend to keep pure in the South, and when once those who are behind this measure succeed in tearing down the poll tax, there will be an attempt to tear down something else and I have an idea what it will be. They will want to tear down some of our social laws. We do not discriminate concerning marriage in the South; we simply do not let the whites and Negroes intermarry. . . . We treat the white the same as the Negro. They simply do not marry. We do not stand for such a thing."

Mississippi's Senator Bilbo asked how the CIO "and other communists" could rant against a tax on voters when on union jobs no one could be hired until he paid the union a fee?

He was interrupted by William Langer of North Dakota, who asked Bilbo what kind of legislation he did favor. "Is he still for the bill he had here before, to send all the Negroes to Liberia?"

Bilbo was delighted to reply. "I introduced a bill to provide the ways and means by which they could be voluntarily settled in West Africa." It was, he insisted, a sensible way to create a "permanent solution of the race question which we have had before us, which we are having now and of which we will have more in the future."

Langer asked him how those sent to Africa would be selected.

"It is not a question of selection. That is merely a question of defining what a nigra is. A nigra is anyone who is ascended from the African race." One drop of African blood would be enough.

Other members of the Senate left the floor, or else squirmed in their chairs and tried to pretend they were not hearing what they were hearing.

Bilbo insisted he had never specified Liberia. "Oh, well," he told Langer, "the senator should not be so technical about some little part of Africa. The senator could have them sent to Santo Domingo if he wants to, or Puerto Rico, or to South America or to Mexico."

"The senator from Mississippi himself does not care where they are sent?"

"No. And if the senator from North Dakota keeps on, we might send them to North Dakota."

"We have some very fine Negro citizens in North Dakota."

"There are some six hundred twenty-four nigras in North Dakota."

"They are very fine citizens, I will say."

"The senator does not know anything about them. That is the trouble."

After speaking for three hours, Bilbo offered a final piece of wisdom: "By the way, the idea of the pending piece of legislation came from Russia. Those behind it saw this as the opening way to make a stab at the very heart of the Constitution of the United States." He sat down, knowing he was a winner.

On May 15, as planned, the Senate's elaborate stagecraft was played out to its final scene. A motion to impose cloture, to end the speeches, was introduced and, as the script called for, it was duly voted down. Curtain. Applause. The poll tax lived.

Who were these wartime congressmen squirming in their seats and staging angry, ugly spectacles because their power to do much more had been largely taken away? An informal study of the 1940s membership, prepared at NBC News, was based on daily observation of their words and their work, on personal acquaintance with perhaps a fourth of them, and on an analysis of their personal and political histories. It revealed a composite member somewhat similar to this:

A lawyer from a small city or suburb, a graduate of his state university where he was a "B" student, active in some sport, a member of the debating team, often with some involvement in dramatics and intensely active in the campus fraternities, clubs, projects, committees. If he practiced law at all he preferred courtroom trial work, which satisfied a need to perform in public and which allowed him to use such oratorical gifts as he believed he had. He had less interest in the duller, if more profitable paper shuffling and telephoning in behalf of corporate clients. His first political campaign likely was for some modest local office, a campaign entered for two purposes—first, to make himself known with billboards and radio commercials proclaiming his high character, and second, to publicize his law practice. By now he had joined the Rotary, Kiwanis, Lions or Ruritan club, and one or more of the Eagles, Elks, Red Men, Odd Fellows or Masons.

Fred Hartley of New Jersey, the Hartley of the Taft-Hartley Act, boasted in his biographical notes that he was "the only living person for whom an Aerie of the Eagles Club has been named." Another told a reporter with some pride that once he had been chosen to be the "uuuh man" in the Toastmasters Club. At its meetings each member was encouraged to learn public speaking by standing and orating while the other members evaluated his performance. The "uuuh man" was assigned to count the awkward, nervous pauses and to fine the speaker five cents for each "uuuh."

This was the usual track: law school, small campaigns for small offices, joining the clubs and shaking the hands and slapping the backs and speaking the small pleasantries, eating or pretending to eat the chicken and peas and making the speeches, observing such religious pieties as the community expected, taking whatever side seemed most beneficial in local controversies (or, when feasible, taking both sides), cultivating party leaders and the givers of campaign money, positioning oneself socially at some point near the middle of the middle class and avoiding too much public association with the rich at the country club. All this, plus at all costs never making a clumsy mistake that invited laughter and ridicule, as did a politician campaigning in New York City who was asked to make a speech in the Bronx and politely inquired, "Where *are* the Bronx?" And, depending on the local sociology, being carefully respectful of any group identifiable by its religion, race, ethnicity, national origin, patriotic endeavor, or any enterprise known or said to be devoted to civic, charitable or educational enterprise of any description, however absurd.

All these restrictions left a candidate free to attack only the most carefully chosen of public evils—communism, high taxes, union bosses except in places where unions had power, government extravagance except where government extravagance was being lavished on some local project, farm prices—too high before urban audiences and too low in farm areas—while in a statewide election involving both cities and farms the preferred object of attack was the greedy, gouging middleman standing between the underpaid farmers and overcharged grocery buyers.

The war years popularized the "ism" speech—the declaration of opposition to communism, Naziism, socialism and indeed to "all isms but Americanism." This pledge of fealty first appeared in speeches in American Legion halls, where it was a guaranteed crowd pleaser. Soon it was everywhere.

Finally, of course, came the attacks on the opponent. Here an easy technique was to ask a question that sounded important and resonated in the air, but was actually completely irrelevant. "What has my opponent ever done to stand up to Joe Stalin? Nothing whatever!" Pause, allow this stunning revelation to sink in, and then, "Wouldn't you like to have a [congressman/senator/governor] who will stand up for you? Who will stand up for America?" Applause and cheers, prompted where necessary by campaign aides planted in the audience. Graceful exit, smiling.

Senator John McClellan recalled with pleasure a political debate on an elevated platform outdoors among the pine trees. His opponent listed every evil known or thought to exist anywhere in Arkansas and charged that McClellan had done nothing about any of them. Pleased with himself, he reached for a pitcher on the platform railing to fill his water glass and while smiling and beaming out at the audience and not watching what he was doing, poured the water not into his glass but over the edge of the platform and down on the head of an elderly, white-haired grandmother in a wheelchair. McClellan waited while his opponent apologized and while people scurried about trying to help the old lady. Then he said, "Do you want a senator who's too dumb to pour water in a glass?" McClellan won.

After years of this kind of preparation, a member of Congress arrived in Washington and moved into the office he had spent half his life pursuing, free to do as he pleased, subject only to the voters' decision or, more likely, indifference. When he took the floor in the Senate he could talk as long as he liked, say anything he liked, however false and however vicious, knowing the constitution protected him against libel suits. He alone controlled his office and his staff and his work schedule, attending sessions or ignoring them as he chose, leaving Washington whenever he liked and returning when he was ready.

Once in office, he was pleased to find that generations of congressmen before him had taken great care to see that election laws and customs were stacked in his favor, to make it as difficult as possible for that most miserable and detested pest, the challenger trying to take away his seat. The incumbent member could raise campaign money more easily than any challenger because those giving money to his opponent took a dangerous gamble. If the challenger lost, the incumbent would never forget who financed his opponent and someday, somehow, retribution would be his. He could use his free postage allowance to mail every voter in his state a "newsletter," a self-serving political document thinly disguised. He could send American flags recently flown over the U.S. Capitol to schools, American Legion posts and Boy Scout troops in his state. Hidden in the basement of his office building, barred to snooping reporters, was a battery of automatic typewriters turning out thousands of form letters in response to mail from the voters, each form letter looking cozy and personal. If an executive agency decided to build a new road, dam, bridge, park or post office in his state or district, the congressman could insist on announcing it first and claiming the credit. The result of all this was that year after year, an average of over 90 percent of incumbent members running for reelection were winners.

That was the system. What kind of men and women did the system send to the wartime Congresses? Among others, these:

Representative Clarence J. Brown, Republican. Blanchester, Ohio: Masons, Elks, Eagles, Junior Order of United American Mechanics, Rotary. As a boy he made money on the downtown corner beside the bank selling popcorn from a baby carriage. He went to law school, but never practiced. Instead, he joined the clubs, slapped the backs and bought a country newspaper with a rigidly Republican editorial line. When the chicken and peas were served, he ate them and asked for seconds. And so when he arrived in the House of Representatives in 1939 after a succession of minor Ohio offices, he weighed 240 pounds, all jowls, jokes, joviality and rimless glasses. Isolationist and anti-union, he called the CIO "a conduit of communism," voted against most New Deal programs and remained in the House until 1965. Each year when the smelt ran in the Great Lakes, bushels of these small fish were shipped to Washington and served to the members of Congress. Brown became the champion when in one strenuous afternoon he ate 168 smelts.

Senator Alben W. Barkley, Democrat. Paducah, Kentucky: Moose, Elks, Red Men, Rotary, Lions. Born in a log cabin just twelve years after the Civil War, the son of an impoverished farmer. His teachers discovered he had a speaking voice that could awaken sleeping hogs in the next county, a valuable political asset in a day before microphones and amplifiers. Along with volume and amplitude, his oratorical gifts lay in delivering rolling epigrams in Biblical cadence and turning a political speech delivered from the bed of a hay wagon into something resembling the Sermon on the Mount, a talent hugely admired in a time and place short of other entertainments. He worked as a janitor to pay for college and law school, and in 1905 campaigned from muleback for county prosecutor. He went to Washington and the House in 1913. He left Congress to run for governor of Kentucky, advocating tonnage taxes on coal, prohibition of whiskey and the abolition of betting on horse races, thus defying the three main industries in the state—coal, whiskey and race horses. They combined to defeat him. But even as a nonsmoker in a tobacco state, an advocate of coal taxes in a coal state, a Prohibitionist in a whiskey-making state and an opponent of gambling in a horse-betting state, he won election to the Senate in 1926. He supported the New Deal and with Roosevelt's help was elected majority leader. When the isolationists were demanding that Europe fight its wars alone, Barkley supported all of Roosevelt's preparedness measures, saying, "The only way to stop Hitler is to defeat him, and if we do not help Great Britain and the other nations to stop him over there, we shall someday have to surrender to him or defeat him here." He supported a Jewish state in Palestine when few others did, ran an investigation of the Pearl Harbor attack and reported that the United States did not "incite" it and that the responsibility was entirely Japan's. Over the years he pursued the politician's God-given privilege of switching from one side to the other, and when after years of advocating Prohibition he called for its repeal, the Republicans in his second Senate election promised to "defeat all four Barkleys—the free trade and the protectionist Barkley, the Wet Barkley and the Dry Barkley." They failed that time as they failed every time, and he stayed in the Senate until he became vice president in 1949. He died of a heart attack seven years later on a college campus platform while making a speech.

Representative Sol Bloom, Democrat. New York City: Child actor, theatrical producer, songwriter and real estate developer who followed none of the political rules of the time. He was not a lawyer and was barely educated at all. He was born in Pekin, Illinois, the son of poor Jewish immigrant parents, went to work at twelve, hung around theaters selling programs until producer David Belasco hired him as a boy actor in *Under the Gaslight.* He began producing for his own stock companies, hired the famous actress Maude Adams in one of them, and promoted outside businesses that made him wealthy enough to move to New York City's Riverside Drive, then in one of the richest congressional districts in the country. In New York he built the Apollo Theater and was hired by the Chicago World's Fair to book midway attractions, including fire-eaters, belly dancers and America's first hootchy-kootchy show. After he helped George Ferris build his Ferris wheel, he developed more New York real estate, made still more money and announced he was "retiring to devote my life to public service." Tammany Hall, as a reward for huge campaign contributions, offered him a seat in the House of Representatives, where he arrived in 1923. He was put on the Foreign Affairs Committee. When war came he supported Roosevelt and voted a liberal line. He wore spats, vests with white piping, pince-nez glasses with a black silk ribbon, and seemed to wish he and his wife, Evelyn, could go out to parties more than seven nights a week. During Prohibition, an admirer sent to his office a trunk made of carved teak and filled with bottles of Canadian whiskey. The U.S. Capitol police, then a motley and unprofessional force of patronage appointees, discovered the trunk, stole it, dragged it down to the furnace room and drank the whiskey. Bloom was furious. He took the floor of the House, demanded better police protection and said his office had been robbed of a trunk filled with documents on the Teapot Dome scandal. He remained in the House until he died in 1949.

Representative Sam Rayburn, Democrat. Bonham, Texas: Speaker of the House, the second most powerful office in government. Grew up in a town so poor it had made no money since it shipped mules to South Africa for use in the Boer War. Rayburn rode barefoot on muleback to hear his first political speech, and found this specialized art form so engaging he began practicing it in the barn to an audience of chickens and cows while his brothers and sisters listened outside and snickered. His University of Texas law degree took him to the legislature, where he wrote the first law in the United States to license and regulate automobiles, and in 1913 to Washington and to Congress, where each new member was paid seventy-five hundred dollars and issued six brass spittoons. Writing home, he called Washington a "sour-bellied place." But he was effective in it, loyally supported Roosevelt, and when Speaker of the House William Bankhead, father of actress Tallulah, died in 1940 Rayburn was elected to replace him and soon became the most admired and trusted speaker in modern times.

In February 1944, General Marshall and Henry Stimson asked to see Rayburn privately, even secretly, in his office. Rayburn called in two other congressional leaders to hear a frightening story: Albert Einstein and others had convinced the president it was possible to build a military weapon of an entirely new type, a weapon of such power one bomb would wipe out a city. The Germans, Stimson said, also were working on it and there was a race between Nazi scientists and American scientists to complete this new and frightful thing. Until then they had financed the work by moving military appropriations from one account to another, but now they needed new money—$1.6 billion. Stimson said, "If Hitler's government perfects it before we do, we could lose the war overnight." When they offered details on the bomb project, Rayburn said, "I don't want to know. If I don't know a secret I can't let it leak out." Nothing more was said. The congressional leaders agreed to find the money. They would just have a word with Clarence Cannon, chairman of the Appropriations Committee. No committee chairman resisted when Rayburn said to him, "I want this done." Rayburn lived quietly, said he did not go to parties much because "These Washington society women never serve chili." He lived at the Anchorage in a two-room apartment with no kitchen and had his meals sent in from a restaurant across the street. Every day, for his health, he dosed himself with cotton blossom honey from Texas. When Roosevelt wanted the arms embargo repealed, two Texans, Connally in the Senate and Rayburn in the House, got it repealed. When Roosevelt wanted a Department of Social Welfare, Congress refused. Rayburn told him if he would change the name to Federal Security Agency he would get it passed, and did. All the while seeing that the portraits of Robert E. Lee on his office wall were kept dusted and clean and facing south.

Senator Robert Alphonso Taft, Republican. Cincinnati, Ohio: The son of President William Howard Taft so disliked the backslapping, chicken-eating, joke-telling and nickel-cigar smoking of the ordinary men's clubs he joined none of them and chose instead the Cincinnati gentlemen's clubs, which held to more rigorous standards of wealth, decorum and social status. From the Taft school in Connecticut, run by his uncle Horace, he went on to Yale and Harvard Law, always standing first in his class. No one ever doubted his intelligence, but there were reservations about his chilly and remote personality and considerable amazement that he ever got elected at all. His campaign photographs showed him in a blue serge suit, shiny black shoes and felt hat, looking unhappy while holding out at arm's length a wild turkey shot by someone else, or standing awkwardly beside a cow and patting her on the head with an elegantly kid-gloved hand. Richard Harkness of NBC wondered if Taft won because people thought they were voting for his chuckling, roly-poly 350-pound father. Nearer to the truth was that Ohio's Republican history was long and vigorous, Taft's name was known, and, perhaps most important, he was married to Martha Bowers Taft, a woman of charm and style and a witty, effective campaigner who traveled the state with him and made the engaging speeches he was unable to make. After the election an Ohio newspaper said, "Bob and Martha Taft were elected to the Senate yesterday." In the Senate, feeling himself one of the Lords Proprietors of the Republican party, he ignored the rule that freshman members be quiet for a year or two, and from the first he charged aggressively into every controversy, speaking in a nasal, twanging, flat, grating voice. He was all classic 1930s Midwestern Republicanism— smaller government, lower taxes, isolationism, dislike of the unions, hatred of the New Deal and of Roosevelt. He voted against extending the draft in 1941, against lend-lease, explaining, "An invasion of the United States by the German army is as fantastic as would be an invasion of Germany by the American army." Late in 1941, when Hitler dominated the European continent, Taft told historian Arthur Schlesinger, Jr., he thought the best solution was a "negotiated peace." In 1943, he was still saying the wisdom of American entry into the war was "debatable." When asked by a newspaper interviewer, he could not name a favorite author, favorite food, favorite music, or favorite anything. He played golf and took his family on camping trips where they sat in the woods and passed the time eating nickel candy bars and playing hearts. A strange man of great ability and total integrity but with a flawed understanding of the world of his time and a limp, flaccid personality that without his father's name and his wife's abilities probably would have kept him practicing law in Cincinnati.

Senator Robert F. Wagner, Democrat. New York City: In his youth he was in the New York Athletic Club not as a member but as a bellhop. He was born in Germany and in 1885 moved with his parents to New York City, where his father became a janitor in a tenement on East 106th Street. Not exactly the material the Rotarians and the downtown clubs were looking for. He worked his way through City College and New York Law School, where he displayed some speaking ability. One day, he walked into the Algonquin Democratic Club in the German neighborhood of Yorkville and asked to be allowed to make a speech in a political campaign. That speech led to others and to an offer from Tammany Hall to send him to the State Assembly. His first act there was to get through a bill to cut the fare on the Brooklyn elevated from ten cents to five cents. The governor vetoed it. Then to the State Senate and the chairmanship of a committee to investigate the fire in the Triangle Shirtwaist factory. He proposed, and the legislature passed, fifty-six industrial safety laws. In 1926 Tammany sent him to the United States Senate, where he wrote, sponsored or pushed into federal law more landmark legislation than any U.S. senator in history. Herbert Hoover vetoed one Wagner bill after another, but when Roosevelt arrived they were signed into law: Social Security, federal aid to the unemployed, bankrupt farmers, the poor, blind, disabled, the Civilian Conservation Corps, the Federal Housing Administration, and the National Labor Relations Act, known to all as the Wagner Act, his monument. Wagner was quiet, industrious and, in the opinions of his colleagues, "affable, intent, persuasive.... [He] never tires of answering questions, never impugns the motives of his opponents, . . . [and] as fast as a committee's digestion permits, pours on the facts." During the war he supported Roosevelt's aid to the Allies fighting Hitler and watched his son, Robert, Jr., move from Yale and Harvard into the New York legislature (he eventually became mayor of New York City). He lived quietly in Washington's Shoreham Hotel and never did much of anything beyond his Senate work and an occasional swim in the hotel pool.

Senator Hattie Caraway, Democrat. Jonesboro, Arkansas: Her husband, Senator Thaddeus Caraway, died in 1931. While Arkansas's politicians fought over a successor, the governor appointed Caraway's wife to fill the remainder of his term and to give the state's courthouse gangs time to decide on a replacement. She arrived in Washington, looked around the Senate, and made her first pronouncement: "The windows need washing." She was a farm wife, a pleasant woman who had made the beds, kept a garden, cooked for the family. It was taken for granted she would not run in the next election, but for reasons still not clear, she became a candidate and Senator Huey Long of Louisiana decided he wanted her reelected. He told her to wear a hat, the same one every day, to wear the widow's black clothes, to say as little as possible and let him bring his formidable political organization into Arkansas and campaign for her. He arrived with a circus of sound trucks, Bibles, a huge staff and in nine days made thirty-nine speeches in thirty counties, attributing to Mrs. Caraway political opinions she had never known she held. To the surprise and fury of the Arkansas political establishment, she won, the first woman ever to be elected to a full term in the United States Senate. After that, Long never again paid any special attention to her. In the Senate, she seldom said a word. "I haven't the heart to take a minute away from the men. The poor dears love it so." She supported Roosevelt, the New Deal and the defense preparations. But she remained a Southerner and voted against ending debate on the poll tax. One of her few legislative initiatives was a bill requiring the airlines to supply every passenger with a parachute. (It was defeated.) She rode to her Senate office on the trolley car, brought her lunch in a paper bag, had milk delivered and set down outside her office door and each night washed the bottles in her bathroom sink and set them out to be collected in the morning. She won another election without Huey Long's help and served until 1944, when she was defeated by J. W. Fulbright. On her last day, the Senate rose in tribute to a plain, unassuming woman who had served her time, cast her votes, said little and irritated nobody. Writer George Creel said, "While talking to her—as nice a way to pass an hour as could be imagined—one expects her to start shelling peas."

Senator Gerald P. Nye, Republican. Cooperstown, North Dakota:

Masons, Knights of Pythias. On December 7, 1941, he was waiting offstage to make an antiwar, isolationist speech to an America First meeting in Pittsburgh. The news of Pearl Harbor came. He made the same speech anyway, adding that "this was just what Great Britain planned for us . . . we have been maneuvered into this by the president." He was a country newspaper editor first appointed and then elected to the Senate. When he arrived in 1925, wearing high-top yellow shoes and a soup bowl haircut, the Senate was uncertain if his governor had had power to appoint him and kept him waiting a month while it argued. While his daughter hoped that soon "they will give Papa a place to sit down," his friends in North Dakota sent him a milking stool. The Senate seated him in what the New York *Times* called "a bad day's work." When Roosevelt arrived, Nye loathed every word he ever said, every idea he ever offered. The NRA's Blue Eagle he called "a bird of prey on the masses." The movie industry, he complained, was producing anti-Hitler films because it was dominated by Jews. "My objection is the film producers are foreign born and are in a position of power to control what eighty million people a week see in our theaters." He was asked if he expected them to make pro-Hitler movies. And did he object to Chinese control of the hand laundries? In 1934, he pressured the Senate into establishing a committee to investigate the munitions industry. Nye presided over the hearings, browbeat witnesses (among them J. P. Morgan), and helped produce a report suggesting that the United States had been tricked into entering World War I by the arms dealers. Two years later, he helped author the first of the Neutrality Acts, forbidding Americans to sell or ship weapons to any belligerent countries. After war broke out in Europe, he opposed every defense measure and said he agreed with Charles Lindbergh that it was the Jews who were eager for war. He opposed aid to Britain, which he called "the greatest aggressor in modern history." And as for helping Russia fight the Nazis, he opposed that too, arguing that Russia was "populated with thieves, human butchers and murderers of religion." In time Nye changed his haircut and changed his clothes to dark suits and white shirts, but he never changed his views. In 1944 North Dakota had had enough and voted him out.

Senator Joseph H. Ball, Republican. St. Paul, Minnesota: On August 31, 1940, a Pennsylvania Central Airlines DC-3 took off from Washington airport in a thunderstorm and made it to Lovettsville, Virginia, where it crashed, killing all aboard, including Senator Ernest Lundeen of Minnesota. In a field in rural Virginia lay the body of one of the U.S. Senate's most virulent isolationists. Governor Harold Stassen of Minnesota appointed in his place a devoted internationalist, Joseph H. Ball, a political writer for the St. Paul *Pioneer Press* who in his first Senate speech denounced isolationism. "We are aware of the ever-growing peril to this nation from the ruthless aggression of the totalitarian states. Only Britain, with her fleet and heroic air force, still stands as a barrier between us and whatever designs Hitler and his allies may have on this continent." His speech, though not so understood at the time, may have marked the end, or the beginning of the end, of Midwestern isolationism in America; few, if any, members of Congress were elected on hard isolationist positions after 1940. Ball's first speech called for repeal of the Neutrality Act, and in March 1941, he voted for lend-lease even though he said his mail from home was twenty-five to one against it. He and his wife had to spend a month touring Minnesota explaining why he had done it. Then he and three other senators introduced a resolution calling for a postwar United Nations and for a system of collective security to keep the peace. Had Lundeen been alive to hear this, he would have choked and turned purple. But Ball never wavered. Isolationism was dying in Minnesota, and in 1942 he was elected to a full six-year term. A world had turned.

There was at least one power that Roosevelt could not take from Congress: the power to tax. And it became clear quickly that the war could not be fought, and certainly could not be won, without new taxes. The war bond drives had been public relations successes but financial failures. The federal budget was soaring to previously unimagined levels: four times the size of the largest New Deal budget, three times the size of the largest World War I budget. Something had to be done. But raising taxes in the 1940s was not as simple as it looked, because the system for collecting them was not equipped for the new burdens about to be placed on it.

The old system, still in place when the war began, was this: Employed people paid taxes, in quarterly installments, not on the current year's income, but on the income they had earned the previous year. Hence, taxpayers began each year in debt to the federal government. It was up to them to find the money when the tax bill came due—to pay last year's income taxes out of this year's income. The system had worked well enough when income taxes were low (and, for most people, nonexistent). But the war, as it pushed the rates ever higher, set a strange series of events in motion. And Congress, without quite realizing what it was doing, found itself approving a measure that would radically change the way American government worked.

It began, curiously enough, in a department store in New York. Beardsley Ruml, a man almost unknown to the public, was an economist and the treasurer of R. H. Macy & Co., owners of Macy's. He noticed that when the store's employees retired and began living on their pensions, they found themselves in immediate financial difficulty. In the first year of living on their lower pension incomes, they had to pay taxes on the last year of their higher employment incomes. Many could not do it. Looking beyond Macy's, Ruml noted that a widow, in the year after her husband's death, had to pay his taxes but did not have his income to pay them with. And looking ahead, Ruml began to wonder what would happen when an employee of Macy's (or any other corporation) would do when he left a $7,500-a-year job and began earning $50 a month in the army. He would owe taxes on his last year of civilian income and would have to pay them with the first year of his draftee's pittance. Clearly this system could not continue.

Ruml's habit, when he perceived a problem, was to lock himself in a room away from distractions—no newspapers, magazines, radio or people—recline for a few hours in a deeply upholstered chair, and allow his mind to float freely in what he called "a state of dispersed attention." Late in 1940, he shut his door and allowed his mind to zoom in and out and around the problem of how government could squeeze more and more money out of people without forcing them into hopeless debt. In the spring of 1941 an idea floated in from somewhere. "Pay-as-you-go," he called it. It was all quite simple, but also revolutionary: let everyone pay this year's taxes this year by having the money deducted from paychecks before he ever sees it. Then, everyone would start each year clean, free of debt.

He introduced the idea early in 1942 by giving a small dinner at the Plaza and explaining his plan to a few of his colleagues in the financial world. (As chairman of the Federal Reserve Bank of New York, he was well connected.) Then he took it to Washington and presented it to the Senate Finance Committee. At that point, it began to encounter opposition— because of an important catch in the proposal. To begin a new year cleanly with a pay-as-you-go system, Ruml argued, it would be necessary to forgive the taxes for the previous year. Otherwise, people would have to pay two years of taxes in one year, an impossible burden for many.

The opposition came less from Congress than from the Treasury and the White House. And it emerged from a very different vision of what the tax system was supposed to do. Randolph Paul, an assistant secretary of the treasury with responsibility for tax policy, was one of the New Dealers who defined liberalism as the constant pursuit of new ways to punish the rich. The purpose of taxation, he believed, was not simply to raise money to support the government, but also to control private behavior. Tax incentives would give government a way to encourage whatever activity it liked and to punish whatever it disliked. Most of all, taxation would be a way to curb the power of the wealthy, to penalize them for making more money than they deserved. Giving rich people a year's tax amnesty was, Paul believed, unconscionable.

Roosevelt had always talked about taxing the rich, but he had seldom done it; most of the new taxes he had approved (including, most prominently, Social Security) had been regressive. But in 1941, Roosevelt was more sympathetic than usual to Paul. He was thinking about proposing a law to limit all individual incomes to twenty-five thousand dollars a year for the duration of the war (a figure the Chicago *Tribune* claimed he had chosen because it was the most money he had ever made himself until he became president). That idea went nowhere, but it suggested that Roosevelt, too, was in no mood for tax forgiveness.

Supporters of the Ruml plan argued that since everyone would continue to pay taxes without interruption, no one would benefit from the amnesty until the last year of his or her working life. But the president was unpersuaded. He seemed convinced that whatever Ruml claimed, whatever anyone claimed, the bill was a trick to benefit the rich. He did nothing to discourage the Treasury Department from attacking it.

For a while, the plan appeared doomed. The Senate Finance Committee voted it down thirteen to three. The House Ways and Means Committee voted it down fifteen to nine. When supporters maneuvered around the committee and brought it to the floor of the House, it lost again. Editorialists were by now writing about the "tax muddle." Gallup polls were reporting that overwhelming majorities—83 percent of Democratic taxpayers and 87 percent of Republicans—supported the Ruml plan. Some members of Congress were charging that the administration was resisting the idea only because the "Treasury didn't think of it first." But liberals continued to balk. "The true content of the proposal," one opponent claimed, was simply to "make the rich richer and the poor poorer." And the president continued to promise to veto any bill that contained a tax-forgiveness clause.

Democracy was at work, producing paralysis. Everyone agreed that the tax system was not working. Everyone (including the president) agreed that the pay-as-you-go system would work better. But bitter disagreements over a one-time (and largely imaginary) "windfall" for the wealthy had brought the whole process to a halt. Finally, Congress produced a bill that included a year's forgiveness for lower-income people, and only a partial forgiveness for the wealthy. Conservatives complained that it discriminated against the wealthy. The president did not mind that at all. He signed it. It took effect on July 1, 1943.

The prolonged battle over the immediate effects of the plan had, apparently, prevented anyone from looking closely at the potential long-range results. For Beardsley Ruml, from his locked room and his overstuffed chair, had produced a revolution in American public finance. When people became accustomed to paying taxes as they had always paid for automobiles—on the installment plan—Congress and the president learned, to their pleasure, what automobile salesmen had learned long before: that installment buyers could be induced to pay more because they looked not at the total debt but only at the monthly payments. And in this case there was, for government, the added psychological advantage that people were paying their taxes with not much resistance because they were paying with money they had never even seen. The term "take-home pay" now entered the language.

The war was progressing in 1943, but no one could yet see the end. And in Congress, a nervous fear was rising among Republicans, and even among some Democrats, that Franklin Roosevelt—using the unfinished war as an excuse—would run for a fourth term in 1944. Would those who detested FDR—an increasing number—ever see the last of him? A president who had already defied a tradition dating back to George

Washington and won a third term? Could he possibly consider a fourth? Could he be defeated if he did? The Republicans did what they could to poison the air. And unable (or unwilling) to criticize the administration's conduct of the war, they turned to other, less momentous issues.

Such as the government purchase of Blair House, a handsome eighteenth-century residence across Pennsylvania Avenue from the White House. Washington was being flooded with important visitors, so many the White House could not accommodate them—kings, queens, presidents, prime ministers; and such others as Vyacheslav Molotov, the Soviet foreign minister, who arrived carrying a suitcase filled with brown bread, sausages and a pistol, and whose first request, after his meetings with the president, was to be driven down to Virginia to tour Luray Caverns. The government had needed a guest house, and it had bought one.

William Langer of North Dakota, known with good reason as "Wild Bill," took the Senate floor and spoke, as he always did, in a furious roar, the spittle flying, the noise bouncing off the ceiling and out the open doors and down the arched and columned corridors. "So we have a president of the United States in the White House but he gives his house away to Mr. [Harry] Hopkins! Mr. Hopkins lives there! So, when some of these kings and queens, dukes and duchesses, ex-dukes and ex-duchesses and all the rest of them come to Washington there was no room for them in the White House. What was to be done about it? That was simple. It was said, 'We will buy another house.' . . . The soldier boys can sleep in Union Station on the floor."

Langer unrolled a copy of the *Saturday Evening Post* and read, "Visiting dignitaries have been encouraged to treat Blair House as they would their own homes, to have breakfast in bed if they feel so inclined. . . . " With one eye on the *Post* and the other on the voters in North Dakota, he went on, "A farmer in the Northwest gets up at four o'clock in the morning and goes out when it is twenty degrees below zero and pulls the cows' teats to get a little milk, a little butterfat, to keep his family alive. He is paying for Blair House so that kings and ex-kings and queens and ex-queens can sleep and sleep . . . and have breakfast in bed if they are so inclined!"

No one paid any attention to Langer. But in January 1944 Roosevelt himself presented Congress with an issue it could pay attention to for weeks and months, and did. In a letter saying he was speaking "as an interested citizen" for people who could not speak for themselves, he expressed concern that most of the eleven million servicemen stationed all over the world would be denied the right to vote in that fall's elections. Congress had approved a few symbolic measures to deal with the problem, but they were, Roosevelt claimed, a "fraud on the American people." What the G.I.s deserved was a simple measure allowing the federal government to send them all federal ballots; working through states and localities would be too cumbersome and too slow. Every member of Congress, the president demanded, should stand up and be counted in a roll-call vote so that when the boys came home, they would know who had looked out for their interests and who had let them down.

There was rage in Congress. One senator said to Allen Drury of United Press, "Roosevelt says we're letting the soldiers down. Why, goddamn him! The rest of us have boys who go into the army and navy as privates and ordinary seamen and dig latrines and swab decks and his go in as lieutenant colonels and majors and lieutenants and spend their time getting medals in Hollywood. Letting the soldiers down! That son of a bitch. . . . "

Senator Taft was convinced that Roosevelt's plan was to march the troops to the polls, and line them up under orders to vote for the only name they knew—his own; to line them up as WPA workers had been lined up at the polls in past elections. Brutal and high-handed interference by the president in the work of the Congress, he said in the iciest tones of a man whose tones were never warm—manipulating the votes of eleven million men to get himself elected to a fourth term and making it appear that if Congress refused it was betraying our men in uniform. "Goddamn him!"

Roosevelt's bill asked that soldiers using the federal ballot not be required to pay any poll tax. That question, already fought out once, had returned to enrage the Southerners again. Particularly John Rankin of Mississippi. He was never sure which he hated most: blacks, Jews, communists or some combination of the three. But he leaned toward blacks, since there were more of them in Mississippi. He stood up in the House, read the names of Jews supporting Roosevelt's bill, and proclaimed, "Now who is behind this bill? The chief publicist is *PM,* the uptown edition of the Communist *Daily Worker* that is being financed by the tax-escaping fortune of Marshall Field III, and the chief broadcaster for it is Walter Winchell, alias no telling what."

Hearing his cue, a conservative Republican asked, "Who is he?"

"The little kike I was telling you about the other day, who called this body the 'House of Reprehensibles.' "

Republicans and Southerners together could not defeat the bill outright, as they would have liked. But they could, they hoped, defeat it indirectly by insisting that state and local ballots be sent to the camps and battlefronts along with the federal ballot. That, everyone knew, would be impossible. Senator Scott Lucas of Illinois explained the problem:

The army and navy have definitely stated that they cannot han-dle the ballots from every state in the Union. We have one hundred two counties in Illinois. We have one hundred two different kinds of tickets in Illinois. If the army and navy are going to carry state ballots in the same manner as they carry the uniform federal ballots, they will have to carry one hundred two Illinois ballots to every camp in this country and every camp overseas . . . sixty days would be required before a directory could be prepared giving [the servicemen's] addresses and at the end of the sixty days six to eight hundred thousand of them would have moved from where they were when the cataloguing process was started. Every day ten thousand men are moving to new locations. All one has to do is ride on a train and see the number of servicemen coming and going everywhere.

Taft, still furious, responded: "I challenge the assertion of the army and navy that they cannot carry by air two hundred fifty tons of ballots. I am told that today nearly ten thousand tons are being carried by air over the 'hump' in China, the most difficult place in the world for flying. Now, in order to conduct an election, they cannot carry two hundred fifty tons by air?"

The truth was less dramatic and less political, and it never was clear where Taft got the figure of 250 tons he kept talking about. In 1944 there were 48 states and within them 3,050 counties, plus the cities, all having their own ballots for mayors, councilmen, sheriffs, governors, state legislators, county commissioners, county attorneys, prosecutors, and beyond that there were uncounted other political entities holding elections—school, water and utility districts—and the total number of ballots from all these elections would surpass 5,000. The military services insisted that it was physically impossible to send each uniformed man and woman an individual set of ballots from his own home state, county and city, and that if instead they had to send each one the entire pile, each set of all these ballots in envelopes with return envelopes would make a stack of paper more than four feet high. And if each ballot with its two envelopes weighed an ounce and a half, they estimated the total weight at 160,000 tons, an impossible load to fly overseas and back.

The argument went on for days and turned nastier by the hour. Republican Senator Edward Moore of Oklahoma made a flaming speech against the bill, to which Lucas responded, "And someday, somewhere, if these boys have not the opportunity to vote, some one-armed veteran from Italy or from some island battle will be running against the senator in Oklahoma and will remind him of the time he was denied the right to vote when he was over there saving his country. He will throw his empty sleeve into his face in that campaign and he will tell him about it. And he will get results."

The measure was amended. The amendments were amended. And at the end, everything of substance had been taken out. The final bill sent to Roosevelt's desk was a squeezed lemon. He was unwilling to sign it and unwilling to veto it, so he did nothing and let it become law without his signature. Most overseas servicemen did not vote—and Roosevelt won his fourth term without them.

There was great lamentation in Washington at the performance of the Congress of the United States. Richard L. Strout in the *New Republic* said,

> The trouble in Washington goes deeper than the men. . . . The basic fact in Washington under the division of powers is the absence of final responsibility. You can never fix the blame. . . . Only a nation supremely gifted in self-government could make a system like this work for 150 years. But now it is in competition with tiger-swift dictatorships. On the answer to the question— can we have efficiency and still have Congress?—may rest the future of democracy in America.

Strout and others advocated some version of the European parliamentary system, where leadership is centered in the majority party and in the party's own choice for head of government and where blame can always be assigned. Yet it was not clear either before the war or after that the European parliaments performed with any greater efficiency. With greater dignity and more fastidious language perhaps, since many of their members were, or said they were, of aristocratic heritage, while the American politician's little joke was that "in this country *everybody* can run for Congress and almost everybody does." And since in European parliaments many members considered public office a part-time duty, while most members of Congress saw it as a career, a job, a living.

Most of them were of modest origins. About 90 percent had been born soon after the Civil War, figures from a Victorian past, among them Southerners still embittered from growing up in a post–Civil War Reconstruction that had only reconstructed them into isolation and poverty. (Mississippi, the state most embittered and the most desolately poor, elected the two most embarrassing members of the wartime Congresses, John Rankin and Theodore Bilbo.) All these nineteenth-century personalities remembered, also in bitterness, World War I, just over twenty years past. Many of them had served in it, and few of them could see where the expenditure of money and blood had produced any benefit to Americans. And all of them, without exception, had grown up in a country where the president of the United States had usually been a remote figure doing little, where Congress had done whatever it wanted to do, which was seldom very much; a country where the churches and the Salvation Army, not the government, fed the poor; where anyone able to make money was able to keep it; where most people's government business was done with people they knew by name at the city hall or the county courthouse, not with a forbidding and unfamiliar New Deal bureaucracy with a staff of a hundred thousand people.

It was not the system that made the wartime Congresses unruly, politicized, argumentative, unresponsive and occasionally vulgar. It was the course of American history.

IX

The Strains of the New

A littered stairway led up from Fourteenth and H streets to the Casino Royal night club where the Saturday night crowd had been asked to leave the dance floor. The show was about to begin. The spotlight came up, doing its best to penetrate the stagnant layers of smoke from the Camels, Lucky Strikes, Chesterfields and Old Golds. The thin beam it was able to force through the polluted air centered on the small stage and the six-piece band. There was a drum roll, rim shots, a trumpet sting and out to the stage, doing a little soft-shoe dance, came Jack "Jive" Shaffer, the comic and bandleader. He was plump, bald, red-faced and all pink and green clothes, rhinestone cuff links and clear nail polish. And showing the wear of too many years in night clubs with the fumes of sweat, smoke and whiskey forcing out the oxygen, years of too many jokes and not enough laughs. He looked up at the man aiming the spotlight and said, "Hey, can't you guys find me a spotlight with hair on it?"

The laughter was thin, scattered and brief, and even then they were laughing not at his joke but at him. But he knew this was an impossible audience anyway. They were not your nice, neat married couples from the tract houses in Silver Spring, in town to spend their carefully calculated entertainment budget. Mostly they were soldiers, sailors and marines from a dozen military stations within a bus ride of Washington, some of the fifteen thousand who poured in every Saturday looking for whatever entertainment they could find before their passes expired on Sunday. They were willing to settle for anything. On Saturday night they hoped to find a bed to climb into, alone if necessary or with an agreeable woman if possible. But now there were rapidly diminishing prospects for both. As for beds, it was already too late. The fairly decent ones in the church basements and the military shelters would all be filled by now. And the Wacs, Waves and women marines they had brought with them to the Casino Royal were required to be back in their quarters in an hour or two. Their time was short, their money shorter and their desperation rising. Soon the women would be gone and unless some other amusement turned up—now increasingly unlikely—they would have to spend the night trying to sleep on the benches in Union Station or in the chairs in hotel lobbies and the YMCA, alone.

"Hey, how about the president's new plan to deduct your taxes in advance? He calls it pay as you go! But after you pay, where can you go?"

Now they were not listening at all, and even when the members of the band tried to laugh it up there was no response. The customers were intent solely on each other, the clock, and the drink the Casino Royal was serving, claiming it was whiskey and charging as if it were. It was something labeled "Scotch type" whiskey, made in Chicago mostly of water and God knew what else, and tasting of brown grocery bags. When the waiter brought a drink, the watery whiskey, and not much of it, had been watered still further with District of Columbia tap water from the Potomac River. The Casino Royal had few problems with drunks.

"Hey, you hear the news? FDR's Christmas present to Hirohito? A deep sea diving suit so he can go down and inspect his navy."

Six sailors and Waves at a table laughed. The soldiers and Wacs at the next table did not. Interservice insults were exchanged. An interservice fist fight started. Other uniformed men ran to take sides and join in. A table was overturned, glasses were shattered, whiskey spilled. The Casino Royal management had dealt with this so often before, night after night, it had its plan to stop fights carefully worked out, put on paper and posted on a wall backstage under the heading "TO STOP DISTURBANCE." The plan was: (1) lower the house lights; (2) turn the spotlight on a large American flag hanging from the ceiling; (3) start up an electric fan aimed at the flag, causing it to flutter; (4) have the band instantly stop playing dance music and strike up "The Star-Spangled Banner"; and (5) call in the military police and the navy's shore patrol.

It always worked. The soldiers and sailors stopped swinging at each other, faced the flag and stood at attention while the band played. There was no way a uniformed military man in wartime could refuse to do this, however angry he was. Before the anthem was finished, the military police and the shore patrol were walking up the steps from Fourteenth Street.

Washington had always been home to many strangers: members of Congress and their staffs, who came to the city on short-term leases from voters and who were often summoned home almost before they unpacked; officials in the executive agencies whose jobs disappeared with every change in administration, sometimes sooner; lobbyists, diplomats, soldiers, sailors, journalists and others who came to Washington because their employers sent them there and who left when their employers told them to leave. The city had been accustomed to transients since its birth in the early nineteenth century, when most members of the government were in town for only a few months of the year and lived crammed into boarding houses on Capitol Hill chafing to get done and return to their families. It had learned to absorb them, even to like them. But it had also learned to ignore them. The "real" Washington, most residents had always believed, was the permanent population: the cave dwellers, the civil servants, the business and professional communities. Their lives moved in the same stable patterns year after year, regardless of the changes in the political tides.

But not even the oldest and most-established Washingtonians could ignore the flood of strangers pouring into the city during the war. Between 1940 and 1945, the population nearly doubled. The town was filling up with men and women far from home—hundreds, even thousands more of them every week—people trying to live and work and, when possible, entertain themselves in a city ill equipped to accommodate them. "Old-timers in Washington know how the Indians felt when the hunters and trappers came to their forests," the New York *Times* commented in 1943, "how the cattlemen felt when the settlers staked claims upon their range." The result was an undercurrent of frustration and anxiety that ran through the community at almost every level and that occasionally burst to the surface. "Washington the capital is running the greatest war in history," one journalist wrote at the time. "Washington the city is a powder keg, waiting to explode."

But it never did explode. Instead, it began to adjust to a new form of existence: more harried, more crowded, more contentious, faster, lonelier, bigger. And while some of the strains of wartime would subside when the fighting was over, the city would never again live by its old rules.

Washington did not give up its small-town ways without a fight. It drew battle lines everywhere, struggled fiercely and usually lost, perhaps nowhere more clearly than in its war against vice.

The terms of that war had been set in part by Franklin Roosevelt. In 1933, as Prohibition came to an end, the president had personally written the new liquor law for the District of Columbia, hoping it would become a model for the rest of the nation. He was intent above all on preventing the return of the malodorous nineteenth-century saloon with its drunks at the bar swaying, stumbling and starting fights. So Roosevelt's law forbade any customer from being served anything alcoholic while standing up. People seated on bar stools could drink beer and wine. For hard liquor, customers had to sit at tables and be served by waiters. And in deference to the churches, the law required all bars to close at midnight on Saturdays.

The law was still on the books, and still enforced, when thousands of soldiers, sailors and marines began flooding into the city on wartime Saturday nights. By midnight, the Casino Royal and places like it were closed. The G.I.s, many of them drunk, all of them restless, poured out into the streets looking for beds somewhere or looking for entertainment and adventure.

On a Saturday night in March 1943, ninety-three city police officers and a detail of military police were assembled in the guardroom at Union Station. They thought they were there to escort an arriving dignitary whose name, because of wartime secrecy, could not be revealed. But at midnight Inspector Harvey Callahan called them to attention and told them that their mission was to raid a hotel near Logan Circle that the police vice squad had discovered was a house of prostitution.

In its prewar years of easy and comfortable torpor, Washington had regarded prostitution as a fairly minor nuisance, and its few feeble attempts to suppress it had been left to a small vice squad, led by Detective Sergeant Roy Blick. Blick used his one good eye to search out prostitutes who broke the rules by accosting respectable businessmen, government officials, members of Congress and diplomats, but only if those accosted complained. His more frequent occupation was to send his squad into men's rooms at Union Station or the bus depots, or on raids of Lafayette Park across from the White House in a clownish pursuit of homosexuals, whom Blick always called "queers."

By 1943, under pressure from the U.S. Army, Blick had discarded these casual tactics and become more aggressive. And on this March Saturday night, the police, after receiving their orders, moved in silence to Logan Circle, parked their cars out of sight, threw a cordon around the hotel, blocked every entrance, broke down a door and charged in. What they found was a crowded, noisy, thriving commercial enterprise in full pursuit of money and sexual adventure—downstairs a blaring jukebox was playing records by the Andrews Sisters, a dice game with what Blick called "mammoth" stakes, beer and liquor were being sold after hours and with no license. There was enough sin here for any taste.

Upstairs, they found a crowded waiting room, and a hallway jammed all the way down to the front door with a line of men, mainly soldiers, waiting their turn. In strode Brigadier General Albert L. Cox, commander of the D.C. national guard, who arrived with the military police. The soldiers standing in line did not yet know it was a raid and thought he was just another customer until, red-faced and furious, he shouted, "You're all under arrest. And goddamn it, why don't you *salute?*"

There was a confused and disorderly retreat, the soldiers kicking and scrambling to get out before anyone could take their names and serial numbers. But it was too late. When they were all rounded up, the police had arrested 171 people, including 52 men in uniform.

Washington's new concern with vice was forced on it by the military.

The army said that across the country it had already lost the equivalent of four divisions because there were sixty thousand men with syphilis or gonorrhea it had been unable to draft. Now it demanded that Washington clean its streets and shut down its bordellos to protect its men from disease. Some commanders hinted that if this was not done, the city might be placed off limits to troops on leave. The capital of the United States off limits to its own army because it was drenched with venereal disease? The humiliation would have been intolerable, an embarrassment of historic dimensions. The police responded with vigor.

Under this kind of pressure, nothing was safe any longer. At 2701 Connecticut Avenue stood an apartment building of dark, heavy stone with the appearance of sober upper-middle-class respectability—a residence for lawyers, substantial merchants and a number of rich widows, a handsome place at a prestigious address. Few residents noticed that in the yellow pages of the telephone book was an advertisement for an establishment at 2701 called The Hopkins Institute. Some sort of health and exercise place, it appeared, offering such health-giving services as massages, steam baths and high colonics. Its clientele included members of Congress and other prominent figures. But disturbing reports began reaching Roy Blick and his vice squad, reports that "patients," as the institute called them, were accepted only on recommendation of other patients, and that a new arrival was given a routine massage and then informed that other restorative services were available at additional cost. The Hopkins Institute was a whorehouse.

Blick raided it and discovered eleven women established in splendidly elegant rooms. And, to the extreme discomfort of a number of men of high position, Blick also found a book listing not only the names of the customers but also the nature of services they preferred and the prices they had paid. When the *Post* reported the existence of the book, terror struck the institute's patrons all over town. The city prosecutor, Jack Fihelly, received frightened telephone calls from dozens of men asking if their names were listed. He declined to answer. And the next question, racing by telephone from office to office was, "Dear God, will it be made public in the trial?" It never was. A judge ordered the book turned over to the FBI, and J. Edgar Hoover added it to his personal and private file of embarrassing evidence and gossip he used when needed for persuasion and threats.

Another and more modest bordello, on the fifth floor of an apartment building on Fourteenth a block or two from Clifton Street, was never raided. Perhaps because it had a business policy not previously known in the prostitution profession—it was closed at night. Its hours were nine to five, and the idea, shrewdly thought out, was that a businessman could leave his office during the day, presumably to call on a client or see his dentist, ride the trolley up Fourteenth Street, pay a visit, return to his office and then home at night with no one, including his wife, any the wiser. Since no customer could return to his office smelling of whiskey, nothing alcoholic was served. Instead there were tea, coffee and chocolate chip cookies baked in the apartment's own kitchen. The waiting room was supplied with newspapers and the *National Geographic.* The place thrived during the war, closed soon after, and the owner retired and lived under another name in a house on Bradley Boulevard in suburban Bethesda, Maryland. Years later she said, "I just thought of myself as a businesswoman, supplying a service to relax some of the tensions of the war. I followed a basic principle of business—keep the store open at hours when your customers can get there. And by closing at night, I avoided problems with drunks and suspicious wives, and Roy Blick never bothered me."

There was a joke that made the rounds of wartime Washington. A man crossing the Fourteenth Street bridge looked down into the Potomac and saw another man drowning. "What's your name and address?" he shouted to him and then ran off to see the drowning man's landlord. He asked to rent the now-vacant room and was told it was already taken. "But I just left him drowning in the river," he protested. "That's right," the landlord replied, "but the man who pushed him in got here first."

Nothing was harder in Washington than finding a decent place to live. Even high-ranking government officials, heads of war agencies, members of Congress and cabinet members had to camp out in hotels. Harry Truman, for example, spent his first Washington years living in a small hotel room across the street from the Capitol while his wife and daughter stayed home in Independence. Jesse Jones, Leon Henderson and at least a dozen other ranking federal officials lived at the Shoreham Hotel near Rock Creek Park. And they were the lucky ones. Owners of private homes were pressured to rent out extra rooms and often charged exorbitantly for spaces little larger than broom closets, with bathroom privileges during certain hours only. Houseboat colonies sprang up along the Potomac turning parts of the waterfront into a sea of shabby vessels with towels and socks and underwear hanging to dry from the masts.

The search for bed and board became an obsession, and at times an adventure. Young men and women new to town stood outside newspaper offices at press time to grab the first editions and thus the first look at the classified ads for rooms for rent. The next task was to decipher the cryptic descriptions of what space and amenities were offered. "Kit priv," of course, meant kitchen privileges. But what else did it mean? Access to the kitchen only at hours specified by the landlord? The use of only certain shelves in the refrigerator? One ad said, "Kit priv no cabbage garlic onions." What other rules would be announced after a homeless supplicant had paid the rent in advance and moved in?

Kenneth Banghart, an NBC radio announcer experienced in the sociology of Washington rentals and landlords, had these suggestions for newcomers: When you answer an ad and go to the house, look most carefully at the bathroom. Ask exactly how many people will be using it and ask about their work schedules. Then look around the bathroom for any little hand-written signs stuck on the wall such as "No clothes drying on the shower rod." Or "No reading in the bathroom," or "50-cent extra charge if light left on." Banghart's advice: "If you see any signs like that, leave. Because you know the landlord is a crabby son of a bitch. He'll pester you all the time. Every day he will announce some silly-ass new rule."

A woman near 35th and O streets in Georgetown advertised a basement apartment for seventy-five dollars. Applicants came by the dozens. She interviewed each one in embarrassing detail, inquiring about personal habits of every description—sexual, religious, social, dietary, working, sleeping. But since housing, any housing, was entirely a seller's market, applicants could refuse to answer her questions only at the risk of having to deal with another landlord even worse—or they could lie. Finally, behaving as if she were awarding the Nobel peace prize, she rented it to a young man named Walter Royen, who did do some lying. He promised to have no pets and no parties, to maintain a monastic silence, total sexual abstinence and complete sobriety, and to pay the rent promptly and in advance. He also agreed to keep her yard cleaned and mowed.

His troubles began when he discovered that the apartment, below ground and windowless, was so damp and airless his shoes mildewed, his typewriter rusted and the wallpaper slid downward off the walls into sticky coils on the floor. The end came when a young woman friend stopped by one morning on her way to work to have breakfast with him. The landlady, always spying, observed her leaving at 8 a.m., had not seen her arrive a half-hour earlier, and quickly concluded that unbridled licentiousness was occurring downstairs under her very feet. She ordered Royen out.

On Wisconsin Avenue at Hall Place, a middle-aged woman and her mother accepted a male roomer, not saying that he had to share the one bath with the two of them. They allowed no radios after 9 p.m., no pets, no use of the kitchen or the telephone and no smoking. When he sneaked cigarettes, they collected the butts and lined them up on a paper towel on his dresser along with threatening notes. In the bathroom the mother's spare set of dentures was always grinning at him from inside a glass of water, and every day her wet, dripping pink bloomers were festooned across clotheslines in the bathroom, making it resemble the inside of a sultan's tent. He had to climb through them to the mirror to shave. He left.

It was not always so nasty. In 1943, a young reporter, new to Washington, answered an ad offering a room for rent in a house on Windom Place. He found it to be one of Washington's typical 1930s houses—pink brick, two-story "colonial" with a patch of grass in front, a concrete walk leading up to a white doorway and two pointy cedars standing symmetrically beside the steps.

Answering the door was an attractive woman in her thirties, red-haired, green-eyed, and hesitant to open the door to a man she did not know. The room offered for rent was upstairs in the back. Her own bedroom adjoined it, a double-width sliding door between them. The door was standing open. While he examined the room she examined him.

"My husband's a major in the army. When I'm here alone I keep that sliding door open. Better air circulation on hot nights."

"It's very nice. How much is the room?"

"Well, I haven't decided exactly. Do you like it?"

As Washington rentals went in the 1940s, it was far better than most. A walnut four-poster double bed, a white candlewick bedspread, a couple of chairs, lamps and a dresser. It had a separate bathroom with no hand-lettered signs in it. Its windows looked out into maple trees. In the background were the sounds of traffic out on Massachusetts Avenue. On the walls were framed and matted arrangements of dried wildflowers. Pretty.

"I made those myself. Sort of a hobby. I grow the flowers out back—gives you something to do when you're alone. My husband's been away two years now, in Europe. My mother had this room until a year ago. She hated Washington. Moved back home to Florida."

She wanted to talk, a lonely woman in a lonely city crowded with new people who did not know each other and would never know each other. She was tense, pacing the room, straightening her wildflower pictures, pulling a corner to straighten a bedspread already straight, turning a lamp on and off and asking who he was and where he came from and what he did. His answers seemed to please her.

"The room is very nice. How much?"

"You know, I don't need the money, really. I've thought a long time about doing this. These classified ads, it's a gamble. You could wind up with some bum in the house. Some slob."

"Then why are you doing it?"

"Roosevelt says it's our patriotic duty," she said with a little smirk. "But, really, it would be nice to have somebody around to talk to, I guess. Soon as we bought this house they sent him overseas and left me stuck here alone. He's been gone two years and he never writes. I don't know anybody in Washington but a few women, all army. Their husbands are away, too. We play bridge, four women, somebody makes a casserole and a salad and I come home and go to bed alone. You understand, don't you?"

"Yes. I can see you don't like to talk about money but if you want to rent the room you have to tell me what the deal is."

She paused, fluffed a pillow, hesitated again, looked out the window. There was no sound but the L4 bus groaning up the Massachusetts Avenue hill toward American University. It was late, half-dark now, the sun descending into Virginia across the Potomac. She had to force herself to say it. "The room is fifty dollars a month if you want total privacy, if you want to keep the sliding door closed and stay to yourself. If you want to leave it open and be sociable, talk to me, it's twenty-five dollars and the whole house is yours and I'll give you breakfast."

She looked almost frightened, as if she had stripped herself naked before a stranger. Her hands shook. She fluffed the same pillow again.

Nobody said anything. He pretended to examine the framed wild violets and yellow asters.

"Suppose your husband comes home?"

"He never comes. Maybe when the war's over. By then you'll have your own apartment. But he won't come. He won't even write. It's not one of your great marriages."

He wondered how many women like this there were in Washington. Was it true, all those cute stories he'd read? All that stuff in *Newsweek* and so on about Washington having ten women to every man? True or not, what if the major did come home on leave and find him alone in the house with his wife? Suppose he arrived, full of military zeal and bravado, carrying in his bag the .45 Browning automatic issued to all officers? Suppose on his way home he stopped at the flower stand in Union Station and bought her a few roses? He considered the possibility of hearing (or even worse, not hearing) a taxi door slam at 2 a.m. out on Windom Place and the major, bearing roses for his wife, striding purposefully up the stairs and into the bedroom. No.

"You are very nice and the room is very nice, but I have another place to look at and I'll let you know."

She knew it was a lie. "My husband will not come until the war is over. He may not even come then. If you like the room you ought to take it."

"Thank you. I'll let you know."

The housing crisis was worst for blacks. Their community was growing at least as fast as that of whites, but the housing stock available to them was actually diminishing. One government committee entitled a report on the problem "Shrinking Negro Neighborhoods" and recounted in depressing detail how the federal government time and again appropriated land on which black homes stood when it needed space for some new structure. Two hundred black families were displaced from buildings that once stood on the site of the Pentagon. When Arlington National Cemetery was expanded in 1943, several hundred more families were forced to move. In Washington itself, black homes were demolished, the same report noted, to make way for "government buildings, highways,

schools and recreational facilities; and no compensating housing has
been built." Virtually all the new housing being constructed in Washington during the war was restricted to whites. The new neighborhoods,
like the old ones, were governed by covenants forbidding owners to sell
or rent to blacks. "In Washington," an official of the National Capital
Housing Authority wrote in 1943,

> the white population is very conscious of Negro expansion into
> areas formerly occupied by whites, but is scarcely aware of white
> expansion into areas formerly occupied by Negroes. . . . The net
> result is the loss of territory by Negroes.

One by one, former black neighborhoods disappeared. "The West
End, known as Foggy Bottom, was once a good-sized Negro community,"
one housing authority wrote shortly after the war. "The Negro population has been steadily reduced. The land has been taken over piece by
piece for white luxury apartment buildings, government buildings, among
them the new State Department, additions to George Washington University, and most recently, the new George Washington University Hospital." Georgetown, once home to hundreds of black families, had by
the late 1930s evolved into the fashionable community it remains today.

Housing for whites did expand, and expand rapidly, throughout the war,
but never nearly fast enough to meet the demand. Private contractors
tried their best to cash in on the need for housing, and new suburban
developments began to spring up so fast that community services could
not keep up with them. Arlington County, home of the Pentagon and
thus of large numbers of defense workers, had the worst problems. "We
live in Arlington," a Mrs. McGuire, mother of a nine-year-old girl, told a
reporter for the Washington *Daily News* in 1943, "but the Arlington
schools are too crowded—they won't take elementary school students."
School officials were touchy. "It isn't any newspaper's business whether
Arlington schools are too crowded," a spokesman for the superintendent
snapped at the same reporter. "Why don't you stop snooping around?"

But it didn't take much snooping for the problems of the exploding
Arlington suburbs to be obvious. The county's sewage system was obsolete even before Pearl Harbor, and local officials were pleading with

Congress to help them pay the several million dollars needed to expand capacity. They got the money, but they could never keep up. In March 1943, county authorities had to evict families from a group of homes in the new Columbia Forest development because, the *Evening Star* reported, they had been "living since January without sewer service on a street pitted with yawning holes filled six feet or more deep with water." Complaints about such conditions even reached Capitol Hill. One representative rose in 1943 to ask, portentously, "Shall we members of Congress submit to such a program of inexcusable disregard of our health and die like flies by reason of infection and contagion? . . . Officers of the Army and the Navy have come to tell me that they are more worried about losing their wives and children from disease . . . than they are about losing their own lives in the front lines of battle."

Even the most conscientious efforts seemed to flounder. Early in 1942, the Defense Homes Corporation—a New Deal–like agency set up to construct government-financed housing for war workers—began construction of an ambitious development: Fairlington, just south of the Pentagon. Acres of farm land were to be the site of Williamsburg-style red-brick garden apartments for 3500 families, a self-contained community with its own schools and services. By the summer of 1943, nearly 1000 families were already in residence, with another 150 moving in every month. They arrived to find no schools, no stores, few paved streets, inadequate garbage pickup and almost no public transportation. The promised sixteen-room school consisted only of a foundation. If all went well, residents were told, two rooms might be open by Christmas. The proposed shopping center was nowhere to be seen. Housewives had to walk up to three-quarters of a mile along unpaved streets and across muddy fields, children in tow, to the town's only bus stop, there to wait for one of the two buses a day that linked the community to downtown Alexandria; all that to buy even as little as a quart of milk. "No matter how you plan, you forget an item or two," one Fairlington resident complained. "I even bought a bike to ride back and forth to the store— but there isn't any store to ride to." Those who worked at the Pentagon or other government buildings had to tramp through the same muddy streets and fields and wait in long lines, sometimes for hours, for the same overcrowded buses; it took them up to two hours sometimes to travel the few miles to work.

Fairlington at least had sturdy, well-designed housing (most of it still

standing today and now expensive townhouses and condominiums).
Much government-financed war housing was shabby, makeshift and
explicitly temporary—the residential equivalents of the dreary temporary buildings that now lined the Mall and surrounded the Washington
Monument. All across the District, spilling into Maryland and Virginia,
emergency housing developments were springing up—known in the
trade as "demolishables," "demountables" and "T.D.U.s" (temporary
dwelling units). "It would be difficult for anyone, whatever his architectural convictions and planning prejudices, to make the grand tour of
Washington's housing without coming out sadder as well as wiser,"
Architectural Forum commented in early 1944.

Major Cannon R. Page of the 1st Army Corps sat in his office contemplating the new decision to allow young women to serve in uniform—
Wacs in the army, and in the navy Waves. "What in hell are we supposed
to do with them?" he complained. "Young girls away from home the first
time and thrown in here with all these horny enlisted men? Does the
army want to send a girl home to her mother with the clap? Or pregnant?
It's going to be a goddamned mess!"

For the most part, it wasn't. The Wacs and the Waves proved valuable,
even indispensable to the military and became a permanent part of the
armed services, paving the way for their full integration in the 1970s
and 1980s. But for them, too, Washington in wartime was a strange and at
times difficult place.

The army and navy began an energetic program of building quarters
("duration residences," they were called) for their new women. On
Nebraska Avenue, across from the Mount Vernon Seminary which the
navy had seized, temporary plywood housing originally designed for
male sailors was, at the last minute, reassigned to the Waves. Young
women arrived from all over America to live in rows of cubicles, about
sixty square feet each, with shelves, lockers for clothes, bunk beds and
little else. The bathrooms were communal, designed for men, and were
outfitted with rows of wall-hung urinals. In each urinal the Waves placed
a potted geranium.

Many years later Vivian Ronca, a wartime Wave, recalled life in
Quarters B on Nebraska Avenue. "The girls complained about being
assigned to Washington because they thought there were no men here.

But there were plenty, an abundance of young men. We'd go down to F Street, the shopping street, and wander around, and there were men all over. We'd just bump into them on the street. A lot of girls whose home towns were boring found Washington exciting. Many of them were married here. I was."

But it was not easy to arrange her wedding in wartime Washington. Her schedule was rigid—after one week at work she was allowed twenty-four hours off, after two weeks forty-eight hours, three weeks seventy-two hours.

"I was married on my seventy-two-hour weekend and then had to be back at work as usual. I had to get special permission to wear a bridal gown and special permission to go away in a white uniform. Always had orders on what we could wear, wedding day or any day.

"After a time our barracks were so crowded they allowed the married girls to move out and live elsewhere. Some of the girls married just to get out of the barracks.

"Some of them came into the navy expecting glamor and fun and games but found hard work and long hours and hated it, wanted to get out so badly. Some of those who wanted out tried to get pregnant and get a bad conduct discharge.

"People would come up to you in the street and say nice things to you. If you were on the street in uniform at 11:30 a.m. and had to be at work at noon, a dozen people would stop and offer you a ride to work. At bus stops, people always stopped their cars and offered rides. On the trolley cars they even wanted to give you their seats. Can you imagine that?"

One day, Eleanor Roosevelt rode out to Quarters B in the president's White House limousine, parked it in front, and invited the Waves to climb in, sit down for a moment, and climb out the other side and let another crawl in. "Write home," she said, "and tell your mothers you've sat in President Roosevelt's limousine."

She wanted to assure them that there was nothing wrong about a woman serving in uniform since, as Vivian Ronca recalled, "At that time there was a stigma in some places, not Washington, as if we were supposed to be prostitutes or something. Eleanor came to encourage us. She even took some of the girls over to the White House and gave them a private tour."

In these navy barracks on one long block of Nebraska Avenue were as many as two thousand young women, and so on summer evenings soldiers, sailors and marines stationed in the city, along with the few young male civilians who were still around, found their way there by the hundreds. They sat on the steps of the barracks, on the curbs or on the grass and leaned back against the trees in the still partly wooded neighborhood. They talked of home and jobs and the war and what they hoped to do when it was over if they survived and their lives were again their own. Then the men began bringing over small radios and long extension cords to run up through the barracks windows to the electric outlets inside. (The transistor had yet to be invented.) They sat on blankets on the grass and listened to the dance bands. Males were not allowed inside the buildings, and so in good weather it became a huge street-and-grass party with the men bringing blankets and paper sacks of fried chicken and potato salad—all patrolled by the navy. From this grassy, wooded area (oddly enough, the future site of the Japanese ambassador's residence) came the sounds of talk, laughter and a radio playing Artie Shaw's Gramercy Five. They were young and away from home and in these hours it was sweet.

"But all in all," Vivian Ronca remembered, "it was a lonely experience, so far removed from anyone you ever knew. Holidays were sad times. In the barracks you'd have Christmas and Thanksgiving dinner all by yourself. But we thought we were ever so much more comfortable than the boys overseas getting shot."

The first Wave commissioned officers came to Washington in late 1942 from navy training at Mount Holyoke College. One of them was Ellen Beckman, a former teacher, now a navy ensign. Years later she remembered. "We arrived just before Christmas and the navy had no place for us to stay. We were sent to the YWCA at Seventeenth and K, and they gave us five days to find another room."

On Christmas Day, the tireless Eleanor Roosevelt came to the YWCA and sat in the lounge and talked to the new officers. What was their most serious problem? Housing, of course. "I wish I could accommodate all of you in the White House," she told them, "but it's jammed with people and half of them I don't even know who they are. One of my sons came to Washington and we had to send him to a hotel."

Before her five-day deadline, Ensign Beckman found a room in a house "run by an old fuddy-duddy and his wife. As a patriotic gesture they kept turning off the heat. I was working in the navy code room all night, eleven at night until seven in the morning, and so I had to sleep during the day. The landlord didn't like it. So I moved.

"In the code room everything was so secret we could not let the janitors in at night and so we had to burn our own trash right there in the office.

"I rode the trolleys home and they kept getting new motormen brought in from out of town, they didn't know the streets and at the switching points at intersections they had to ask the passengers which way the car was supposed to go. We told them.

"The navy paid me thirty dollars a month for meals. It wasn't enough. I had to eat at People's Drug Stores lunch counters. So it helped to get invited out. There was a rule against officers dating enlisted men, but that broke down completely and nobody tried to enforce it. I think the admirals were kind of amused by the girls."

Lorraine Inman sat at a typewriter in the Army Exchange Service, headquarters for the PX's (post exchanges) on army bases around the world, and there, like thousands of other young women newly hired, she fought Washington's paper war, sometimes typing reports with twenty carbons and having to erase all twenty to correct every mistake. Fifty-four hours of this every week for twenty-eight dollars. Her immediate task was to issue tobacco allocation cards entitling officers to buy a set number of cigarettes a week, and to issue allocations for refrigerators for officers' housing and such other items as condoms and hair straightener. It was hard work at low pay in an expensive city, but she was luckier than most of the new women hired by a wartime government. She had always lived in Washington, had gone to work for the army when she graduated from Eastern High School in 1942, and so had escaped the fears and pains of all the women moving in from other places—principally the pain of finding decent housing.

Women in uniform had an advantage over civilians such as Lorraine Inman. The military housed their own—poorly and clumsily, perhaps, but they did it. The civilians usually had to fend for themselves. A government agency called the Defense Housing Registry tried to help. Women arrived at its offices just off the train or bus, walked up to the counter and said, "I want a suite with private bath within walking distance of the Munitions Building." They learned quickly. "NEWCOMERS DISCOVER

PRIVATE BATHS WENT OUT WITH HITLER," the Washington *Post* reported. "Walking distance," it added, applied only to cross-country runners.

President Roosevelt—who managed still to fancy himself an architect even after looking out the White House windows at the hideous temporary buildings on the Mall he had helped design—tried his hand at devising a solution to the housing crisis for young women. He drew up plans for temporary residential buildings along the Mall, row after row of drab two-story dormitories as dreary as the office buildings they would adjoin. His designs called for a central hallway with ten small cubicles on each side. In each cubicle he sketched a cot, a dresser, a mirror and a curtained closet in a corner. At one end of the corridor he drew in a single bathroom for the twenty occupants and at the other end a lobby surrounded by alcoves, each just big enough to hold a bridge table and four players. Across the back, he drew in a cafeteria. These rooms, he said, could be rented for fifty cents a day. What did his housing experts think of it?

They thought it was terrible. For one thing, the partitions between the rooms stopped short of the ceiling. No one could play a radio without disturbing her neighbor and residents could not adjust the temperature to suit themselves. Roosevelt protested that when he was at Groton, expensive a private school as it was, the boys lived in cubicles with eight-foot partitions. The open space at the top had improved the circulation of air. Anyone who had to have the temperature adjusted so meticulously was some kind of sissy.

But this just wasn't up to modern housing standards, they told him. Each woman should have her own washbasin. Roosevelt replied that each woman could put on her lipstick in her own room. Thousands of students all over the country, even in the best schools, did not have separate bathrooms and washbowls. "I want a common washroom with about five showers, five toilets and with twenty tin basins and twenty tooth mugs in a row." The Hudson Valley squire, the Groton alumnus, the ultimate patrician. It was good for the soul—particularly other people's souls—to live simply, to suffer a little.

Roosevelt's housing plan was a failure. Nobody liked it. It would, he was told, be an eyesore out there on the grass among the trees and monuments. Roosevelt gave up, sighing over "these fancy people." Other and even more hideous temporary buildings for military offices were built on the Mall, but not his twenty-cubicle barracks. Instead young women had to live in even worse eyesores, some almost slums, in downtown Washington near the government offices.

District of Columbia housing officials inspected a typical rooming house for women and described their findings in a report Dickens would have understood. It was dark red brick with three stories and basement, nineteenth-century gas light fixtures still in place even though electricity had been installed. In its twelve rooms were two bathrooms, ancient toilets with the yellow oak water tanks mounted high on the walls and flushed with brass pull chains. All walls, floors, stairways painted in dark Victorian browns. The paint was peeling, the stairs sagged. In it lived nineteen government employees—fifteen women and four men—and uncounted rats and cockroaches. Two of the men were in two basement spaces separated by beaverboard from a coal furnace. Each had an iron cot, a table and a chair. Each man paid $17.50 a month. And from the basement to the third floor, every room except a small foyer was crammed with beds. In most, two women shared a room, and paid $21.50 a month each, three clean towels and one clean sheet a week included. The landlady was somewhat less greedy than most, since she allowed clothes to be washed in the bathrooms if one could ever be found unoccupied. She levied no additional charge for hot water. Hand-written signs in the bathroom were plentiful, but even with all its squalor, the house was always filled because the roomers could walk to their jobs.

Still the women came. The Army Service Forces combed the country, mainly in rural areas, recruiting young women to take clerical jobs in the military services, showing them enticing pictures of a bustling wartime city and talking about salaries of $1,440 that in the small towns seemed a fortune. In the town of Alma, Arkansas (population 776), one-fourth of the girls in the 1944 high school graduating class signed up to leave for Washington, and several of their teachers cast aside their low-paid jobs and went with them, all of them climbing aboard a Pullman car for their first train ride, looking for more excitement and money than they had any reasonable expectation of finding in Alma.

And so Washington became a city crowded with women. Sally Reston in *The New York Times* quoted a young typist working for the navy: "The men may have started this war but the women are running it." When the agencies shut down in the late afternoons, the streets looked like a women's college campus between classes. When the department stores finally realized that their women customers now worked all day and no longer had time to shop, they agreed to stay open late on Thursday nights and found this so successful they never stopped it.

But the story that had spread around the country—that in Washington women outnumbered men by ten to one—was always false. Young women did outnumber young civilian men, but at all times, day and night, the city was crowded with men in uniform as far from home as the women were and just as lonely. Many of them had military desk jobs in the city and were always available for dates, dances, and picnics. On slow news nights United Press reporter Douglass Wallop could look out the windows of the National Press Building and across Fourteenth Street into the windows of the Willard Hotel where couples lucky enough to find hotel rooms were too busy to lower the shades.

They were called "government girls," and they helped break a taboo that had kept women largely out of federal jobs for a century and a half. In the nineteenth century, government agencies in Washington had, almost without exception, flatly refused to hire even one female. The Patent Office had once recruited a few women to do the tiresome hand work of copying patents, but they were instructed to work at home and mail in their copies, and never to appear in the office. Their salaries were sent to them in the names of male relatives, since a female name could not appear on the official payroll. The first woman actually to work in a government office was the wife of a clerk in the Treasury, who came in to do her husband's job while he was out sick. When he died, she was allowed to take his place permanently, but at significantly lower pay and only by appearing on the payroll under her brother's name. Even when Congress voted finally to allow women to work in government jobs, there was a vicious antifeminist campaign. In the Treasury, when some paper money was found to be missing, male officials (who had never wanted the women in the first place) charged that the new employees were stealing it by hiding it under their skirts. They were ordered to remove their skirts at the end of each day and shake them out before leaving the building.

The government girls of the 1940s had different problems, but often no less serious. They were paid far less than almost any men working for the government in a city whose living costs were high. They were far from home. They were lonely. Occasionally the war agencies tried to help. Leon Henderson used his own money to set up a no-interest loan fund at the OPA for young women who ran out of cash awaiting their first pay check. Other offices appointed what on a college campus might have been called a dean of women, whose job it was to talk with new women employees, some of them as young as sixteen, and counsel then on how to deal with their problems: homesickness, fatigue from working at boring, repetitive jobs six days a week while spending evenings in small rooms stumbling over their roommates' suitcases strewn around the floor.

Hollywood director George Stevens, in a comedy called *The More the Merrier,* managed to find laughs in the Washington spectacle of twelve women in bathrobes, curlers, toothbrushes and lipsticks in hand, standing in line for a turn in the bathroom, and standing in line to use the pay telephones in the hallways, agonizing at the possibility that some man calling to ask for a date would give up because the phone was always busy.

There was a good deal of that, but Washington was still small-townish enough and still Southern enough to feel it had to try to keep the women entertained. Through an organization called the Women's Battalion, the armed services sent trucks and buses to take them to dances at military bases. There was the USO, the Stage Door Canteen, the YWCA, the churches and synagogues. And every day, it seemed, some group in town set up yet another committee to arrange trips, parties, picnics, boat rides on the Potomac, bicycle trips in Rock Creek Park and hot dog roasts on somebody's lawn.

They were young. Washington was an experience they had never had before and surely would never have again. Although the housing and money problems persisted, they survived them. And they went on to type and file and mimeograph the United States of America through its greatest war.

Harold Ickes, who had once been director of the Chicago branch of the NAACP, was glowing with pride in January 1943 as he welcomed Marian Anderson to his Interior Department building. The occasion was the dedication of a mural commemorating Anderson's famous 1939 concert at the Lincoln Memorial, a concert Ickes had been instrumental in arranging. The singer was, he now said, an "apostle of her race." The next night, she sang for the first time in the DAR's Constitution Hall at a United China Relief benefit. "One almost believed," NAACP director Walter White wrote of that concert a few days later, "that he could see a gleam of the brotherhood for which men fight and die on battlefields today all over the world."

And there were, in fact, glimmerings of change in the city's race relations. The number of blacks working for the federal government had increased substantially—from 8 percent before the war to 18 percent now. More significant, perhaps, about half of them were in white collar jobs. In the 1930s, blacks in positions of real responsibility had been so few that virtually all of them were members of the small "Black Cabinet." Now, such a cabinet would number over two hundred. And important institutions in the white community were beginning to take notice of racial problems. The Washington *Post* editorialized against discrimination repeatedly and ran stories detailing the problems of the black community. Several interracial community organizations had formed to address black grievances. The president himself had endorsed some of them.

Still, the optimism was hard to sustain. William Hastie, who had been the first black ever to become a federal district judge (in the Virgin Islands), served as a civilian aide to Henry Stimson advising the War Department on racial issues. In January 1943 he resigned with a public blast at racism in the armed services and at his own inability to do anything about it. "Reactionary policies and discriminatory practices," he wrote in the Chicago *Defender,* "were the immediate cause of my resignation. . . . My views were disregarded." As indeed they were. The military had assembled a few black units, put them under the command of white officers and relegated them to largely menial tasks. Secretary Stimson was writing privately, "The Negro still lacks the particular initiative which a commanding officer of men needs in war . . . and the social intermixture of the two races is basically impossible." Things would be just fine, he added (perhaps in reference to Hastie), "if a little group of agitators . . . would only keep their hands off." Robert Patterson, Stimson's undersecretary, responded huffily to Hastie's demands: "It would seem that Negroes might be inspired to take pride in the efficiency of Negro units in the Army, as representing their own contribution to the armed forces." Dwight D. Eisenhower looked into black complaints and found that American generals in the field, along with

commanders in the other Allied armies, were unanimous in their opposition to taking time out from fighting the war to engage in what they
called "social experiments."

Hastie's resignation struck a nerve. The NAACP presented him with
its highest honor—the Spingarn medal—as a reward for his "courageous
and principled" stance. And in Washington, the episode reminded the
black community that a segregated military was defending a segregated
city in a war to defend freedom. For on the whole, Washington remained
in 1943 what it had always been—a city coldly divided by race and, it
seemed, determined to stay that way. Foreign visitors were often aghast:
The "capital of the free world" was home to a rigidly circumscribed
community that one Czech diplomat called (rather overstating the case)
"a Nazi ghetto."

Richard Wright came to Washington for the opening of an Orson
Welles stage adaptation of his novel *Native Son*. He tried to enter a
restaurant with the white producers, was refused, and had to eat outside
sitting in his car. Harold Ickes ordered an end to racial discrimination on
the golf courses in federal government parks. When several black golfers
tried to take shelter in the clubhouse in East Potomac Park during a
sudden downpour, the whites inside refused to let them in. The local
Red Cross organized a blood drive for wounded men at the front. Blood
donated by blacks was kept separate from blood taken from whites.
When the NAACP objected to this practice as having no scientific basis,
Representative John Rankin took the House floor to chastise the
"crackpots, communists and parlor pinks in this country . . . trying to
browbeat the Red Cross into taking the labels off the blood bank. . . . That
seems to be one of the schemes of these fellow travelers to try to
mongrelize this nation." And William Hastie, a few days after his
resignation, agreed to meet columnist I. F. Stone for lunch at the
National Press Club to discuss the controversy. The club management
refused to serve him. Stone and Hastie sat defiantly in the dining room
for nearly an hour conducting their business, while the black waiters
stood uncomfortably aside, under orders to not so much as pour a glass
of water for the judge.

Returning from Casablanca early in 1943, Roosevelt had stopped
briefly in Liberia for "coffee and doughnuts" and a chat with President
Edwin Barclay, a staunch friend of the United States. Later that year, at
the president's invitation, Barclay came to Washington for a short state

visit. It was an awkward moment. Roosevelt invited him to stay at the White House, and he became the first black (other than servants) ever to spend a night there. But when he accepted an invitation from several senators to appear briefly in the Senate chamber, all but two of the Southern members walked out.

He was the first black to speak before the Senate since Reconstruction. "I wish to express to you," he told the remaining members, "my high appreciation of the courtesy shown me in permitting me to observe for a few moments the processes of lawmaking in the United States." He then sat down and waited for the ritual words of welcome in response. Silence. Vice President Wallace squirmed uncomfortably in his chair on the rostrum. No one rose. The clock ticked. Senator McKellar took the floor and yielded to Senator Taft. Taft said nothing, then yielded to Senator Thomas of Utah, who was also speechless. Finally, after what seemed like an interminable pause, the Senate's sergeant-at-arms stepped forward and quietly asked Barclay if he would like to walk across the Capitol and visit the House chamber. As he departed, the sighs of relief were audible in the visitors' gallery.

By the middle of 1943, tensions in the Washington black community were becoming almost palpable. One source of frustration was the performance of the FEPC, which Roosevelt had created with such fanfare two years before to forestall A. Philip Randolph's proposed march on Washington. From the start, the FEPC had been a bureau-cratic orphan, bounced from one agency to another, lacking the author-ity to subpoena witnesses and with no power to enforce its decisions. It had begun under the auspices of the Office of Production Management, within which it at least retained control of its own budget. But in a 1942 reorganization, it was shifted to the War Production Board, where even its budgeting authority was lost. Later it was moved to the War Manpower Commission, which was under the direction of Paul McNutt, a former Indiana governor who nursed presidential ambitions and who showed a marked disinclination to pursue any case or offend any potential constituency. When McNutt ordered the committee to "postpone" con-sideration of a controversial case involving the major railroads, the chairman and two members resigned. "Crucified, dead, but never buried," Charlie Cherokee, columnist for the *Defender,* wrote at the time, "the President's Committee on Fair Employment Practices rots slowly, a stark malodorous warning that prejudice reigns supreme."

A particular bone of contention in Washington was Capital Transit, the privately owned company that ran the city's bus and trolley system. Capital Transit staggered through the war with a chronic labor shortage, its drivers and mechanics drafted into the army or moving off to better-paying jobs elsewhere. At times, it was so short of drivers that it had to cancel or curtail service. Even so, the company refused to hire a single black. Capital Transit's president, E. D. Merrill, wiping his rimless glasses with a tissue and looking thoughtfully at the ceiling, explained that "members of the Negro race have not yet had enough years of cultural growth . . . whereas white people have had generations and generations of experience in this sort of thing."

The black community appealed to the FEPC, and in 1942, under pressure from the commission, Merrill hired one black driver. The white drivers walked out. Merrill fired the black and vowed never to hire another. The FEPC made no response. By the summer of 1943, frustrated local residents had organized a biracial Committee on Jobs for Negroes in Public Utilities and sent groups out to picket bus and trolley stops. A "Capital Transit Trek" was announced—a mass march followed by a demonstration at Franklin Square. The city was so alarmed by this unprecedented activism that wild rumors began spreading: The march would be accompanied by a race riot, perhaps as violent as the terrible Detroit riot a few weeks earlier, in which thirty-four people had died. There were predictions, the *Daily News* noted, of "up-ended street cars, up-turned buses, shootings, mass fights in the Pentagon Building and so on." Others reported fears "that a gang of 800 'roughnecks' had been imported from New York to invade downtown theaters and hotels" and that "every bank in Washington will be robbed." For days, all the major papers ran editorials denouncing "rumor mongering" and appealing for calm. And in the end the march, with the chief of the metropolitan police marching at its head, went off peacefully. The FEPC in response bestirred itself to appoint an "expert" to study the attitudes of white bus drivers, then "temporarily" shelved the Capital Transit case. By the end of the year over 15 percent of the city's buses were idle because there were not enough drivers to operate them. But still not a single black was hired—a record that remained intact thirteen years later, when the company was sold to new owners.

In August (perhaps in response to growing rumors that A. Philip Randolph was again contemplating a march on Washington), the president disbanded the FEPC and organized a new one, this time with bureaucratic independence.

The Capital Transit demonstrations were only one sign of a growing militancy throughout the city's black community. In February 1943, three Howard University students—all women—sat down at a segregated soda fountain in a United Cigar Store and ordered drinks. The waitress refused to serve them; they refused to leave. Management finally filled their order for three hot chocolates, then gave them a check for seventy-five cents—more than double the normal price. When the students refused to pay the overcharge, six D.C. policemen rounded them up and took them to jail—where they were searched, interrogated and housed in a cell with prostitutes until, hours later, the dean of women at Howard secured their release.

The United Cigar Store incident outraged the Howard campus and inspired the Washington chapter of the NAACP to launch a "direct action" campaign against segregated establishments throughout the city. A law student, William Raines, suggested wider use of the technique the three women students had used at the lunch counter, a technique some labor unions had found effective in the 1930s—what the unions had called a "sit-down," and what Raines called a "sit-in":

> If the white people want to deny us service, let them pay for it.
> Let's go downtown some lunch hour when they're crowded. . . .
> We'll take a seat on a lunch stool, and if they don't serve us, we'll
> just sit there and read our books. They lose trade while that seat
> is out of circulation. If enough people occupy seats, they'll lose
> so much trade they'll start thinking.

In mid-April twelve Howard students staged such a sit-in at the Little Palace Cafeteria at Fourteenth and U streets. Outside, pickets circled carrying signs: "Our boys. Our bonds. Our brothers are fighting for you. Why can't we eat here?" The owner finally shut the restaurant, eight hours early. "I'll lose money," he explained, "but I'd rather close up than practice democracy this way. The time is not yet ripe." Months later, there was a more celebrated demonstration in Thompson's Restaurant at 11th Street and Pennsylvania Avenue. It was surrounded for days by picketers while black students sat patiently inside waiting to be served. At one point, six black soldiers (unconnected with the demonstrators) joined the students at tables inside and refused to leave even when M.P.s arrived and warned them that the incident might "embarrass" the army. Finally, the restaurant management gave in, and for several days—as local reporters watched—blacks were served without incident. When the reporters left, the old Jim Crow restrictions returned.

There were more demonstrations at movie theaters, stores and restaurants. Much of the black community began mobilizing to support the students—contributing money to the Civil Rights Committee they formed, signing petitions on behalf of the "Equal Rights Bill for the District of Columbia" they submitted to Congress, and at times joining them on picket lines. In the end, though, the direct action campaign never had the impact its organizers had hoped for. Demonstrations were relatively few; successes were even fewer.

But the city—and the nation—were at least beginning to grope about for methods by which to confront America's oldest social injustice. Blacks in Washington, even if barely noticed at the time, were helping show the way.

X

Endings and Beginnings

I n 1943 a young reporter at his first White House press conference had his first look at Franklin Roosevelt from a few feet away. It was a shock, unnerving. Here was the most famous face in the world, one he had seen a thousand times. In newspaper and magazine and newsreel pictures it was the face of a handsome man with strong, well-formed features displaying a smiling, good-natured manner, chin tilted high, ivory cigarette holder pointed to the sky. Those were the pictures. Here was the reality—a man who looked terribly old and tired. No doubt youth was too quick to notice the effects of age, but this man's face was more gray than pink, his hands shook, his eyes were hazy and wandering, his neck drooped in stringy, sagging folds accentuated by a shirt collar that must have fit at one time but now was two or three sizes too large.

In private, Press Secretary Steve Early was asked why the president didn't buy new shirts that fit. Collars hanging so loosely made the president look even more shrunken and drawn.

"That damn Dutchman is so tight he won't buy new shirts until the old ones are ready to use for cleaning rags."

"What's the matter with him?"

"He's just tired. Running a world war is a hell of a job."

The new Statler Hotel, having escaped seizure by the U.S. Navy, had become Washington's headquarters for the ceremonious dinners where speeches were made, plaques were awarded, backs were slapped and hands shaken and where ill-fitting rented tuxedos stood away from the backs of the wearers' necks, like horse collars. The Statler attracted all these affairs because, with the advice and guidance of the White House Secret Service detail, its architects had designed the new hotel's Presidential Room for the safety and convenience of a crippled president. A driveway from the street led directly into a huge private elevator able to lift the president, in his limousine, up to the mezzanine level where he could be helped out and into his wheelchair in private and then rolled out to the head table. The Statler was the only hotel ever designed this way in Washington or anywhere else, since no other country had ever elected a political leader unable to stand or walk, and it was one of the few public places in Washington the Secret Service thought secure enough for the president to enter. And so any group—political, business, union, news media—planning a dinner and expecting the president to attend had to reserve the Statler's Presidential Room.

At the Democratic party's annual political ritual and rain dance, the 1944 Jefferson-Jackson Day dinner of unrationed chicken at one hundred dollars a plate, Vice President Wallace rose at the head table, looked out over the Presidential Room and declared the New Deal was "ageless," and—red in the face—shouted, "The president has never denied the principles of the New Deal and he never will. Roosevelt, God willing, will in the future give the New Deal a firmer foundation that it has ever had before." Applause.

In spite of the growing doubts about his health and appearance, the campaign for Roosevelt's fourth term had begun.

When the Southern Governors Conference, all Democrats, came to Washington for their annual meeting in January 1944, they went to the

Statler even though they did not expect Roosevelt to attend any of their sessions. He did not like the Southern leaders much, and they liked him even less; too liberal, they thought, spending too much money, too close to Sidney Hillman and the CIO and the communists. But a presidential election was coming up in November and the party convention in July would have to choose a Democratic candidate. The governors wandered the Statler hallways, chewing cigars, holding small meetings in one room and then another, drinking a little bourbon, complaining that the hotel served no grits for breakfast, talking endlessly about finding a candidate for president they could all support. In the end, the governor of North Carolina came out and said to reporters lounging in the hallway and waiting for news, "We go into meetings to cuss him out, but we just can't figure out any other answer than Roosevelt in 1944."

The Democratic National Committee, meeting in Washington the same week, wasted little time discussing candidates. It voted unanimously and with loud cheers to "solicit" Roosevelt to serve another four years as "the great world leader," announced that the party's nominating convention would be on July 19 in Chicago, and chose a new National Committee chairman, Robert E. Hannegan of St. Louis, described as "a handshaker de luxe, a thorough believer in organized politics, devoted to the art of making friends." One committeeman said he was "sick of all those goddamned Democrats in Congress who are always sniping at the New Deal and then coasting into office on Roosevelt's coat tails. Now they'd better come around."

But from the beginning of 1944 through the spring and into the summer, Roosevelt refused to acknowledge the campaign for his fourth term, refused even to say he would accept the nomination if offered. Week after week at his press conferences the reporters tried to pry something out of him, anything. They got nothing. On February 8 they asked him, "Would you accept a fourth-term nomination?"

He replied, "There is no news on that today."

In May: "Mr. President, Chairman Hannegan made a very direct statement that it was his personal judgment that you were going to be the candidate in 1944 for the Democratic ticket."

"Oh, look—look. . . . I am not going to talk about it now any more than I did before. And number one, I didn't read what he said. And number four [sic] if I did read it I'm not going to talk to you about it."

"Well, Mr. President, there are only seventy-one days before the

Democratic National Convention. [Laughter.] Would you give us some clue when you will be ready?"

"My God! Have you been counting?"

"Yes, sir. On the calendar."

"I haven't. Bad habit."

"Anything about the vice-presidential nomination?"

"No. I don't talk about that either."

On June 13: "Is there any place we could go, Mr. President, to find out about your fourth-term intentions?"

"My what?" [Laughter.] "Well," he said in a whisper, "I don't know. I want to be helpful. . . . "

"We'd all appreciate it."

"So would I." [Laughter.]

"How about the Democratic Convention, sir. Would that be a good place to go to find out?"

"I don't know."

"Mr. President, maybe you will tell us about your vice-presidential intentions, then."

"Maybe I could get you on a plane, send you out to China [Vice President Henry Wallace was flying to China that day], the only thing I can think of."

Not until a few days before the Democratic Convention would he give the press even a dry crumb of news about his plans for the next four years.

In fact, he had long since decided to run again. He liked being president, liked being the center of attention, liked the crowds and the adulation. But beyond that, he and his staff and his family believed that with the end of the war somewhere in sight—two years or less, they thought—it was essential that he remain in office to finish it off, disarm Germany and Japan, help the world back to its feet, and then pursue the dream he had dreamed since his days of service with Woodrow Wilson. Wilson had inflamed him and people around the world with his vision of an international organization to abolish war forever, a vision so pure and sweet that peasants in rude cottages across central and southern Europe had hung Wilson's picture on their walls, genuflected before it and burned candles beneath it. Wilson's war to end war had not ended all wars, but conceivably Roosevelt's could. If he hoped to leave behind a monument more substantial than a granite slab with his name on it, no monument could be greater than the promise of permanent peace. A new president—someone like Thomas E. Dewey—might also pursue Wilson's dream. But then again, he might be more intent on destroying the New Deal.

Roosevelt also feared that after the war—when press censorship ended, when the news of the inevitable wartime waste and blunders and the stratospheric debt would become public, when the American people heard for the first time of the huge cost in lives and broken bodies—after the war, when all these ugly facts became known, the old isolationists might rise again. They might demand that the country once more withdraw into itself, leaving Europe prostrate in such destruction and poverty as to invite yet another dictator. Roosevelt knew he would oppose this, but he could not be certain others would. So, yes, he would run again. But he would withhold his announcement as long as possible so as to delay the shower of poisoned arrows his enemies would aim at him the moment he became a candidate, among them the arrow most favored by Republicans—that he wanted to make himself a dictator, the country's first permanent president.

On July 11, 1944, toward the end of a press conference, Roosevelt told reporters, "I have got something else."

"Is it an announcement about your fourth-term intentions, Mr. President?"

"Well, you can't tell. You are guessing again. You have done it before. This time, this time you are right."

"Good."

"Well, there are two letters here, one that I got yesterday from Mr. Hannegan." He read aloud Hannegan's letter: " 'I desire to report to you that more than a clear majority—' Wait a minute," Roosevelt interrupted himself. "I want a cigarette." [Laughter.]

He took out a Camel, and Steve Early lit it for him.

"Unfortunately, this is not a Murad." [Laughter.] A brand of cigarettes called Murad had a famous advertising campaign urging smokers caught in awkward or embarrassing situations to "Be nonchalant. Light a Murad."

He continued reading Hannegan's letter: " . . . a clear majority of the delegates to the National Convention are legally bound by the actions of their constituents to cast their ballots for your nomination as president."

"Louder!"

"In view of the foregoing, I would respectfully request that you send to the convention or otherwise convey to the people of the United States an expression that you will again respond to the call of the party and of the people."

A reporter from NBC noticed that FDR's hands were trembling and he was scattering cigarette ashes all over his desk and into his lap. But why shouldn't they tremble? Here was a man in declining health agreeing to take on four more years of burdens that seemed certain to shorten his life, if not end it. Now Roosevelt was reading his reply to Hannegan's letter:

"Dear Mr. Hannegan:

. . . If the convention should nominate me, I shall accept. If the people elect me, I will serve. . . .

"At the same time I think I have the right to say to you and to the delegates of the coming convention something which is personal, purely personal. For myself, I do not want to run. . . . After many years of public service . . . my personal thoughts have turned to the day when I could return to civil life. All that is within me cries out to go back to my home on the Hudson River, to avoid public responsibilities, and to avoid also the publicity which in our democracy follows every step of the nation's chief executive . . . such would be my choice.

"But we of this generation chance to live in a day and hour when our nation has been attacked, and when its future existence and the future existence of our chosen method of government is at stake.

"To win this war wholeheartedly, unequivocally and as quickly as we can is our task of the first importance. To win this war in such a way that there will be no further world wars in the foreseeable future is our second objective. To provide occupations and a decent standard of living for our men in the armed forces after the war, and for all Americans, are the final objectives.

"Therefore, reluctantly, but as a good soldier, I repeat that I will accept and serve in this office if I am so ordered by the commander-in-chief of us all, the sovereign people of the United States."

* * *

One question had been answered. But outside the White House, in the hot, steamy political world beyond the president's office, there were other questions: questions about his running mate, questions about his opponent and questions about his health.

The question of a running mate was of particular concern to party leaders. This was not, they realized, an ordinary vice-presidential nomination. And they were determined that the incumbent, Henry Wallace—whom they had accepted only grudgingly in 1940 and whom they now considered impossibly liberal and controversial—be replaced. Given the state of Roosevelt's health, it was likely the Democratic convention would be nominating two men for president. Few leaders wanted to see a President Wallace.

Early in July Roosevelt met with Hannegan, Ed Flynn, and other Democratic powers in his second-floor study at the White House. Everyone conceded that Wallace had to go, but at first there was no agreement on who would replace him. The president seemed to want William O. Douglas, whom he had appointed to the Supreme Court five years earlier. Douglas was very young, very liberal—just what the party men didn't want. Some pressed for James Byrnes, but Byrnes was a Southerner and a fallen-away Catholic and would alienate too many groups. There was talk of Alben Barkley. He was too old, they decided. The name they kept coming back to was Harry S Truman, senator from Missouri, whose conduct of the committee investigating war industries had impressed them all. Roosevelt seemed unenthusiastic, even uninterested. But he agreed.

Characteristically, though, he could not bring himself to tell either Wallace or Byrnes that they were now out of the running. He saw Wallace at the White House a few days later and, as the meeting broke up, threw his arm up over the vice president's shoulder and said, "I hope it's the same team again, Henry." He even wrote a letter to the convention stating that if he were a delegate, he would vote for Wallace—although he carefully avoided instructing the real delegates to do the same. When he met with Byrnes just before the convention, Roosevelt insisted he had endorsed no one and encouraged Byrnes to keep his candidacy alive. He even began talking about Douglas again.

Hannegan arrived at the Chicago convention with a letter from Roosevelt saying he would accept either Truman or Douglas as a running mate. (Originally, the letter had listed Douglas's name first, until

Hannegan prevailed on Roosevelt to reverse the order.) But Truman, who had still heard nothing from the president, was committed to Byrnes and refused to allow his own name to be put in nomination. The night before the balloting, Hannegan summoned Truman to his hotel suite and took a call from Roosevelt in Washington. The two men were sitting on the edge of the bed, and Hannegan was holding the receiver away from his ear so Truman could listen to the president's words:

"Bob, have you got that fellow lined up yet?"

No, Hannegan answered.

"Well, you tell him if he wants to break up the Democratic party in the middle of a war, that's his responsibility." Then a click, and silence.

Truman looked like a man utterly defeated. He got Byrnes to release him from his pledge of support, and the next day—after Hannegan spent a long night calling the heads of delegations—he became the Democratic nominee for vice president. (Roosevelt had been nominated by acclamation the day before.) Truman spoke before the convention, appearing conspicuously ill at ease, and accepted the nomination. A few minutes later, he left the hall surrounded by bodyguards, photographers and autograph-seekers. The candidate and his wife clung to each other, looking dazed and suddenly very frightened. Mrs. Truman turned to her husband as they walked to their car and asked, "Are we going to have to go through this all the rest of our lives?"

Thomas E. Dewey, nominated by the Republicans on the first ballot, was already out on the stump speaking in his round, resonant baritone voice—a voice so pure and mellifluous that in his younger years he had considered a career as a singer until he had decided he could not trust his future to a fragile pair of vocal cords and had chosen law and politics instead. Now, as a candidate for president, he spoke so euphoniously that each word emerged polished and glowing like a jewel resting on its own little velvet pillow.

In public Dewey came across as pompous and cold. And for good reason. He was both. Columnist Samuel Grafton had said of him during his 1940 campaign for the presidency, when Dewey was thirty-seven years old: "If a young man is as cold as this at thirty-seven he will reach absolute zero at fifty."

Dewey's reputation rested primarily on his success as a special prosecutor pursuing criminals in New York City. Among those he sent to prison were gangsters extorting money from prostitutes, the Nazi Fritz Kuhn, Wall Street swindlers, tax evaders and subway employees caught stealing nickels from the fare boxes. Now he traveled the country campaigning against Roosevelt, displaying his voice, his flawless tailoring, his black Homburg hats and his little black moustache. His appearance prompted Alice Roosevelt Longworth to stick a label on him he was never able to peel off. He looked, she said, like "the little man on the wedding cake."

His pomposity and condescension annoyed reporters. At five feet eight he was around average height, but somehow he seemed smaller. He once announced a press conference in a hotel meeting room, and a circle of chairs was set up for reporters with a single chair in the center for the candidate. When he walked in, he found a thick telephone directory lying on the seat of his chair. He refused to sit.

Dewey's task seemed all but impossible: a young and not particularly appealing challenger confronting the most popular president of his time in the midst of a war over which that president had presided and which the United States was about to win. He had only one real issue—Roosevelt's health—and he dared not use it, at least not directly. Even in a political campaign where the rules of courteous discourse are lax when they exist at all, attacking an opponent as an invalid with degenerative diseases would be unacceptably crude. But Dewey did imply. Over and over he described the administration as a used-up, burned-out gang of "tired old men." According to the Democrats, Republicans began spreading rumors that Roosevelt had undergone major surgery while on vacation in South Carolina, that he had suffered several strokes, that he was showing signs of senility. And they circulated copies of a news picture that made the president look particularly terrible: pale, wasted, hollow-eyed, his mouth drooping.

The Republican tactics evoked expressions of outrage. Marquis Childs of the St. Louis *Post-Dispatch* wrote in the midst of the campaign:

Something like an organized effort seems to be behind the spread of rumors about President Roosevelt's health. . . . There is a type of frustrated individual who actually seems to get a malicious pleasure by hinting that he, or she, has inside information that Roosevelt is suffering from some kind of serious ailment. . . . The

President's physician during his three terms in office has been Admiral Ross McIntyre . . . who said recently that his patient was in as good condition as a man of 62 could be. . . . The canards about the President's health are below the belt.

Below the belt, perhaps, but not false. Admiral McIntyre, an ear, nose and throat specialist who after twelve years as physician to the president was now more courtier than doctor, was misleading both the public and the president about the true condition of his patient. Roosevelt was, in fact, in desperately poor health. He had gallstones, and was on a low-fat diet that caused him to lose weight and to look shrunken and drawn. That, however, was far from the worst. Dr. Howard G. Bruenn, a cardiologist in the Navy Medical Corps, gave the president a thorough physical in March 1944, four months before he announced he would run for a fourth term. Bruenn discovered that Roosevelt had a badly enlarged heart, that he was suffering from hypertension and hypertensive heart disease, that he was experiencing cardiac failure in the left ventricle and that he had contracted acute bronchitis. Clearly he did not have the strength and stamina to preside for another four years over the end of a world war and the complexities and dangers to follow it. It is probably not too much to say that he was already dying.

But Roosevelt himself seemed unconcerned. He showed no interest in the examinations, never asked Bruenn for the results and submitted passively to some, but never all, of the regimen the doctor prescribed for him. And when he began hearing reports of the rumors Dewey and the Republicans were spreading, he grew incensed. For months he had seemed withdrawn and depressed, taking little interest in anything, unwilling to contribute more than a written statement now and then to his campaign. But for a moment in the fall of 1944 he regained his strength, driven by his hatred for Thomas E. Dewey.

On September 23 he appeared before a meeting of the Teamsters union at the Statler Hotel in Washington, a friendly audience in a familiar place with microphones carrying his words out over the radio networks. "Well, here we are," he began, "here we are again—after four years—and what years they have been! You know I am actually four years older, which is a fact that seems to annoy *some* people. In fact . . . there are millions of Americans who are more than *eleven* years older than when we started to clear up the mess that was dumped in our laps in 1933."

By now the audience was roaring with approval, and Roosevelt was beaming—the old smile, the upturned face, the vigorous voice, the familiar wit which he could use with savage effect:

These Republican leaders have not been content with attacks on me, or my wife, or on my sons. No, not content with that, they now include my little dog Fala. Well, of course, I don't resent attacks, and my family doesn't resent attacks, but—Fala *does* resent them.

You know—you know—Fala's Scotch, and being a Scottie, as soon as he learned that the Republicans had concocted a story that I had left him behind on an Aleutian Island and had sent a destroyer back to find him—at a cost to the taxpayers of two or three, or eight or twenty million dollars—his Scotch soul was furious. He has not been the same dog since.

A few weeks later, Roosevelt seemed to refute any remaining doubts about his health by riding for four hours in a driving rain through the streets of New York while perhaps two million people strained to see him. That night, in a speech to the Foreign Policy Association at the Waldorf-Astoria Hotel, he delivered a stinging attack on Republican isolationists and a vigorous defense of his plans for a postwar international organization. "Peace," he said, "like war, can succeed only where there is a will to enforce it, and where there is available power to enforce it."

On election night, Roosevelt sat, as he had three times before, with family and staff at the small dining-room table in the Hyde Park house, gathered pencils and paper, ate scrambled eggs and waited for the election returns. By midnight, it was clear he had won, but it was not the landslide he had known in past elections. Of about 48 million votes cast, Roosevelt got 25 million and Dewey 22 million, the smallest popular vote margin since Woodrow Wilson in 1916. He won 432 electoral votes to Dewey's 99. It was not the tremendous victory of 1936, but it would do. Roosevelt had no great love for Southern politicians, but it was notable that his largest majorities by far were in the states of the former

Confederacy. In Mississippi he won about as big a margin as it was possible to get—93.6 percent of the vote.

Late into the night, Dewey still had not sent the usual polite message of congratulation to the winner. And so Roosevelt finally went upstairs to bed, riding up in the small elevator originally installed in the house to carry the family's trunks up and down. He said of Dewey, "He's still a son of a bitch."

In 1801, as Thomas Jefferson waited for his inauguration as president, he lived in a boardinghouse on New Jersey Avenue. On his inauguration day, he walked the three blocks from there to the U.S. Capitol, took the oath of office as president of the United States, walked back to the boardinghouse, and sat down to a table with the other boarders and ate a little mutton. That was it.

In the years that followed, inaugurations gradually came to resemble Roman circuses. There were bands, flags, receptions, fireworks and musical entertainments with singers, tap dancers and symphony orchestras. There were parades past temporary grandstands along Pennsylvania Avenue. There were architects' competitions to design a presidential reviewing stand in front of the White House to be used only once, for a few hours, but required to be heated and bulletproof. First there was one inaugural ball. That became too big and unwieldy, and eventually there were six or eight balls, entertaining the president and the first lady, politicians, diplomats, justices, generals and admirals, political leaders or bosses of cities, counties, states, givers of campaign money, union leaders and business tycoons, the exact composition of the crowds dependent on the political philosophy of the president being installed. All of them, along with their wives, husbands, lovers and mistresses, spent a gaudy, hectic four days in a city without enough hotel rooms, restaurant tables, taxis, tuxedo rentals, hairdressers, or limousines, even though the livery companies brought in every Cadillac, Lincoln and Imperial up and down the East Coast, and the automobile manufacturers sent in hundreds of their new cars hoping they would be seen in the news pictures hauling dignitaries.

In 1944 Roosevelt wanted none of it. A lavish inaugural would, he said, be inappropriate in wartime. What he did not say was that he also wanted to spare himself a physically taxing ordeal. He simply didn't have the strength to endure the traditional four days of ceremony and revelry.

When he returned to Washington from Hyde Park on a rainy day shortly after the election, he rode in an open car through the city streets to the White House (flanked by Harry Truman and Henry Wallace, both of whom looked uncomfortable) past large, cheering crowds. That was his parade. A few days later a reporter asked if there would be the usual military procession on inauguration day. Roosevelt responded, "Who's here to parade?" The armed services were too busy fighting a war to take time to march down Pennsylvania Avenue. There would be no ball, no entertainments, only a simple ceremony on the south portico of the White House, looking out over the wintry lawn toward the Washington Monument and across the Potomac to Virginia.

A few hundred people, perhaps the smallest inaugural crowd in history, came to stand on the snow-covered grass below the portico. Roosevelt stood under an awning, took the oath and then delivered a short inaugural address, about five minutes long. Then, as his eldest son, James, later described it, he went inside and said, "I have to go to a reception now and shake hands with a thousand people, and I don't think I can do it."

"Then don't do it."

"I have to do it. It would look bad to bow out." He added, "There's a bottle of bourbon up in my room. If you'll go up and sneak it down to me and I can get some inside of me, I think I can get through this."

Then he said something more ominous, something he needed to tell James now because he might not have another chance. He had selected him to be an executor of his will. When the day comes, he said, "There is a personal letter in my safe that I have addressed to you which contains my instructions for my funeral. Among other things, I want you to have the family ring I wear. I hope you will wear it."

With the help of a little bourbon he did get through a luncheon and a reception. He had asked for chicken à la king for lunch, but White House housekeeper Henrietta Nesbitt, ever the tyrant, said it would be too much trouble to keep it hot and so the menu was chicken salad with more celery than chicken, rolls without butter and cake without frosting.

For an hour and twenty minutes, guests filed in to shake hands with Mrs. Roosevelt, Mrs. Truman, and then the president, who sat in the Red Room at a luncheon table, while the thirteen grandchildren, there at Roosevelt's insistence, swarmed all over the White House.

James wondered later if the president wanted them there out of some fear he might never see them all together again. Mrs. Roosevelt held a bouquet of violets grown by a neighbor in Hyde Park. The food at lunch, she said, was "very slim." Sculptor Jo Davidson held Grace Tully's lunch plate while Helen Keller ran her hands over Miss Tully's hat and admired its feathers. Bernard Baruch stood and watched. All the Cabinet came, all the ambassadors, the leaders of Congress, the Supreme Court. From the Oyster Bay branch of the Roosevelt family, a few Democrats came but no Republicans. In the receiving line, Mrs. Roosevelt was heard giving Mrs. Truman pointers on how to relax her knees to make the standing and handshaking less tiring. After lunch, a tea for the members of the electoral college, 250 more handshakes, and finally Roosevelt was through with social rituals. His next task, forty-eight hours later, was to leave Washington by train for Norfolk, Virginia, to board the navy's cruiser *Quincy* and cross the Atlantic for a secret meeting with Winston Churchill and Joseph Stalin on the Black Sea coast of Russia, at Yalta.

As William D. Hassett saw it, Roosevelt had "achieved every political ambition a human could aspire to." Now "there remains only his place in history. That will be determined by the service which he renders to all mankind. So F.D.R. will win his niche or pass into the oblivion which in a quarter of a century has swallowed all the statesmen of the First World War." It was at Yalta that Roosevelt hoped to win that niche.

Jonathan Daniels, who was acting as White House press secretary in the president's absence, had the melancholy task of leafing through the black-and-white photographs flown back every day from Yalta and trying to choose a few to be handed out to the press when the time came for news of the Yalta meeting to be made public. He looked for pictures that did not make Roosevelt look like an aged, fading, dying man. He could not find any.

On February 12, about three weeks after the inauguration, the public finally learned that the president was in Yalta with Churchill and Stalin. A communiqué issued simultaneously in Washington, London and Moscow said the three leaders had agreed on their strategy for crushing Germany and enforcing an unconditional surrender, had agreed to form some kind of international organization, probably to be called the United Nations Organization, and had agreed to cooperate in keeping the peace when the peace was won. It announced that the Curzon Line, a legacy from World War I, would be the boundary between Poland and the Soviet Union. And in pale, thin diplomatic prose which said little and implied much, it noted that Stalin was to have "influence" in Yugoslavia. In other words, the Soviet Union would have control in Europe from the Vistula River to the Adriatic Sea. Since even those who despised the Soviet Union conceded that the Russians had to get something out of the war in return for the loss of twenty million lives, the announcement from Yalta was received in Congress and the press with grudging approval.

The next day, a second communiqué from Yalta announced the names of those Roosevelt had chosen to attend a conference in San Francisco to establish the United Nations Organization. It was clear he was trying to avoid the mistakes Woodrow Wilson had made in 1919 when he tried to create the League of Nations. Wilson's delegation had included no Republicans. Roosevelt's would. And the president would go to San Francisco himself to make the opening address.

Roosevelt came back from Yalta aboard the *Quincy,* docking at the Norfolk navy yard, and then proceeded by train to Washington and the underground siding at the Bureau of Engraving and Printing. He arrived at 6 a.m., but stayed in bed, as was his habit, even though he was in a railroad car twenty feet under the trolleys, buses, taxis and morning commuter traffic above him on Fourteenth Street. He lay there drinking coffee and reading the newspapers until 9 a.m., when he came above-ground into the daylight and rode to the White House. He spent the day working on a speech he was to make to Congress the next day, March 1, in which he would report on his meeting at Yalta.

It was one of the poorest speeches of his life. It was too long, more than an hour. He kept wandering away from the written text and ad-libbing lines that to an NBC reporter in the radio gallery on the balcony made no sense. His voice was weak and quavering. Dean Acheson of the State Department called it "an invalid's voice." He was even willing, as he had never been before, to refer in public to his physical disability. In the past he had made his speeches standing and holding on to the House Chamber's podium, supported by the steel braces on his legs attached to a wide leather band around his waist. This time, he told Congress and the radio audience, he would speak from a chair on the floor of the House Chamber because, he said, after a long trip it was easier not to have the weight of ten pounds of steel around his legs.

His speech was meant to do what Woodrow Wilson had failed to do: persuade Congress to support an international organization he hoped would prevent war in the future: "Unless you here in the halls of the American Congress, with the support of the American people, concur in the general conclusions reached at a place called Yalta, and give them your active support, the meeting will not have produced lasting results."

The applause in Congress was substantial and prolonged. All the members, including even his most relentless critics, joined in a long, profuse, shouting-and-whistling standing ovation, though it had been a pedestrian speech, poorly delivered and containing not a single memorable phrase. What they were applauding was not the speech itself but its substance. Here was an issue that seemed far removed from the ordinary cheap maneuvering for political advantage. Here was a speech marking a great moment in American history: the imminent victory of the Allies and a plan that would, if it worked, save their grandchildren from ever again having to endure what they had endured, the agony of seeing fathers, sons, husbands, brothers shipped home from foreign wars in flag-draped coffins.

It seemed the applause would never end. As Roosevelt was wheeled out, those near him saw tears in his eyes. He was home, the victorious leader of a victorious nation. For a moment, partisanship was forgotten. He was a hero.

The next day in the White House, it was the old routine. He held a press conference and told reporters that when the war was over he would not object to sending German soldiers into Russia to help rebuild some of what they had destroyed. He received news that John L. Lewis, who had bedeviled him throughout the war, was now demanding that his United Mineworkers Union receive a royalty on each ton of coal its members mined, the money to be used to finance welfare programs for the miners; and that Lewis was demanding, too, that mine owners supply their workers with free helmets, lanterns, goggles and shoes. There were proposals from the OPA for changes in meat-rationing. There was a bill to be signed permitting Congress to resume after the war its familiar trips to the pork barrel for money to finance dams, rivers and harbors in their home districts. There was a meeting with Assistant Secretary of State Joseph C. Grew, who said the conference in the Dumbarton Oaks mansion in Georgetown, to design a United Nations Organization, was going well and that the alternative to its success was "international anarchy." Roosevelt held a Cabinet meeting and then announced he wanted to go to Hyde Park the next day, Saturday.

Over the weekend at home, he piddled with the mail flown up from Washington, agreed to receive several visitors in the next few weeks, including William L. Mackenzie King, prime minister of Canada, who had sent word ahead that while in Washington he wanted to hold a press conference. Bill Hassett told Roosevelt the press would not much welcome this. They had never found King very communicative and said of him,

> *William Lyon Mackenzie King*
> *Never tells us a goddamn thing.*

The president returned to the White House for a few days that were mainly spent receiving titled foreign visitors. With the war winding down, they were able to travel again, and they required substantial time and attention. Toward the end of the month Roosevelt, looking extremely tired, said he had had enough of entertaining visitors and would leave on Thursday, March 29, for Warm Springs, Georgia, for two weeks, maybe longer.

As he left, the day was pleasantly warm. The summer's heat and damp had not yet arrived. Washington's splendid cherry trees were in bloom, the wisteria was draping its lavender clusters over the fences and brick walls. His train to Warm Springs left the Fourteenth Street underground track at 4 p.m., crossed the Potomac into Virginia and headed south toward Georgia and his little wooden cottage and the warm spring water he had once hoped would help him strengthen his leg muscles and allow him to walk again.

Dr. Bruenn, always at his side now, listened to Hassett saying the president's health was deteriorating: "He is slipping away from us and no earthly power can keep him here." For months, Roosevelt had seemed simply not to give a damn about anything, even his own reelection. Had Dewey not started what he considered a particularly dirty campaign, the president might never have campaigned at all. Now, when Hassett gave him papers to sign, the bold, assertive signature of the past was gone. In its place was a feeble scrawl, trailing off into nothingness and ink splotches at the bottom of the page.

Dr. Bruenn was alarmed too. His patient had lost twenty-five pounds, had no strength and no appetite, could not taste his food, and looked worn, drawn, exhausted. But Roosevelt had enough strength to insist that even though everyone was trying to talk him out of it, he would be in San Francisco to address the opening of the United Nations Conference on April 25. Nothing, he said, could stop him from going.

On the first floor on the House side of the U.S. Capitol, a locked, unmarked, unnumbered door opened into a room with a mildly fragrant reputation. For a generation or more it had been the private preserve of the speaker of the House. House members knew it informally as the "board of education" room, so called because the speaker occasionally took recalcitrant House members there to "educate" them in why they should vote his way. The methods of persuasion, cajolery or coercion varied from one speaker to the next. They included threats to withhold party campaign money in the next election, promises of good committee assignments certain to produce publicity or even promises of closer, more convenient parking spaces in the House garage, some of the most valued currencies in congressional life. At other times, the board of education room was the scene of a good deal of drinking. John Nance Garner, when he was speaker, usually needed a little whiskey to get him through a strenuous legislative day and by around 5 p.m. he sometimes had to ask his friends to help him down to the first floor and lead him to the board of education room for a daycap, always available. Even during Prohibition, it was said, the room never ran dry. When Sam Rayburn (whose taste ran to bourbon and what he always called "branch water") became speaker, the board of education room remained busy in the late afternoons. The talk, gossip, smoke and whiskey still flowed. Old friends, all politicians, all in the same line of work, all members of the club, all congressional insiders, all white males, enjoying each other's company and the reassurance of whiskey warming their bellies.

In the room were black leather couches and chairs, a desk, telephone, refrigerator and a bar stocked mainly with Kentucky bourbon. Most members never saw the inside of the room. Rayburn invited only those he liked and trusted, and his invitations were coveted. And so it was that Harry Truman, newly installed as vice president, was pleased and honored on April 12, 1945, when he heard that Rayburn had invited him to come to the board of education room when the Senate adjourned.

Lounging in the room that day, rattling ice and pouring themselves drinks and waiting for the invited guests to arrive, were Rayburn and Lewis Deschler, parliamentarian of the House. The telephone rang—a little surprising, since almost no one knew the private number. It was Steve Early at the White House asking Rayburn to have Harry Truman call him immediately on his arrival. A few minutes later, the Senate adjourned and Truman came in, a pleasant but unprepossessing man, pink-faced, gray-haired, wearing his usual double-breasted suit with the lapels pressed flat, along with a few touches befitting a former haberdasher, such as the white handkerchief carefully folded flat in his breast pocket with three little peaks showing. It was a style that could only be called spiffy. His thick glasses magnified his eyes and made him look a little owlish. He was a politician no one really disliked. He was straightforward and without pretense, always did what he said he would do and what he thought was right as far as he could figure out what it was. The other congressmen trusted him as being pretty straight and pretty reliable and unlikely ever to do anything embarrassing.

For a few minutes, they forgot to tell him about Early's call. When someone remembered, he phoned the White House and heard Early say in a tense, tight voice that he must come immediately and quietly. Quietly? Truman wasn't sure what that meant. But he quickly excused himself, telling Rayburn, "Something is happening over there."

At the White House, Truman rode up the elevator to the family sitting room on the second floor where Eleanor Roosevelt was waiting, quiet and controlled. She put her hand on his shoulder and said, "Harry, the president is dead."

In the press offices at the "Little White House" in Warm Springs and in the real White House in Washington, all was confusion. Jonathan Daniels was so distraught he could barely speak. So it was Steve Early, the old professional, who arranged a conference call to the three wire services and told them in a strained, quiet voice: "I have a flash for you."

A "flash" was the wire services' designation for news of the most shattering urgency. It was always followed by ringing the bells on the teletypes ten times to alert inattentive editors. The International News

Service got the news out first, at 5:47 p.m., perhaps the briefest news story ever written: "FDR DEAD."

Within minutes, the news was being relayed around the world. Editors worked frantically to reset their front pages and get out special editions. Radio stations cancelled their commercials. In Chicago, Colonel McCormick ordered his *Tribune* to report the death straightforwardly. McCormick himself had planned to have champagne served at dinner that night, but he did not want it said he had toasted the president's passing, so "we drank Montrachet instead." Cissy Patterson had the *Times-Herald* fill its entire front page with a black-bordered photograph of Roosevelt, with no headline and no words. Inside, she ordered, the paper would turn its attention to the new president. "Truman's the news now."

From London came a message so phrased its author would have been evident even if he had not signed it:

I FEEL SO DEEPLY FOR YOU ALL. AS FOR ME, I HAVE LOST A DEAR AND CHERISHED FRIENDSHIP WHICH WAS FORGED IN THE FIRE OF WAR. I TRUST YOU MAY FIND CONSOLATION IN THE GLORY OF HIS NAME AND THE MAGNITUDE OF HIS WORK. CHURCHILL.

For a while, Truman wandered about the West Wing almost aimlessly, waiting for his wife and daughter to arrive from their apartment on Connecticut Avenue, waiting for the chief justice to arrive, waiting for someone to find a Bible somewhere on the White House bookshelves— waiting to be sworn in as president of the United States. People began to gather in the cabinet room: the presidential staff, the cabinet, others, all stunned, many in tears. Most of them barely knew Harry Truman. A few had never met him. For a while no one seemed to notice him, a virtual stranger sitting alone in a big leather chair to one side of the room. One cabinet member later remembered glancing at the new president and thinking, "He looks like such a little man."

Less than an hour later, he held his first Cabinet meeting and looked out on a group of officials about whose work he knew virtually nothing. He had been vice president for only two and a half months. Roosevelt had ignored him, told him nothing, seldom even spoke to him. The meeting was tense and awkward, and about all Truman could find to say to the Roosevelt Cabinet, now suddenly and strangely the Truman Cabinet, was that he intended to continue his predecessor's policies and that he hoped all of them would remain in office, at least for a while, because he needed their help. The meeting ended, and the members drifted in silence out into the night.

Secretary of War Stimson stayed behind. He had a "most urgent matter" to discuss with the new president. And that night, for the first time, Truman learned of the development of the atomic bomb.

The details of the president's death became public slowly over the next several days. He had been sitting at the rickety card table he always used as a desk in his modest wooden cottage in Warm Springs when he pressed a hand to his temple, said "I have a terrific headache," and collapsed. Dr. Bruenn had climbed out of the swimming pool, come running in and tried to revive him. Nothing worked. He had suffered a massive stroke, a "cerebral hemorrhage" the doctors called it. He was dead in the afternoon.

The plan was for Roosevelt's remains to leave Warm Springs by train the next day, Friday, to reach Washington and the White House for a funeral service in the East Room on Saturday and then to go on by train to Hyde Park for burial in the garden behind the family's house on Sunday. But the logistics were massive and difficult. Warm Springs, a tiny town, could not supply a coffin, an embalmer, an undertaker or a hearse. All these had to be ordered hurriedly from Atlanta. A hearse bringing the bronze coffin broke down with a flat tire on the highway. A coffin could not be carried in through the door of the railroad car—the turn inside was too tight. One of the car's windows had to be removed and then replaced. The coffin would weigh 760 pounds and would require some kind of wooden ramp to get it up from ground level to the railroad car window. Time was short. A local carpenter said he could build a ramp during the night if he could find some helpers. It was built. A train had to be put together in haste at the Southern Railway yards in Atlanta and brought to Warm Springs during the night, and had to come in backwards since in the little town there was no place to turn it around. The coffin would be so heavy it would take at least ten muscular men to lift it up the ramp and through the window and ten more in the car to pull it inside and set it in place.

In Washington, the U. S. Army chief of staff, General George C. Marshall, personally took charge and assembled a group of officers to organize a funeral. Some men would be needed in Warm Springs, they said. The little town could not handle this alone, nobody there could deal with all the complexities. The local people loved Roosevelt and would do anything for him, but this was too much for them. Within an hour the army had two thousand men from Fort Benning, Georgia, loaded in trucks and carrying their dress uniforms, guidons with black mourning bands added to their battle streamers, and tents and field kitchens for overnight on the ground at Warm Springs. The marines came with a detail from the navy. A military band arrived in town, its brass instruments glittering in the sun as they were unpacked on a too warm day.

The undertaker finished his work and asked, "Is there a bier?"

"A what?"

"A bier. A platform inside the railroad car for the coffin to rest on."

No. There was no bier. Nobody had thought of it.

Back to the carpenter who had already worked all night. For Roosevelt, he would go on working. He built a bier. They covered it with a blanket borrowed from the marines.

It was a strange-looking train that rolled in. A steam locomotive painted in the Southern's green livery pulled it in rear end first. On the other end, soon to become the front end, were two other handsome steam locomotives. They had been pulled in backwards from Atlanta, and when the train was ready to leave for Washington they would pull it out, the engine on the rear end being uncoupled and left behind. No one in town had ever seen anything like this before, but there was no other way to get a train in and out.

The last car on the train, to carry the body, was a private car, the *Conneaught,* supplied by the Southern. It would carry the president's coffin and a four-man military honor guard standing at attention at the four corners of the bier. Immediately in front of it was the old, familiar car on which in life he had traveled thousands of miles, the *Ferdinand Magellan.*

Up through the South the train rolled at twenty-five miles an hour. The family asked that it be moved slowly because all along the way, throughout the afternoon and throughout the night, people lined the tracks to see it pass. In darkness, the *Conneaught* was softly lit, the shades raised, and people outside could see the American flag atop the coffin, the honor guard in dress uniforms and, occasionally, Mrs. Roosevelt sitting there. The people stood along the tracks beside tobacco and corn and peanut fields, in the cities and towns. Even at 3 a.m. they were out there. They held their children up to see. They cried. They knelt. They sang hymns. No one could count the people lining the track through town and country from Warm Springs to Washington. Some guessed two million.

The new president—accompanied by Henry Wallace and James F. Byrnes, either of whom, but for Bob Hannegan's maneuverings the previous summer, might himself have been president now—met the funeral train at Union Station. Many in the crowd outside the station recognized Wallace before they recognized Truman.

A slow funeral cortege—a horse-drawn caisson, a squadron of motor-cycle policemen, armored troops, the marine band, the navy band, a battalion of midshipmen from Annapolis, a detachment of service women, a line of black limousines—moved through the streets of Washington between columns of soldiers at attention. Two dozen army fighters roared across the sky in tribute. An elderly black woman sat on the curb in front of the White House, rocked back and forth, and cried out as the procession went past her through the gates, "Oh, he's gone. He's gone forever. I loved him so. He's never coming back."

Two days later, Roosevelt left Washington for the last time, to be buried in his mother's rose garden in Hyde Park.

On the morning of April 13, 1945, the New York *Times* ran a banner headline. Three lines:

> *PRESIDENT ROOSEVELT IS DEAD;*
> *TRUMAN TO CONTINUE POLICIES;*
> *9TH CROSSES ELBE, NEARS BERLIN.*

Not even the shock of Roosevelt's death could draw attention away from the imminent Allied victory in Europe. The last desperate Nazi offensive, the Battle of the Bulge, had been turned back (though at terrible cost) in December. Now British, French and American troops were sweeping toward Berlin from the west while Soviet forces moved in from the east. On April 30, Adolf Hitler—who two weeks before had celebrated Roosevelt's death as his deliverance—shot himself in his bunker as shells from Russian guns landed outside around him. On May 7, what remained of the German government agreed to surrender.

False reports of victory had been flowing into Washington for weeks. When the real news came in on the morning of May 7, it seemed almost anticlimactic. President Truman, speaking over the radio in his still unfamiliar, flat midwestern voice, urged restraint: "This is a solemn but glorious hour.... If I could give you a single watchword for the coming months, that word is work—work and more work. We must work to finish the war. Our victory is only half won."

In New York, half-a-million people flooded into Times Square to celebrate. In Washington, the streets were quiet. V-E Day was not even a holiday. Government employees were ordered to report to work as usual to set an example for those who might wish to return to their peacetime sloth. Some workers brought radios to their offices to listen to the president's speech, but many bosses forbade them to listen ("a childish performance," the Washington *Post* commented). The Brentwood Terrace Citizens Association invited an official of the American Legion to speak at a ceremony marking the victory; his patriotic message was that the war with Japan should be shortened by the use of poison gas.

But there was at least one moment when the task still ahead was forgotten. The next day, May 8, the formal documents of surrender were signed. And at 8:30 p.m., moments after Truman made the official announcement, the lights on the United States Capitol were lit. For the first time since December 9, 1941, the great white dome gleamed splendidly in the night sky.

Early in August, the new president was in the middle of the Atlantic, sailing home aboard the U.S.S. *Augusta* from a conference with Stalin and Churchill in Potsdam, Germany. It had not been a happy occasion. Churchill, in the midst of the meeting, had gone home for Britain's first election since before the war. He had not returned. Clement Attlee, leader of the victorious Labour party, had replaced him as prime minister and replaced him in Potsdam. But it was Stalin whom Truman had found most troubling. "I cannot understand that man!" the president said of him in frustration toward the end of the meeting, after Stalin had refused to compromise on any important issue. The trip home was a somber one, Truman wondering what would come of their failure to resolve the question of Germany, the question of Poland, and many other troubling controversies. On August 6, he was having lunch in the wardroom with the ship's officers when he received a radio message: the United States had successfully detonated an atomic bomb over the Japanese city of Hiroshima. "This is the greatest thing in history," he cried as the sailors around him cheered.

In the White House press room, quiet in the president's absence, a young staff assistant broke the news to reporters at 10:45 a.m. and gave them a statement Truman had prepared in advance: "It is an atomic bomb. It is a harnessing of the basic power of the universe. The force from which the sun draws its power has been loosed against those who brought war to the Far East." Three days later, on August 9, there was another announcement: a second bomb had been dropped on Nagasaki.

Not many people understood what the atomic bomb was. No one, certainly, fully understood what it would mean for the future. But everyone understood that this might be the thing that ended the war, and for days the anticipation and the anxiety and the rumors grew. All over Washington people stayed close to their radios, waiting for an announcement. Crowds kept a vigil in Lafayette Park. Shopkeepers began boarding up windows downtown to protect them from the celebrations they knew would soon come. On Sunday, August 12, the radio networks broadcast news that the Japanese had surrendered, then discovered the story was false and retracted it. There were a few brief celebrations, quickly squelched.

At 7 p.m., August 14, White House reporters entered the Oval Office to find the president standing in front of his desk, flanked by James Byrnes, Cordell Hull and perhaps a dozen other officials. Japan had surrendered, he said, then he broke into a broad smile. The war was over. A few minutes later, he could hear the blare of automobile horns and the roar of happy crowds from the streets outside. Washington, having planned and directed the war and forced the American people to sacrifice their lives, their comforts and their money to pay for it, felt at last it was entitled to celebrate.

The streets filled with people shouting, singing, running about not certain what to do but looking frantically for ways to express their relief and their joy. A crowd on F Street spontaneously sang "The Star-

Spangled Banner." Churches rang their bells. Boys set off firecrackers. Trucks intentionally backfired. Young servicemen embraced and kissed women they passed in the streets. A few couples copulated standing up inside the half-dark doorways of office buildings. There was a good deal of drinking. At Fourteenth and New York, a young sailor staggered up to a mailbox, opened its lid and vomited into it.

Across from the White House, the crowd in Lafayette Park formed a conga line, then streamed across the street and chanted, "We want Harry!" The president came out on the front lawn and reached through the iron fence to shake hands with those he could touch, then made a speech from a hastily assembled sound system under the portico:

> This is the great day. This is the day we have been looking for since December 7, 1941. This is the day when fascism and police government ceases in the world. This is the day for the democracies. This is the day when we can start on our real task of implementation of free government in the world.

Slowly, in the weeks and months after V-J Day, some of the strains of wartime life in Washington began to subside. The first new cars appeared in dealers' showrooms—all Fords, all of them slightly reworked 1942 models. The OPA cancelled an order for the printing of 187 million ration books for food, gasoline and shoes. The Agriculture Department ordered the release, without ration points, of 12 million pounds of salt pork for the Southern states, where it was a dietary staple, explaining, "It was a question of letting the pork go or not getting the cotton crop harvested." A few nylon stockings appeared in Murphy's store on F Street and were sold instantly. The hosiery industry said it would be months before they were plentiful again. Mrs. Ira Eaker, wife of an air corps general, had carefully nursed just five nylon stockings, two and a half pairs, through the entire war. "Do you know," she said, "in army circles on V-J day there was more talk about nylons than anything else?"

At a ceremony at the Capitol, a thousand people—members of Congress, military leaders, Cabinet officers and others—gathered to see the tattered American flag the marines had raised on Iwo Jima, a moment preserved in a historic photograph by Joe Rosenthal of AP. The flag had come to Washington to be flown over the Capitol. A young marine said to a reporter, "A hell of a lot of people died to get that up there."

A few weeks later, the navy arranged a tribute to sailors who had died at sea. Their friends and relatives were invited to send flowers and notes to Washington to be flown fifty miles out and dropped into the Atlantic. The plane left Washington carrying more than a ton of flowers and tokens and scattered them across miles of ocean. Among them was a single yellow blossom with a card written in a child's scrawl: "To my brother, from Bill."

By early September, the free Watergate concerts were back. Near the Lincoln Memorial, a marble amphitheater looked out over the Potomac and over a large band shell on a floating barge, where the military bands and the National Symphony Orchestra played concerts on summer evenings. Some young couples rented canoes from Fletcher's Boathouse in Georgetown, paddled down to the Watergate, tied their boats up to the ropes mooring the barge and reclined on pillows to listen to the music.

The Washington *Post* ran a story on its "women's" page: "WAR'S END MAY REVIVE SOCIAL ERA." According to society reporter Marie McNair:

> The lights will gleam again from the crystal chandeliers in the White House East Room. There will be state receptions with dancing, maybe, later in the evening.... Perhaps the Cabinet wives will resume their afternoon "at homes," discontinued along with all other official entertaining after Pearl Harbor when the world and his wife would go calling on those afternoons when the doors of Cabinet residences were open to the public.

Other things seemed to be returning to normal too. A month after V-J Day, a citizens committee on race relations issued a report on the status of the city's lunch counters, which the black community had mobilized to desegregate a year before. "Large cafeterias and public restaurants still do not accept Negro customers," it concluded. "Not long ago Negroes were denied service at lunch counters at dime stores in Washington. Today they are allowed to eat only at those counters having no seats. At the counters with seats, they will not be served." Black people could eat the flimsy ham sandwiches at Woolworth's, but only if they were standing up.

The Daughters of the American Revolution, like the dime stores, quickly reverted to normal as well. Marian Anderson had finally been allowed to sing in the society's auditorium in 1943, but now it was peacetime. Hazel Scott, a black jazz pianist married to Congressman Adam Clayton Powell of Harlem, asked to perform in Constitution Hall. The DAR said no. Whites only.

The war had ended so suddenly that official Washington was not ready for it. The bureaucrats assigned to plan for the postwar period, knowing nothing of the atomic bomb, had assumed the fighting would last another year or two. When it was over, ready or not, they quickly sent the White House a sheaf of hastily prepared economic forecasts— all of them gloomy and pessimistic and all of them wrong. Truman had appointed his friend, John Snyder, a St. Louis banker, to run what was now called the Office of War Mobilization and Reconversion. He reported to Truman two weeks after V–J Day that "There should be no mincing of words," because it was clear the end of war production would dislocate the economy and cause unemployment to rise to eight million by the spring of 1946. Nothing like this happened. Millions of women who had held war jobs left the labor force and returned home, many of them married women who said they wanted to be there when their husbands returned from the military. Thousands of ex-servicemen chose to use their military benefits and to go to college first and look for jobs later. The defense plants turning back to making civilian goods needed their employees and kept them at work in the same plants. Government employment in Washington declined briefly but soon began rising again. As for private business in the city, there were three jobs awaiting everyone looking for work.

Snyder, new in town, and most others trying to forecast the economic future, did not understand the basic nature of government. They did not see that with the wartime innovation of the withholding tax, previously unimaginable amounts of money were being extracted from the American people with relatively few complaints. Federal tax collections in 1940 had totaled $5 billion. In 1945, $49 billion. And it was all spent. The war was over, yes, but its expenses were not. There was the cost of occupying Japan, of pacifying Europe, of loans to allies bankrupted by the war. And with Joseph Stalin violating every day the agreements he had made at Yalta, and creating one nasty little incident after another, Washington was uneasy about his intentions. In one dispute, the Russians placed the U.S. embassy in Moscow under an embargo, allowing no supplies to be shipped in from the United States. The U.S. retaliated, and at the Soviet embassy in Washington blocked a shipment from Moscow of eighty-three crates of furniture, Russian sausage and brown bread, and twenty-six cases of the ambassador's favorite mineral water. Irritations like this, one after another, led Harry Truman in private to call Stalin a "lying son of a bitch" and to decide that money had to be spent to maintain American military power.

These were the reasons why John Snyder's forecast was wrong. A flood of new tax money collected and quickly spent caused the American economy to expand and create jobs so rapidly that postwar unemployment was inconsequential. There were 139,000 government jobs in Washington in 1940. In 1945, 265,000. Not long after V-J Day, employment was higher than at the height of the war and there was a labor shortage.

The Senate Finance Committee, three weeks after V-J Day, listened unhappily to Snyder's and others' predictions of massive postwar unemployment and possibly even social disorder. It also heard Emerson P. Schmidt of the U.S. Chamber of Commerce offer the only prediction that turned out to be correct. He said that with all the savings people had accumulated during the war when there had been nothing to buy, and with government money being spent in massive amounts, "a great boom is impending. I am not predicting its indefinite continuation but I think it will continue for several years." The committee members, remembering the Depression of the 1930s, did not believe him; they feared that instead the end of the war would dump the country back into depression and unemployment. The presumed Keynesian virtues of huge spending and borrowing and piling up debt were not yet clearly understood by the lawyers and small businessmen who made up most of Congress.

Harry Truman, meanwhile, was struggling. He was contending with massive strikes in steel, railroads, automobiles, rubber—the largest work stoppage in American history, with the unions demanding pay increases of 30 percent and more. Inflation reappeared. Truman and Chester Bowles wanted price controls continued. Senator Taft and his friends did not. They slashed the OPA until it was nearly impotent. During the entire war, prices had risen a total of 30 percent; now they rose 20 percent in one month. Returning veterans complained that there was no housing for sale or rent; when controls on building materials were lifted, the bricks, nails and lumber went not into low-priced housing but into more profitable racetracks, bowling alleys, nightclubs and stores.

With Roosevelt gone, the Chicago *Tribune* turned its vitriol on Truman. Even New Dealers were openly contemptuous, calling him "Herman Truman" and "Uncle Fud." All the old and familiar Washington jokes about dumb, fumbling politicians were revived and applied to him. Who, it was asked, wanted a pocket full of dimes with Truman's face engraved on them? Or postage stamps or dollar bills? To those accustomed to Franklin Roosevelt, he simply did not look like a president. "If you want a friend in Washington," Truman once remarked to a White House visitor, "buy a dog." And toward the end of 1945, he said in a speech to the Gridiron Club, "Sherman was wrong. *Peace* is hell."

With the strikes, the inflation, a cranky Congress unwilling to tolerate another New Dealish president, and Senator Taft rasping that some of his ideas were communist, it was hellish for Truman. But he hung on, did his best, finally came to be seen as what he was—a plain but intelligent, tough and honest man—and his reputation outlived his enemies.

In the first months of peace, it came to be clear that the war had awakened Washington from its long afternoon nap and turned it into a busy, growing city. With the piles of money it was now spending, government expanded rapidly into areas where it had never ventured before, and soon business and industry, from automobile makers to grinders of cattle feed, discovered that they absolutely had to have their own offices and representatives in Washington to keep them advised of what the bureaucrats might do next—do for them or do to them. And so Washington lobbying offices, usually named National Associations of something or other, came to number well over a thousand. This, along with the expansion of government itself, attracted still more lobbyists, lawyers, consultants, think tanks, journalists, accountants. Offices and housing for all these people spread outward into Maryland and Virginia for miles beyond the old boundaries. In time, New York's expensive stores opened branches and thrived. Every four corners seemed to have five banks. New restaurants appeared, even some good ones. Finally, and late, America's "Our Town" began to look like a real city—traffic jams, pollution, street crime, dirt, high taxes, expensive housing, insufficient parking, and it was all perfectly splendid.

The city had come out of the war as the capital of the only major country in the world on the winning side, or any side, to survive without a scratch. But those looking for a return to the quiet, easy Washington life they had known in peacetime would not find it. That world was gone. It was replaced by a world that demanded American military power to occupy Japan and to save what was left of western Europe. Therefore, even with the war over and won, the armed services still filled the Pentagon and spilled over into dozens of other buildings all over town.

Three months before his death, Franklin Roosevelt had sent a memorandum to his budget director, Harold Smith, suggesting something of what he thought would happen to the city when the fighting was over. They were among his last thoughts about the city of Washington in the postwar period. "It has been my thought," he wrote, "that after the war is ended all the personnel records of the armed services should be placed in the Pentagon. . . . The War Department will doubtless object to giving up the . . . building, but it is much too large for them if we get a decent peace."

At almost the same time, however, officials in the War Department were making other plans for the Pentagon—plans that would, like Roosevelt's, never be implemented, but plans that more accurately predicted the shape of the postwar city and the postwar world. In February 1945, reports were leaked to the press of the military's proposal not to vacate but to expand the world's largest building. A new (and ugly) twenty-four-story office tower would rise out of the Pentagon's six-acre interior courtyard. It would house some (but not all) of the workers who would be needed to maintain the nation's peacetime forces. On top of the building would be an eternal flame: a symbol of the nation's great victory and of the new American imperium over which Washington would preside.

A Note on Sources

Much of what I recount in this book is based on my own memories of wartime Washington. But I have relied as well on interviews with others; on various archives and manuscript collections; and on a range of published sources.

Particularly helpful were the reminiscences of a number of men and women who lived in Washington during the war and were kind enough to agree to share their thoughts about those years with me. They include: Ellen Beckman, one of the first Waves; Herbert Blunck, the manager of the new Statler Hotel; Sherman Briscoe, one of the few black employees of the Department of Agriculture; Mrs. Richard Coe, a writer for the Washington *Post* and various women's magazines; the Reverend Clarence Crawford, pastor of a Baptist church; Olivia Davis, who owned the Merryland Night Club; Alan Dickey, an architect on the Pentagon project; Ymelda Dixon, who (with her husband George Dixon, the newspaper columnist) chronicled and participated in the wartime party frenzy; William Donohoe, a Pentagon public information officer at the time of Pearl Harbor; Mrs. Henry Grattan Doyle, a personnel officer in the Treasury Department who helped the frightened and bewildered girls who came to Washington to work; John Kenneth Galbraith, who was director of price controls in OPA during the war; Mrs. Mibray German, a public school teacher; David Ginsburg, general counsel to the OPA and a friend of Leon Henderson; Gilbert Hahn, of an old Washington merchant family, whose stores sold rationed shoes; Colonel West Hamilton, one of the few high-ranking black officers in the World War II army; Loraine Inman, a "government girl" manning an army typewriter; Professor Elmer Kaiser of George Washington University, an adviser to the navy on maritime history; Sam Jack Kaufman, conductor of the pit band for the Capitol Theater stage shows; Pat King, a member of the staff of the British embassy; William Lind, a G.I. stationed in

Washington during the war, later a member of the staff of the National
Archives; C. J. Mack, manager of the Mayflower Hotel; Harry McAlpin,
a black journalist and government official; Leila McKnight, who worked
on the Board of Economic Warfare; Hope Ridings Miller, society colum-
nist for the Washington *Post;* Clarence Mitchell, of the NAACP; James
Nabrit, of the Howard University Law School; Dr. Harold Pinkett, an
archivist and an expert on the history of the Washington black community;
James Powell, a member of the District of Columbia police force; Paul
Scott Rankin, a member of the staff of the British embassy; Joseph L.
Rauh, Jr., a New Deal lawyer who wrote the presidential order establishing
the FEPC; Reginald Redmond, a bellman at the Mayflower Hotel;
Edward Reese, an employee of the Pentagon during the war; Vivian
Ronca, who lived in the Wave barracks on Nebraska Avenue; Thomas
Saltz, of Lewis & Thomas Saltz, men's clothiers; Alfred Edgar Smith,
Harry Hopkins's "Negro adviser" and a columnist for the Chicago
Defender; William Traxler, a bellman at the Sheraton-Carlton Hotel;
Frank Waldrop, editorial page editor of the Washington *Times-Herald;*
Mary Warfield, a Washington housewife left alone in the city with her
children while her husband served in the army; Paul Young, owner of
the Connecticut Avenue restaurant that once bore his name.

Records in the National Archives of the following agencies and
organizations were also useful: the Office of Price Administration (Record
Group 188), the Office of Civilian Defense (171), the Office for Emer-
gency Management (214), the War Production Board (179), the National
Capital Planning Commission (328), the Alley Dwelling Authority (302),
the Department of State (59), the National War College Library (334), the
Fair Employment Practices Commission (228), the District of Columbia
Government (351), the Army Services Decimal Files (328), the Office of
Public Buildings and Grounds (42).

A great variety of collections at the Franklin D. Roosevelt Library in
Hyde Park contain material relating to the impact of the war on life in
bureaucratic Washington as well as to the social climate of the city. I
have made use of material from the presidential papers themselves as
well as from the collections of Adolph A. Berle, Frederic A. Delano, the
Democratic National Committee, Stephen T. Early, Leon Henderson,
Harry Hopkins, and Samuel I. Rosenman. Also of value are the following collections in the Manuscripts Division of the Library of Congress:
Raymond Clapper, Tom Connally, Joseph E. Davies, Elmer Davis, Felix

Frankfurter, William Hassett, Harold Ickes, James Landis, Evalyn Walsh McLean, Eugene Meyer. Important material on the Washington black community is available in the Moorland-Spingarn Research Collection at Howard University; among the relevant collections are those of Marian Anderson, Charles Burch, Jeannette Carter, Thomas Clark, Charles Drew, Edwin Henderson, Howard University, Charlotte Hubbard, Campbell Johnson, Pauli Murray, the Promethean Collection, the Civil Rights Documentation Oral History Project. An extensive and valuable collection of newspaper clippings is available in the Washingtoniana Room of the Martin Luther King Memorial Library.

The four daily newspapers published in Washington during the war—the *Post*, the *Evening Star*, the *Times-Herald*, and the *Daily News* —are, naturally, an invaluable source. Additional material has been drawn from other newspapers, including the New York *Times*, the Chicago *Tribune*, *The Crisis* and the Chicago *Defender*, and from many magazines, among them *Time*, *Newsweek*, *Life*, *Fortune*, *The New Republic*, *The Nation*, *The New Masses*, *The New Yorker*, *The Saturday Evening Post*, *The Atlantic*, and *U.S. News & World Report*. The *Congressional Record* is, of course, the basic source for the proceedings of the House and the Senate.

A complete list of the books and articles that have contributed to this book would be unwieldy, but I do wish to mention several volumes that were particularly helpful to me. James MacGregor Burns, *Roosevelt: The Soldier of Freedom* (1970), is an invaluable chronicle of the war years from the president's perspective. John Morton Blum, *V Was for Victory* (1976), is a rich source of material on both politics and popular culture during the war. Robert J. Donovan, *Conflict and Crisis* (1977), is the standard account of the first years of the Truman administration. Jim Bishop, *FDR's Last Year* (1974), and Bernard Asbell, *When F.D.R. Died* (1961), contribute as well to the picture of the last year of the war. Scott Hart, *Washington at War* (1970), is a lively narrative that covers some of the same events I have discussed here. James Borchert, *Alley Life in Washington* (1980), and two books by Constance McLaughlin Green—*Washington: A History of the Capital* (1962), and *The Secret City: A History of Race Relations in the Nation's Capital* (1967)—are important for their portraits of the black community.

Of the many memoirs and other firsthand accounts by men and women who spent time in Washington during the war, I found particularly useful Jonathan Daniels, *Frontier on the Potomac* (1946) and *White House Witness* (1975); H. G. Nicholas, ed., *Washington Despatches, 1941-1945: Weekly Political Reports from the British Embassy* (1981); Chester Bowles, *Promises to Keep* (1971); James Roosevelt, *My Parents: A Differing View* (1976); Michael F. Reilly, *Reilly of the White House* (1947); W. M. Kiplinger, *Washington Is Like That* (1942); Allen Drury, *A Senate Journal, 1943-1945* (1963); Donald Nelson, *Arsenal of Democracy* (1946); and *The Memoirs of Cordell Hull* (2 vols., 1948).